The Curse of
the Marquis de Sade

The CURSE of the MARQUIS de SADE

A NOTORIOUS SCOUNDREL,
A MYTHICAL MANUSCRIPT,
AND THE BIGGEST SCANDAL
IN LITERARY HISTORY

Joel Warner

 CROWN
NEW YORK

Published in the United States by Crown, an imprint of Random House, a division of Penguin Random House LLC, New York.

CROWN and the Crown colophon are registered trademarks of Penguin Random House LLC.

Library of Congress Cataloging-in-Publication Data
Names: Warner, Joel, author.
Title: The curse of the Marquis de Sade / Joel Warner.
Description: First edition. | New York: Crown, [2023] |
Includes bibliographical references and index.
Identifiers: LCCN 2022026391 (print) | LCCN 2022026392 (ebook) |
ISBN 9780593135686 (hardcover; alk. paper) | ISBN 9780593135693 (ebook)
Subjects: LCSH: Lhéritier, Gérard. | Sade, marquis de, 1740-1814. 120 journées
de Sodome. | Manuscripts, French—Collectors and collecting—
Case studies. | Swindlers and swindling—France—Case studies.
Classification: LCC HV6699.F8 W37 2023 (print) | LCC HV6699.F8 (ebook) |
DDC 364.16/30944—dc23/eng/20220728
LC record available at https://lccn.loc.gov/2022026391
LC ebook record available at https://lccn.loc.gov/2022026392

Printed in Canada on acid-free paper

Map copyright © 2022 by David Lindroth, Inc.

crownpublishing.com

2 4 6 8 9 7 5 3 1

FIRST EDITION

Book design by Simon M. Sullivan

For EMILY, GABRIEL, and CHARLOTTE—
who enjoy a good story as much as
they love a grand adventure

In the end, Sade taunts his executioners;
He has passed beyond the waves of the black sea.
But in spite of you, oh infernal pedants,
Despite your cries, his honest works
Will go without you to the temple of memories.
He's done enough to earn glory
And far too much to earn his rest.

—The Marquis de Sade,
"My Epitaph"

Friend Reader (as they said in the prefaces of old), if you know how to appreciate good old books, and amusing characters, do me the favor to accompany me.

—Alfred Bonnardot,
The Mirror of the Parisian Bibliophile: A Satirical Tale

CONTENTS

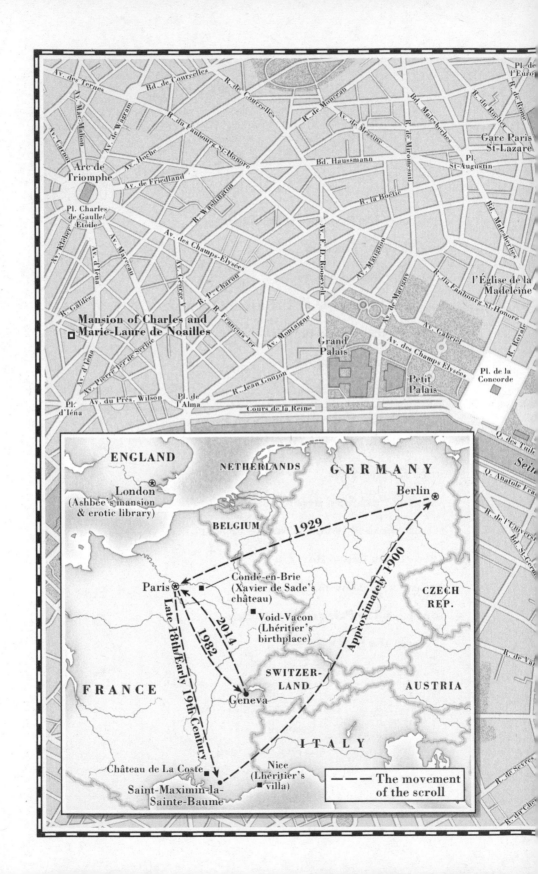

Arc de Triomphe
Pl. Charles de Gaulle/ Étoile

Av. des Ternes
Bd. de Courcelles
R. de Courcelles
R. de Monceau
Bd. Malesherbes
R. du Rocher
Pl. de l'Europe

Av. de Wagram
R. du Faubourg St-Honoré
Av. de Messine
R. de Miromesnil
Gare Paris St-Lazare

Av. Mac-Mahon
Av. Carnot
Av. Hoche
Bd. Haussmann
Pl. St-Augustin

Av. de Friedland
R. la Boëtie
Bd. Malesherbes

Av. Kléber
Av. d'Iéna
Av. Marceau
Av. des Champs-Élysées
Av. F. D. Roosevelt
Av. de Marigny
l'Église de la Madeleine

R. Galilée
Av. George V
R. Washington
R. du Faubourg St-Honoré
R. Royale

R. Pierre 1er de Serbie
R. V. Charon
R. François 1er
Av. Montaigne
Grand Palais
Av. des Champs Élysées
Av. Gabriel

Mansion of Charles and Marie-Laure de Noailles

Pl. d'Iéna
Av. du Prés. Wilson
Pl. de l'Alma
R. Jean Goujon
Cours de la Reine
Petit Palais
Pl. de la Concorde

Q. des Tuil.
Seine
Q. Anatole Fra...
R. de l'Universit...
Bd. St-Germ...
R. de Va...

ENGLAND
London
(Ashbee's mansion & erotic library)

NETHERLANDS

GERMANY

Berlin

BELGIUM

1929

Approximately 1900

CZECH REP.

Paris
Condé-en-Brie (Xavier de Sade's château)

Void-Vacon (Lhéritier's birthplace)

Late 18th/Early 19th Century
2014
1982

SWITZER-LAND
Geneva

AUSTRIA

FRANCE

R. de Var...

Château de La Coste
Saint-Maximin-la-Sainte-Baume

Nice (Lhéritier's villa)

ITALY

R. de Sèvres
R. du Ch...

------ The movement of the scroll

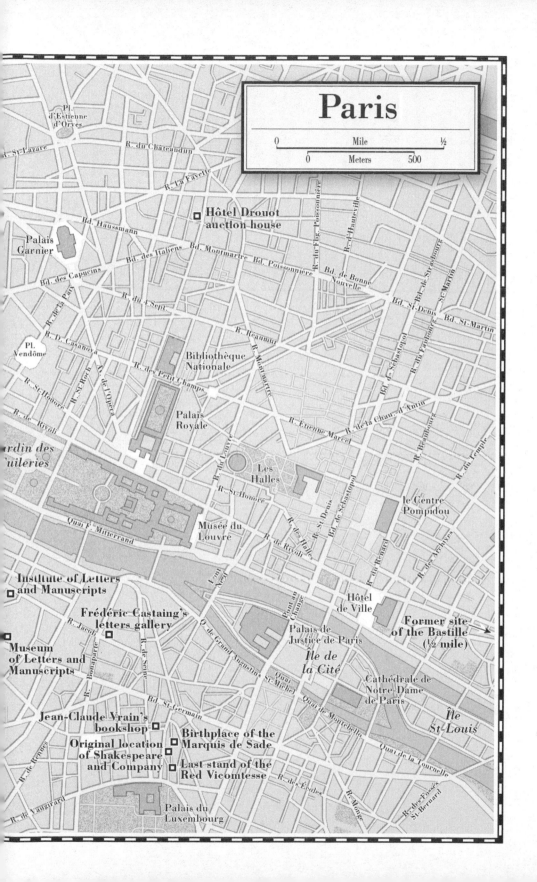

Paris

0 ——— Mile ——— ½

0 ——— Meters ——— 500

Pl. d'Estienne d'Orves

R. St-Lazare

R. du Châteaudun

R. La Fayette

Bd. Haussmann

Hôtel Drouot auction house

R. du Fbg. Poissonnière

R. d'Hauteville

Palais Garnier

Bd. des Italiens

Bd. Montmartre

Bd. Poissonnière

Bd. de Bonne Nouvelle

Bd. St-Denis

Bd. de Strasbourg

St-Martin

Bd. des Capucins

Bd. St-Martin

R. de la Paix

R. du 4 Sept.

R. Réaumur

Bd. St-Denis

R. du Fbg. St-Denis

Pl. Vendôme

R. D. Casanova

Bd. de Sébastopol

R. des Petit Champs

Bibliothèque Nationale

R. Montmartre

R. St-Honoré

R. St-Roch

R. de l'Opéra

R. de Rivoli

Palais Royale

R. Etienne Marcel

R. de la Chau.-d'Antin

R. Beaubourg

R. du Temple

rdin des uileries

R. du Louvre

Les Halles

R. St-Honoré

R. de Rivoli

R. des Halles

R. St-Denis

Bd. de Sébastopol

R. du Renard

le Centre Pompidou

Quai F. Mitterrand

Musée du Louvre

R. des Archives

Institute of Letters and Manuscripts

Pont au Change

Pont Neuf

Hôtel de Ville

Frédéric Castaing's letters gallery

R. Jacob

R. Bonaparte

R. de Seine

Q. de Grand Augustins

St-Michel

Palais de Justice de Paris

Former site of the Bastille (½ mile) →

Museum of Letters and Manuscripts

Île de la Cité

Jean-Claude Vrain's bookshop

Bd. St-Germain

Quai St-Michel

Quai de Montebello

Cathédrale de Notre-Dame de Paris

Île St-Louis

R. de Rennes

Original location of Shakespeare and Company

Birthplace of the Marquis de Sade

Last stand of the Red Vicomtesse

R. des Écoles

R. Monge

Quai de la Tournelle

R. des Fossés St-Bernard

R. de Vaugirard

Palais du Luxembourg

CAST OF CHARACTERS

Sade

Donatien Alphonse François, the Marquis de Sade: An eighteenth-century French aristocrat who produced numerous libertine writings, including *120 Days of Sodom*

Louis Marais: A police inspector who tracked Paris's prerevolutionary sex market

Jean-Baptiste Joseph François, the Comte de Sade: An aristocratic French diplomat and Sade's father

Marie Éléonore de Maillé de Carman: A French noblewoman and Sade's mother

Jacques François Paul Aldonse, the Abbé de Sade: A Provençal intellectual and Sade's uncle

Renée-Pélagie de Montreuil: Sade's wife

Marie-Madeleine de Montreuil: Sade's powerful mother-in-law, known as "the Présidente"

Anne-Prospére de Launay: Sade's sister-in-law

Gaspar François Xavier Gaufridy: Sade's lawyer and notary

Marie-Constance Quesnet: An actress and single mother who became Sade's companion after the French Revolution

François Simonet de Coulmier: Director of the Charenton mental asylum outside Paris in the early nineteenth century

Louis-Marie, Donatien-Claude-Armand, and Madeleine-Laure de Sade: Sade's three children

Gilbert Lely: A Surrealist poet and Sade biographer

Xavier de Sade: A mid-twentieth-century aristocrat and Sade's great-great-great-grandson

Thibault de Sade: A government adviser and Sade's great-great-great-great-grandson

The Scroll

Arnoux: A French citizen from the Provençal town of Saint-Maximin-la-Sainte-Baume who found *120 Days of Sodom* in the Bastille

Hélion de Villeneuve, the Marquis de Villeneuve-Trans: A nineteenth-century Provençal aristocrat who collected erotic literature

Jules-Adolphe Chauvet: A French erotica illustrator

Frederick Hankey: A notorious erotica collector who smuggled obscene books from France to Victorian England

Henry Spencer Ashbee: A Victorian bibliophile who amassed one of the world's largest collections of erotica and authored a three-volume bibliography of erotic literature

Iwan Bloch: An early-twentieth-century German sexologist

Magnus Hirschfeld: A colleague of Bloch's who founded Berlin's Institute for Sexual Science

Marie-Laure de Noailles, the Vicomtesse de Noailles: An influential Parisian arts patron

Charles de Noailles, the Vicomte de Noailles: Marie-Laure's husband

Maurice Heine: A French writer and Sade devotee

André Breton: Leader of the Surrealists

Nathalie de Noailles: Daughter of Marie-Laure de Noailles

Jean Grouet: A radical French publisher

Gérard Nordmann: A Swiss billionaire and erotica collector

Carlo Perrone: Grandson of Marie-Laure de Noailles and Italian media baron

Jean-Jacques Pauvert: A young French publisher who openly published Sade's works in the 1940s, challenging the country's longtime ban

Martin Bodmer: The heir to a Swiss industrial fortune, known as "the king of bibliophiles"

Florence Darbre: A Swiss paper and papyrus conservation expert

The Empire of Letters

Gérard Lhéritier: Founder of Aristophil

Jean-Claude Le Coustumer: A major investor in Aristophil

Kenneth Rendell: A leading U.S. letter and manuscript dealer

Frédéric Castaing: A prominent Parisian manuscript dealer and onetime president of France's association of rare-book sellers

Jean-Claude Vrain: One of France's biggest rare-book dealers and Castaing's archnemesis

Alain Nicolas: A major Paris manuscript dealer

Bruno Racine: Onetime president of the Bibliothèque Nationale de France

Jérôme Dupuis: An investigative reporter at the French newsmagazine *L'Express* who covered the book industry

Claude Aguttes: Founder of the French auction company Aguttes

Emmanuel Boussard: A wealthy French investment banker

The Curse of
the Marquis de Sade

The Prisoner in the Tower

OCTOBER 22, 1785

AS THE SETTING SUN SLIPPED BELOW THE TILED ROOFS OF LATE-eighteenth-century Paris, a solitary convict leaned over his desk in the Liberty Tower of the Bastille and began to write:

> The extensive wars that Louis XIV had to wage throughout the course of his reign, while exhausting the state's finances and the people's resources, nevertheless uncovered the secret to enriching an enormous number of those leeches always lying in wait for the public calamities they provoke rather than quell in order to profit from them all the more. . . . It was towards the end of this reign . . . that four among them conceived the unique feat of debauchery we are about to describe.

The man's fine-tipped quill moved quickly across the narrow sheet of paper, filling the page with delicate, almost microscopically small letters, the lines of brown ink crammed so close together to save space that the descenders of his *j*'s, *p*'s, and *y*'s stabbed like lancets into the line below. As he wrote, the light from his shaded candles flickered about the whitewashed stone walls of his cramped octagonal cell, the air rank from the waste that poured from the sewer pipe under his window into the moat below. Past his cell door, the prison echoed with the creaks of doors, clattering keys, and bolts slamming into place, the only signs that he wasn't completely alone.

In the cold evening, shadows played across the trappings allowed to a prisoner of his aristocratic stature: Shelves sagging with six hundred books, with titles by Homer, Newton, and Shakespeare, as well as works on the existence of God, the motion of fluids, and the history of vampires. Expensive bottles of eau de cologne, fine linen towels, velvet cushions, and colorful tapestries stretched across the walls. And a prized collection of dildos, fashioned from rosewood and ebony, crafted to exacting specifications by a prominent Parisian cabinet maker.

The cell's occupant was one of the most notorious criminals in eighteenth-century France. He had spent the bulk of his forty-five years reveling in depravity: engaging in blasphemous acts with a prostitute, torturing a beggar, poisoning whores, hiding in Italy in the romantic company of his sister-in-law, locking away girls and boys in his château for his own sexual designs, and narrowly surviving a bullet fired at his chest. For years, he had evaded the law—breaking out of an Alpine prison, dodging a military raid on his home, absconding from the clutches of a police squadron, and eluding his own public execution.

His name was Donatien Alphonse François de Sade, but most people knew him as the Marquis de Sade.

Sade's exploits had come to an end with his capture in 1778. He had first been assigned to the Château de Vincennes, a royal residence turned prison in a hunting preserve outside Paris, where he had briefly been interned as a much younger man. For six years, he had lived in a damp and rodent-infested cell whose narrow windows provided only the faintest hint of daylight. Then, in 1784, authorities had shut down Vincennes and transferred him to an even more dismal facility: the Bastille. Located near the heart of Paris, the Bastille was one of the most notorious prisons in all of Europe. With his arrest warrant signed by the king, Sade had been locked away with no charges, no trial, no possibility of appeal. For all he knew, he might never be released.

The time behind bars had taken its toll on Sade's once-fine figure. Inactivity and a penchant for delicacies sent to him by his wife—eel pâté, chocolate cakes, bacon-wrapped thrush—had left him obese. He was plagued by migraines, gout, nosebleeds, breathing problems, dizzy spells, and hemorrhoids so painful he needed a special leather cushion to sit at his desk. With his eyesight nearly ruined, he'd taken to wearing strange masklike leather goggles. In his mounting delusion, he'd come to perceive a secret code of numerical signals concealed within his monotonous existence—the number of days he'd been imprisoned, the number of letters and packages he received, the amount of times he'd stimulated himself sexually in his cell. He believed that these ciphers, once cracked, would reveal the date of his release. At other times, he concluded that he was going mad.

Sade had developed one obsession that eclipsed all others: a need to put quill to paper. "It is impossible for me to turn my back on my muse," he wrote in a letter. "It sweeps me along, forces me to write despite myself and, no matter what people may do to try to stop me, there is no way they will ever succeed." He composed endless letters, essays, plays, and novellas, launching a literary career whose reputation would linger long after he was gone, resulting in a body of work so violent and obscene that its author would be variously described as "the freest spirit who ever lived," an "apostle of assassins," and "a professor emeritus of crime." Thanks to his writing, Sade would be so deeply associated with cruelty and perversion that his name would become synonymous the world over with deriving pleasure from pain.

But nothing would match the vulgarity of the effort he began this October evening. Experts would come to call the results "one of the most important novels ever written" and "the gospel of evil." The work was titled *120 Days of Sodom, or the School of Libertinage*.

The novel tells the story of four wealthy degenerates—a duke, bishop, judge, and financier—who engage in a four-month orgy, for which they gather thirty-two subordinates: their four young wives, eight virile men, four elderly female prostitutes, and, as the prime targets of their crimes, sixteen boys and girls, ages twelve to fifteen, selected from a group of several hundred children kidnapped from their homes. In the telling, the four nobles and their retinue retreat to a mountaintop château in the depths of central Europe, a heavily fortified citadel called Silling Castle. Thanks to walled-up exit gates, impassable chasms, and impenetrable snowdrifts, there is no hope of escape. As the duke, the most domineering of the four, tells several of the prisoners, "You are already dead to the world and it is only for our pleasures that you are breathing now."

In Silling Castle, amid sumptuously furnished apartments, sound-proof compartments, and torture chambers buried deep in the earth, the four noblemen subject their young victims to 120 days of escalating depravity. The first day involves one of the old prostitutes recounting a story tying together priests, pedophilia, and body fluids. It is the tamest episode in the novel. Day after day, as the perversions escalate, the descriptions become ever starker, with all semblance of narrative falling away. Eventually, all that remains is a blunt list of horrors: incest, bestiality, coprophilia, necrophilia, starvation, disemboweling, amputation, castration, cannibalism, and infanticide. By the end of the novel, the château is awash in blood and body parts.

The very act of reading the story from end to end seems to exact a physical toll. In 1957, the French philosopher Georges Bataille declared, "Nobody, unless he is totally deaf to it, can finish *120 Days of Sodom* without feeling sick." The Sade publisher Jean-Jacques Pauvert admitted that his and his colleagues' work on the novel "made us profoundly uneasy for several weeks, the atmosphere broken by outbursts of unexpected, truly crazed laughter." Austryn Wainhouse, the American author who first translated the book into English, in the 1960s, wrote, "Sometimes it happens that reading becomes something else, something excessive and grave; it sometimes happens that a book reads its readers through." In the 1980s, the Surrealist literary critic Annie Le Brun compared the task of analyzing the text to "being sucked into a seemingly limitless erotic quagmire." And most recently, the British professor Will McMorran began work on an updated English version, only to note on his blog that "translating felt like a struggle for agency—sometimes it felt like I was acting on the text, sometimes it felt like the text was acting on me." McMorran would come away from the experience believing that *120 Days of Sodom* was the worst thing ever written.

The novel's onslaught of violence and debauchery made its very existence a mystery. Why would someone have written something so appalling that it was all but unreadable? Why would anyone have bothered with such a herculean effort at a time when the results could never be published? And who exactly was the man behind it? Was Sade a revolutionary, working to expose the rotten core of the aristocracy to which he had been born? Was he a radical philosopher, aiming to lay bare humanity's most cruel and twisted desires? Or was he simply an unrepentant criminal, chronicling his own atrocities, committed or simply dreamed of?

There is also the puzzle of the manuscript itself. Sade worked on the text from seven to ten o'clock each evening, since its content was far too scandalous for him to be caught composing it during the day. When he reached the end of a sheet of paper, he pasted another below it, creating an ever-lengthening roll. After twenty-two nights, he flipped the document over and continued to write. The result, after thirty-seven days of work, was a scroll formed from thirty-three sheets of paper fastened end to end, measuring just over four inches wide and stretching nearly forty feet. Both sides were covered with words—157,000 in total—the text so tiny it was nearly illegible without a magnifying glass.

In the years to come, the scroll would embark on a centuries-spanning odyssey that would take it across Europe. It would endure revolutions and world wars; land in the epicenter of scientific, artistic, and literary upheavals; and become the focus of an audacious heist and international court battles. As it bore witness to hundreds of years of tumultuous history, the fragile text would move from one extraordinary owner to the next—and manage to outlast them all.

Finally, in 2014, one of the most powerful men in France would purchase *120 Days of Sodom* for €7 million. The price made it among the most valuable manuscripts in the world, comparable to original copies of the Gutenberg Bible, the *Canterbury Tales,* and Shakespeare's First Folio. The scroll settled into its new home just in time for a year-long national celebration of the bicentennial of Sade's death, the final step of a mass reevaluation of the once-banned writer that led some French intelligentsia to declare that Sade was France's version of Shakespeare.

But within a few months of its homecoming, the manuscript would be snatched away again, this time by French authorities. The ensuing scandal would bring to light festering vendettas at the highest levels of the French government, multimillion-euro manuscript sales derailed by sabotage, and shady financial deals in the shadow of Monaco's Monte Carlo Casino. The affair would involve feuding antiquarian booksellers and auction houses beset by theft, and it would culminate in allegations of a decade-long, continent-spanning, billion-euro con, the specifics of which, if true, would make it one of the biggest financial crimes in French history.

The fallout would rock the world's most celebrated book and manuscript market to its core, raising a question with far-reaching implications for everyone who cherishes the written word: As the age of handwriting comes to an end, what is the value of the original texts left behind?

Some would conclude that it wasn't a coincidence that the upheaval began just after the return of *120 Days of Sodom*. The development, after all, was only the latest example of how nearly everyone who had sought or possessed the scroll over the centuries had seen their fortunes dashed, their prize snatched away. To many observers, the evidence was clear: *120 Days of Sodom*, in all its ugliness and infamy, had to be cursed.

The manuscript's modern-day reputation would surely have pleased its author. When Sade began *120 Days of Sodom* that October evening in 1785, he knew exactly what he was writing. As he noted in the novel's introduction, "The time has come, friendly reader, for you to prepare your heart and mind for the most impure tale ever written since the world began."

CHAPTER ONE

Relic of Freedom

JULY 14, 1789

THE SUMMER SKY ABOVE PARIS HUNG HEAVY WITH CLOUDS AS A PLUME of smoke rose east of the city center. The scent of gunpowder wafted through the muggy afternoon air, while the crackle of musket fire and battle yells echoed through the cobblestoned streets.

Four years had passed since Sade had written *120 Days of Sodom*. Beyond the walls of the Bastille, the world carried on in one of the largest cities in Europe, a crowded metropolis of 810 streets and twenty-three thousand houses that more than a half million people called home. By many measures, by the late 1780s Paris had come a long way toward achieving Louis XIV's declaration a century before that the French capital should rival the glories of ancient Rome. The old walls that ringed the city had come down, replaced by victory arches and graceful boulevards. The bridges over the Seine had been cleared of the medieval houses that had clogged their thoroughfares and left them on the verge of collapse. Colossal new public squares like the Place Vendôme and the Place de la Concorde provided the capital with new civic spaces, while a long stretch of open fields and kitchen gardens on the city's western fringe had been transformed into a grand boulevard called the Champs-Élysées. In posh suburban neighborhoods like the Faubourg Saint-Honoré and the Faubourg Saint-Germain, palatial mansions had gone up to house the swelling number of wealthy bourgeois, boasting recently minted fortunes and new noble titles awarded or sold to them by the crown.

But in the cramped center of the city, conditions remained intolerable. The maze of dark, narrow streets festered with filth and crime, barely penetrated by the *réverbères,* or metal oil lamps, installed throughout the capital. On either side of muddy lanes, in shabby row houses of wood, limestone, and plaster that reached four, five, and six stories high, the families of Paris's servants, laborers, and artisans crammed into three-room apartments, many of which lacked a dedicated kitchen, much less a toilet or bath.

Recently city dwellers had seen the price of bread, the main staple of their meager diets, consume an ever-larger portion of their shrinking incomes as years of costly wars, poor harvests, and the timid leadership of the current monarch, King Louis XVI, led to financial crises. Desperate measures by the crown, such as a new wall around Paris to enforce tolls on goods entering the city and a trade agreement that allowed British goods to flood the market, plunged the nation further into debt. Many lost their jobs, and nearly two hundred thousand Parisians came to depend on religious assistance or government handouts. As the drought-ravaged fields around the city deteriorated, troops patrolled the markets to deter riots over bread. And as radical new philosophical movements championed egalitarianism and an upstart middle class jockeyed for political power, the people watched the nobility continue to revel in opulence.

The final provocation had arrived that summer. An attempt by the king to raise revenues and quell dissent by summoning a convention of the Estates General, an assembly of representatives from the country's various social classes, had collapsed amid political infighting over who should have the most say in the nation's affairs. Struggling to afford food and fearful of an aristocratic conspiracy to undermine the middle and lower classes, commoners had taken to the streets. Factories and wealthy monasteries were ransacked, and most of the new customhouses at the city's toll gates were burned to the ground. Around the city, army regiments moved into battle positions.

With rumors spreading of a crackdown, Parisians girded for battle. Theaters and cafés shuttered their doors, and the call went out to erect barricades, gather provisions, and, most important, marshal arms. Early that rainy morning, a mob of citizens raided the army barracks at the Invalides military hospital, coming away with thousands of rifles and several cannons, but very little ammunition. Hundreds of barrels of gunpowder, they learned, were being stored elsewhere: in the Bastille.

The gray stone hulk's eight medieval towers dominated the city skyline and loomed large in the public's imagination. This was where numerous state convicts had rotted away, including the legendary Man in the Iron Mask, a mysterious criminal forced to hide his face and who would eventually die in his cell before anyone could uncover his identity. Tales of prisoners emerging from the citadel fueled a cottage publishing industry, generating page-turners detailing filthy cells, dangerously inadequate rations, and corpse-filled subterranean dungeons. And now, according to reports, somewhere deep in its bowels lurked the infamous criminal the Marquis de Sade.

While Versailles, with its sparkling fountains and mirror-lined halls, epitomized the opulence of the monarchy, the Bastille had come to represent the iron rule that underpinned it all. So early that afternoon, when hundreds of cabinet makers, locksmiths, joiners, cobblers, hairdressers, tailors, wine merchants, and wig makers took up pikes, knives, and muskets and cried out, "To the Bastille!" they weren't simply looking to requisition gunpowder. They were mounting a direct attack on the tyranny of their king.

In the Bastille, the prison warden waited nervously, as he had for several days. He was well suited for his position, having been born in the fortress during his father's tenure as warden. But as a government functionary through and through, he knew little of the ways of battle. It didn't help that many of the hundred or so guards and soldiers under his command were elderly or infirm veterans. Over the past few nights, he had taken to peering from the ramparts, mistaking the trees below for agents plotting the citadel's demise.

Now the warden's worst fears were coming true. As the morning rain let up, soldiers standing guard atop the Bastille's towers watched a mob stream past the neighborhood's workshops and factories, their caps decorated with chestnut leaves as a symbol of their cause. Upon reaching the bounds of the citadel, an agile carriage maker clambered over a wall and cut the chains to the fortress's outermost drawbridge. As the gate crashed down, the revolutionaries charged into the courtyard, where they faced their remaining obstacles: a twenty-five-foot-deep dry moat and, beyond that, another raised drawbridge blocking entry into the Bastille.

The battle began in earnest. The revolutionaries traded musket fire with soldiers on the battlements above, ducking for cover behind nearby walls and the prison's kitchen buildings. For further protection, the assailants wheeled up several straw-filled carts from a nearby brewery and set them alight, the billowing smoke obscuring their movements. Soon the revolutionaries were reinforced by a contingent of royal soldiers who had defected to their side, along with several cannons. The artillery opened fire on the castle, but the eight-pound balls glanced off the fifteen-foot-thick stone walls. Shifting strategies, the revolutionaries turned their cannons on the wooden drawbridge. Inside, troops moved their own siege guns into position just beyond the entrance. Now both forces had heavy artillery trained on their foes, with just the wooden slats of the drawbridge between them.

Before either side could open fire, a drummer on the tower beat out the call for a cease-fire. Through a hole in the drawbridge came a note from the prison warden. He asked the revolutionaries to allow him and his men to evacuate with their lives. If the attackers refused, he would use the twenty thousand pounds of gunpowder in his possession to blow up the fortress and everything in the vicinity.

The revolutionaries refused to yield. Cries of "No capitulation" and "Lower the bridge" continued. Just as the crowd prepared to resume fire, the soldiers inside relented. With a clanking of chains, the drawbridge came down. The revolutionaries surged into the stronghold, disarming the troops. They found that only one of the castle's defenders had been killed in the fighting, while ninety-eight attackers lay dead outside.

The warden and his men were marched out of the fortress and toward city hall, where the provisional government would decide their fate. The fury of the revolutionaries and the jeering populace lining the streets could not be held in check, and along the way, several of the captives were killed. Then, at the foot of city hall, the crowd lost control. They attacked the warden and one of his officers, stabbing them with swords and bayonets, then unloading their pistols into the bodies. The mob erupted as two bloody pikes rose into the evening sky, crowned with the severed heads of the victims.

Later that night at Versailles, a long carriage journey away from the city, an adviser told Louis XVI that the Bastille had fallen. "Is it a revolt?" asked the king. "No, sire," he was told. "It is a revolution."

Back at the prison, the revolutionaries seized gunpowder stores and ransacked the archives. They threw open the cells but found only seven prisoners, none of whom appeared to be particularly mal-treated. Their number included four convicted forgers, a man sus-pected of a royal assassination plot decades earlier, an unremarkable aristocrat locked away for incest, and an insane Irishman who some-times believed he was Julius Caesar and at other times God. Sade was not among them.

While locating the marquis was not a major priority, his absence was baffling. Ascending the spiral staircase to the prison turret that had been mockingly titled the Liberty Tower, the revolutionaries paused at the sixth floor, where they came upon the double doors to the cell that had long held the Marquis de Sade.

They found a small room filled with a dizzying profusion of luxu-ries. Above all else, the chamber overflowed with paper: letters and notes and essays and numerous handwritten manuscripts in various stages of completion. But its occupant was nowhere to be found, though the cell had been so recently inhabited that dust hadn't yet settled over the furnishings. There were no indications of a planned departure or escape, since nothing in the cell had been organized or removed. Even the clothing remained undisturbed. It was as if Sade had vanished into thin air.

IN THE DAYS following the battle of the Bastille, an item was discov-ered wedged between the whitewashed stones of the wall of Sade's cell: a tiny, tightly wound scroll, covered in minuscule handwriting. The top edge bore its title: *120 Days of Sodom, or the School of Liberti-nage*. The manuscript had clearly been among the prisoner's most prized possessions, since it had been hidden well. It had escaped no-tice during the looting that broke out after the siege, when numerous papers were tossed into the prison yard and consumed by bonfires. Nor had it been uncovered during the Parisian government's more systematic collection of documents in the wake of the raid.

Instead, the manuscript came into the possession of a man named Arnoux. Perhaps he was one of the many curious onlookers who toured the prison after its downfall. As a member of one of the tour groups led through the fortress by certified guides with a flair for embellishment—old suits of armor became iron maidens and printing press equipment was transformed into torture machines— Arnoux could have noticed the scroll tucked away in Sade's room. Or maybe he discovered it while passing an evening in the tower chamber, since visitors could pay to spend a night in one of the cells, among the rats and chains.

Most likely, Arnoux was one of the laborers hired to tear down the Bastille. The effort began within hours of the prison's downfall and grew until an army of hundreds of masons, stonecutters, sawyers, carpenters, clerical workers, and supervisors were swarming the site. Along the ramparts, teams of hammer-wielding workers knocked stones into growing debris piles below, while others trundled blocks to worksites throughout the city, to be reused in the construction of new bridges and guardhouses. The seven-story walls quickly receded, the vaulted ceiling beams emerging into the open air by the end of the month. Entrepreneurs, meanwhile, set about memorializing the victory through commodification of the fortress itself. Paris workshops were soon converting remnants of the fortress into "Relics of Freedom": shackles adapted into inkwells, prison records woven into folding fans, building stones fashioned into scale models of the Bastille, complete with functional drawbridges and minuscule artillery.

If Arnoux was part of the Bastille demolition team, he probably uncovered the scroll while dismantling Sade's cell. The find was ready-made to be included among the Relics of Freedom. The manuscript's tale of noblemen using an impenetrable castle to engage in horrors fit perfectly into the myth of the Bastille and the idea that the aristocracy that controlled it had become too corrupt to stand. But when the document emerged from hiding in Sade's room, no one announced the discovery. However Arnoux came to acquire it, amid the chaos of the demolition, it was easy for him to pocket the scroll and smuggle it away.

Arnoux hailed from Saint-Maximin-la-Sainte-Baume, a small community tucked at the foot of a mountain ridge that rose like a gray stone bulwark from the hills of central Provence. The township was best known as the location of the thirteenth-century discovery of what was believed to be the tomb of Mary Magdalene. It's possible that Arnoux had left Saint-Maximin just prior to the launch of the French Revolution, fleeing the devastating harvests and political upheaval that had led to food riots, military reprisals, even a reported hanging of one of its rebellious residents earlier that year.

Whatever his reason for relocating to Paris or his occupation once he arrived, Arnoux did little to draw attention to himself. He wasn't among the 954 citizens awarded the prestigious title *vainqueurs de la Bastille* for storming and capturing the prison. His name would never appear in state records or court files, not even the municipal registers of Saint-Maximin. But he was without a doubt enterprising and shrewd. He knew that amid the revolutionary tumult, the engines of commerce would carry on. The document he discovered would fetch a handsome price, provided he could find someone who appreciated its worth.

At some point, months or years later, Arnoux returned home, the scroll tucked among his possessions. There, in the neighboring town of Brignoles, emerged an interested party: Charles-André de Beaumont. Born in 1762, Beaumont was the scion of a prosperous Provençal family that had earned a noble title the century before. During the early years of the French Revolution, he served as mayor of the nearby village of Cabasse, then fled the country as the radicalization of the new French Republic placed his life at risk. Once the turmoil abated, he returned, and in 1796 he settled in his hometown, where he used his wealth to acquire a nearby deconsecrated Cistercian abbey. He also made another purchase: the manuscript of *120 Days of Sodom,* offered by Arnoux or one of his progeny. He must have considered the scroll the perfect addition to his collection of rare books.

Ensconced in the Beaumont library, the scroll remained unknown to the wider world. Whatever Beaumont made of the manuscript, he kept his thoughts to himself. As the years stretched into decades, the world beyond convulsed with upheaval. The revolution gave way to the rise of Napoleon, followed by decades of mayhem and war as France swung back and forth between empire, monarchy, and republic. While much of Provence, with its rugged landscape and isolated communities, remained largely suspended in time, elsewhere in France railway tracks and telegraph lines crisscrossed the land, and great iron-hulled ships steamed out of the nation's ports for French colonial outposts in Africa, Indochina, and the South Pacific. In Paris, cramped medieval neighborhoods gave away to grand boulevards lined with modern white-limestone apartment blocks crowned with steep mansard roofs.

All the while, *120 Days of Sodom* remained in Beaumont's possession, until the day his literary collection passed to his son-in-law Raimond de Villeneuve. The scroll traveled east, passing fields of grapevines and dusty hilltop villages, until it reached the Château de Valbourgès, the Villeneuve family's longtime Provençal estate. There, it likely came to rest in the château library, placed among the family records and mementos Raimond was carefully accumulating, piecing together the remnants of a noble line that had been battered by the revolution. The efforts marked the last gasp of a dying breed. The French aristocracy, stripped of its lands, privileges, and way of life, was slipping into obsolescence.

Thus *120 Days of Sodom* might have remained moldering away in this remote Provençal villa, if not for its next owner: Raimond's son, Hélion de Villeneuve. Born in the nearby city of Draguignan in 1827, Hélion inherited the title of the Marquis de Villeneuve-Trans, among the oldest and most distinguished names in all of France. The lineage was related through marriage to many other noble houses, including the Sades. The last prerevolutionary Marquis de Trans, Louis Henri de Villeneuve, blamed the Sade family for the legal wrangling that deprived him of an inheritance left to him by the aunt of the Marquis de Sade.

From a young age, Hélion harbored a progressive streak, cheering on the 1848 revolution, which replaced the country's constitutional monarchy with a democratic republic, and, later, rallying behind the radical socialist Paris Commune, which briefly seized control of the capital in 1871. And like his father and grandfather before him, he lost himself in the formation of an exceptional library. The Marquis de Villeneuve-Trans, in other words, was a bibliophile.

THE TERM "BIBLIOPHILE," first used in early-nineteenth-century France, meant someone who loved books, especially someone who collected them. But bibliophiles didn't just adore books; they perceived of them differently than everyone else did. Most people viewed books as simply conduits of information—things to be read, referenced, or skimmed, then forgotten about or discarded. Bibliophiles, however, saw books as treasures in their own right.

In truth, many of the works they sought were objects of startling beauty. As books had become ever cheaper and easier to produce in the centuries since Johannes Gutenberg's 1440 invention of the movable-type printing press, the finest examples had adopted ever more embellishments as they became symbols of status and wealth. Leather bindings of calf- and goatskin were pressed, rubbed, polished, and dyed to minimize or accentuate their natural grain, then ornamented with hand-tooled motifs, gold-leaf borders, embedded portraits, and, in rare cases, fine gems. Spines developed ornate trimmings and multicolored cloth headbands. Pages were enveloped in marbled endpapers and watered-silk doublures, their edges beautified with vibrant pigments, debossed patterns, even hidden paintings that revealed themselves when one fanned out the sheets.

For most collectors, a book's contents also mattered a great deal. Along with its condition, a tome's appeal depended on its author's reputation, plus the renown and scarcity of its title. Personalized touches, such as revisions, notations, or inscriptions by the author, boosted a volume's worth. In general, first editions had the highest value, but most prized of all would be an original manuscript, written in the hand of the author. For bibliophiles, these one-of-a-kind documents were living remnants of the moment of literary creation, as precious and divine as fragments of the True Cross.

By the time Villeneuve-Trans emerged as a major book collector, in the second half of the nineteenth century, France was brimming with bibliophiles. The number of bookshops in the country skyrocketed, accompanied by soaring prices for rare tomes. Auction houses drew crowds with literary sales, and materials like publishing catalogs, book reviews, and bibliographies became commodities. Some collectors, if they had the funds, partnered with publishers and illustrators to produce limited-edition volumes of their own devising. Others preferred old books, gathering together at literary dinners where they fawned over first editions and illuminated medieval manuscripts.

Writer and book collector Octave Uzanne declared that France had become "the new Bibliopolis." And within this new Bibliopolis, the tastes of Villeneuve-Trans turned out to be especially particular. Perhaps, as in his politics, he chose to rebel against the genteel history of his noble lineage. Or maybe his inheritance of *120 Days of Sodom* inspired unusual inclinations. For whatever the reason, the marquis found himself gravitating toward bibliophilia's most shadowy realm: the world of erotic books.

At the time, as thousands of government-licensed prostitutes plied their trade in Paris's officially sanctioned *maisons de tolérance*—and thousands more prowled the streets illegally—an open-minded French nation was in the middle of an erotica boom. Publishers furtively churned out works like *Gamiani, or Two Nights of Excess, The Kama Sutra of Vatsyayana,* and *The Legend of the Sexes: Hysterical and Profane Poems by the Sire de Chambley,* many of which came ornamented with graphic illustrations. They reissued classic works of pornography like *L'Escole des Filles* and *Le Parnasse Satyrique,* which in previous centuries had led their authors to be burned in effigy and, in rare cases, sentenced to death. The materials were snatched up by prominent collectors like author Charles Nodier, playwright Guilbert de Pixérécourt, and architect Eugène Emmanuel Viollet-le-Duc, responsible for the restoration of the city walls of Carcassonne and the Notre-Dame cathedral. While some collectors relegated illicit works to special corners of their libraries, hidden behind curtains or in triple-locked cabinets, others made them the centerpiece of their collections. When French authorities attempted to crack down on the matter—seizing and destroying stockpiles of contraband tomes, arresting publishers and booksellers for violating good morals and jeopardizing the public interest—erotica dealers relocated to Brussels or Amsterdam and continued their trade.

Collectors in this world were akin to hunters on a safari, seeking out scarce and mythical species. Underground editions of known writings by the Marquis de Sade were particularly attractive quarries. As one observer noted in the 1830s, "He is in all bookstores, on certain mysterious and hidden shelves, which are readily discovered." These works were imbued with hints of danger. Some claimed Sade's notorious novel *Justine* had served as the black scripture of the French Revolution, and that Maximilien Robespierre, architect of the Reign of Terror, had turned to Sade's writing "whenever he found that his blood lust needed fortifying." One critic went further, reporting that a young boy had been overcome with seizures and aged twenty years after reading one of Sade's books.

A young Gustave Flaubert, soon to become one of France's most celebrated novelists, became obsessed with tracking down the marquis's works. He wrote to a colleague that figures like Sade "explain history for me, they are its complement, its apogee, its morality. . . . They're great men, immortals." The distinguished French poet Charles Baudelaire felt similarly, noting in his journal that "to understand evil, one must always return to de Sade, that is, to *natural man*."

Villeneuve-Trans likewise became enamored with Sade's work. He worked closely with Jules-Adolphe Chauvet, the era's most prominent French erotica illustrator, hiring the artist to produce original indecent drawings for many of his prized volumes. He financially supported Gay et Doucé, a prolific underground publishing house, as it hopscotched across Europe to evade the law. And employing the services of a craftsman from Marseille, he fashioned a suggestive wooden capsule with a phallic screw-on lid to hold *120 Days of Sodom*.

Villeneuve-Trans lived the decadent life of a bachelor, and his profligate tendencies cost him dearly. At the death of his father in 1857, he and his sister split what was left of the family's wealth. Less than a decade later, the struggling marquis sold his château for six hundred thousand francs, relinquishing a property that had been in his family since 1201. By 1878, his money troubles had grown so dire that he auctioned off part of his beloved library. Three years before that, he had resorted to what he likely considered an even more drastic measure: He'd decided to sell *120 Days of Sodom*.

He offered the manuscript to two major book dealers in Paris, but neither wanted to purchase it outright, preferring to take it on deposit while they searched for a buyer themselves. Uninterested in that arrangement, Villeneuve-Trans enlisted the help of the illustrator Chauvet, who knew his way around the underground book trade. To find a potential buyer, the two turned their attention to what had become one of the biggest erotica markets in Europe: Queen Victoria's England.

UNLIKE THEIR MORE freewheeling French counterparts, the guardians of Victorian mores considered sex extremely dangerous. Men who succumbed to the tug of their sexual appetites, it was believed, risked sapping the vitality needed to maintain the glorious British Empire. Women were counseled to present themselves as beacons of chastity, even within the bounds of marriage. The suggestive swells of the female body were buried within corsets, bustles, petticoats, and crinoline cages. Piano legs were swathed in drapery to conceal their evocative curves. Even the queen's English had to be purged of hazardous temptations. Breasts turned into "bosom," sexual organs into "unmentionables." References to pornographic writings were hidden behind euphemisms like "top-shelf" or "out-of-the-way" books, "curious" or "facetious" texts, and "literary kruptadia."

Despite such efforts, in nineteenth-century London, a flourishing sex industry had taken root. Amid the belching smokestacks, dung-smeared streets, and crowded tenements of the largest city in the world, disreputable cock-and-hen clubs, titillating *tableaux vivants,* unofficial street-woman promenades, same-sex bordellos, private drag shows, and flagellation salons all catered to a worldly clientele with time on their hands and money to burn. In the middle of it all, located at the confluence of Fleet Street, Kingsway, and the Strand and suffused with the aromas of the nearby sewage-clogged Thames, stood Holywell Street, a thin, crooked lane that doubled as the epi-center for the country's pornography trade. Along the cobblestoned street, leaded windows beckoned to passersby with displays of explicit prints and lewd placards. Inside, dimly lit shelves held pricey limited-edition volumes like *Adventures of a Bedstead, The Stories of a Dildoe,* and *Raped on a Railway,* not to mention reprints of the eighteenth-century British mainstay *Fanny Hill.* Stacked amid prostitute directories and guides to gay nightlife, tomes of pornographic verses offered up lewd stanzas and songs.

England's erotica market was the perfect place for Villeneuve-Trans and his colleague Chauvet to unload an unpublished manu-script of the Marquis de Sade's. Their first choice was the individual responsible for moving much of that pornography to England, a man named Frederick Hankey. Born to a well-placed English diplomat in 1821, Hankey had settled at a fairly young age in a posh neighbor-hood of Paris, where he spent his days tracking down choice selec-tions of erotica. To deliver these materials to his contacts on Holywell Street and elsewhere, he had friends transport his finds covertly across the Channel—smuggled in courier bags, tucked into embassy attaché cases, even strapped to the back and hidden under the clothes of an accommodating colleague.

But Hankey wasn't just a middleman. He was a collector and a connoisseur of debauchery. He cultivated a small but select collec-tion of obscene books, which he had clad in explicit designs evoking sex, death, and torture. He bragged that he once engaged the services of a prostitute while attending a public execution, likely to reenact an endeavor described in the eighteenth-century memoirs of Gia-como Casanova. He yearned to have selections from his library bound in human skin, preferably taken from a living young woman. After meeting him in 1862, Edmond and Jules de Goncourt, two brothers who had taken to chronicling the literary life of nineteenth-century Paris, concluded in their journal that they had encountered "a mad-man, a monster, one of those men teetering on the abyss."

With his elegant blond hair and blue eyes, Hankey was said to bear an uncanny resemblance to his favorite author: the Marquis de Sade. Knowing his reputation, Chauvet approached Hankey in 1875 and, under Villeneuve-Trans's direction, offered to sell him *120 Days of Sodom* for five thousand francs, nearly three times what the typical Paris laborer earned in a year.

After examining the manuscript, Hankey demurred. In his stammering diction, he told Chauvet he wasn't interested in a forty-foot-long scroll covered in what he considered illegible scribbles. If Chauvet went to the trouble of making a readable copy of the novel, he'd reconsider.

Perhaps, as Hankey insisted, he had no interest in an artifact as ugly and awkward as the scroll. He often seemed more concerned with the aesthetics of his collection—beautiful if obscene bindings, exquisitely crafted lewd illustrations—than the specifics of the texts. More likely, he simply didn't have the money for it. Around that time, he sold several valuable selections from his library, probably to stay afloat.

In the years that followed, Hankey continued to prowl the bookshops of Paris, even after gout left his gait so deformed that some whispered he had cloven feet. He would die choking in his apartment in 1882, not long after hearing a visitor at his door and crying out in delirium that it must be a bookseller delivering a rare Sade edition.

UNDAUNTED BY HANKEY's rejection, Chauvet continued to search for a buyer for the scroll. He turned to another English bibliophile, one with a more sterling reputation: Henry Spencer Ashbee. Equipped with a strong sense of propriety and a limitless capacity for hard work, Ashbee had assembled a distinguished literary collection and boasted all the trappings of a pillar of British society. Born to a gunpowder mill manager on the outskirts of London in 1834, he had vastly improved his prospects by marrying into a prosperous German mercantile clan and becoming senior partner of the family's London division. With a cigar, top hat, and full rounded beard accentuating his youthful good looks, he could often be spotted taking his children for rides in his carriage amid the chestnut trees of London's Bushy Park or attending meetings of prestigious organizations like London's Royal Geographical Society and Paris's Les Amis des Livres.

But while establishing a company office in France, Ashbee had fallen into a pursuit that would eclipse his other interests: erotic literature. In an out-of-the-way apartment not far from his stately home, he had used his wealth to amass what many believed to be the largest private collection of pornography in the world.

Aware of his interests, Chauvet wrote to Ashbee on April 22, 1875, hinting that he would soon be able to offer him "an unedited manuscript of the Marquis of Sade!," underlining his words for emphasis. A week later, he sent Ashbee additional details: "I saw the famous manuscript! It is undoubtedly authentic and unpublished! It is a scroll made up of sheets stuck together written on the front and back in characters of a delicacy to defy the best eyes, that can only be deciphered with a magnifying glass."

Ashbee, however, turned down the offer. At the time, his focus lay elsewhere. The Victorian obsession with collecting and classifying everything had inspired him to embark on an ambitious endeavor: a comprehensive bibliography of erotic literature. The effort demanded daunting detective work, since the underground nature of the business meant that nearly every detail of these works was difficult to ascertain. Books were published anonymously in limited numbers and quietly passed around. To evade the police, publishers omitted or falsified publication addresses and print dates, and often lied about publication numbers and printing histories in order to inflate their prices. And the vast majority of these illicit materials were surreptitiously enjoyed and then destroyed, before anyone could make note of their particulars.

Undeterred, Ashbee spent two years on the endeavor. In 1877, he privately published the results: a 544-page compendium of illicit books, pamphlets, anthologies, essays, magazines, prints, poems, dramatic pieces, and manuscripts under the name *Index Librorum Prohibitorum,* a title borrowed from the Catholic Church's official list of heretical books. Over the next decade, he would put out two expansions of his work: *Centuria Librorum Absconditorum* ("A Hundred Books Deserving to Be Hidden") and *Catena Librorum Tacendorum* ("A Chain of Books Which Should Not Be Spoken Of"). To protect his reputation, he published all three under the pseudonym "Pisanus

Fraxi," an anagram of the Latin words for "ash" (*fraxinus*) and "bee" (*apis*), one with none-too-subtle scatological undertones.

"My object," he noted in the introduction to his first tome, "is to collect into a common fold the stray sheep, to find a home for the pariahs of every nation." His bibliography would prove to be a milestone, capturing the dark underbelly of nineteenth-century Western literature, which would otherwise have been lost to time. Thanks to sources like Chauvet, whom Ashbee hired to design the frontispiece for his first tome, *120 Days of Sodom* was included among the pariahs. While he hadn't viewed the manuscript himself, Ashbee made note of "an unpublished work of the Marquis de Sade," describing its unusual appearance and convoluted provenance. This would prove to be the first published mention of the scroll, nearly one hundred years after it had been written.

Ashbee insisted that he aimed to examine, not revel in, the wickedness of his subject matter. He wrote that he hoped his efforts would no more excite his readers than "the naked body of a woman, extended on the dissecting table." But it was clear from the vivid descriptions of works like *120 Days of Sodom* that he wrote with the passion of a true enthusiast.

Yet Ashbee again declined to purchase the scroll when Chauvet once more mentioned the manuscript in 1877, a few months after the release of *Index Librorum Prohibitorum*. While Villeneuve-Trans had increased the manuscript's price to six thousand francs, the cost shouldn't have troubled a rich man like Ashbee. Perhaps the bibliophile had little interest in the marquis's particular blend of depravity. But there were indications that Ashbee might have had more in common with the scroll's author than he ever dared to admit.

In the late 1880s, a Dutch erotica publisher began printing, in extremely limited and well-crafted editions, an anonymous English memoir titled *My Secret Life*. The work would eventually stretch to eleven volumes, totaling forty-two hundred pages. The books, which allegedly came to be prized by occultist Aleister Crowley and silent film star Harold Lloyd, detailed the life of a Victorian gentleman who went by "Walter" and his sexual dalliances with prostitutes, courtesans, and hundreds of other women all over the world. Fictional or not, in its sexual tabulations and endless accounts of debauchery, the tale unknowingly echoed *120 Days of Sodom*. While the author of the mysterious *My Secret Life* would never be conclusively unmasked, the work very well could have come from Ashbee's hand. Both Ashbee and Walter enjoyed ample fortunes and traveled widely. Both employed similar word choices, sentence structures, and particular turns of phrase. And both cataloged sexuality with a fanatical zeal.

Whether or not Ashbee and Walter were one and the same, the two shared another resemblance: Both of them were so caught up in their erotic obsessions that they ended up unfulfilled and alone. In 1891, Ashbee's wife and two of his three children abandoned him. Ashbee had become increasingly conservative in his politics, and perhaps his outspoken attitudes had triggered rifts too great to heal. Or perhaps his family had discovered the true nature of his furtive pursuits. Whatever the reason, Ashbee would never again speak to most of his family. He died in 1900, leaving his mainstream literary treasures to the British Museum, but on one condition: The institution also had to preserve his erotica, which now included the greater part of Hankey's collection, since Ashbee had acquired many of the materials after his colleague's death. The museum agreed, and ended up confining the volumes in its "Private Case," a selection of illicit works kept under lock and key and accessible only by special permission. If either Ashbee or Hankey, the two greatest erotica collectors of their time, had obtained *120 Days of Sodom,* the scroll would have ended up there, locked away in the heart of one of the largest museums in the world.

But the manuscript never made it to England. Even as Ashbee's celebrated bibliography spread rumors across Europe of a long-lost Sade manuscript, the scroll remained unsold. When Villeneuve-Trans passed away in Provence in 1893 without marrying or producing an heir, the relic fell into the possession of his extended family or perhaps a local bookseller. There it resided, awaiting the right person to claim it.

CHAPTER TWO

Par Ballon Monté

SPRING 1985

FOR GÉRARD LHÉRITIER, IT ALL BEGAN WITH A LETTER.

This particular letter stood out as Lhéritier, dressed in a mid-1980s power suit, flipped through the binder of rare stamps and envelopes. Having come to Paris on a work trip for the investment company he owned, the thirty-six-year-old businessman had stepped into Roumet, among the most prominent of the stamp shops that surrounded Hôtel Drouot, an esteemed Paris auction house that handled many high-end philately sales. In the tiny, cramped storefront stocked floor to ceiling with boxes and albums of postage stamps, Lhéritier told Roumet's owner he was looking for some interesting pieces for his son Fabrice's collection. Lhéritier, just over five foot five, had a boy-ish look about him, with his dark curly hair just starting to thin around his temples, and he likely came off as a bit naïve. It was an attribute he often used to his advantage.

The proprietor handed him a file, the contents meaning little to Lhéritier as he glanced through the pages. But one letter struck him as unique. Its old, yellowed envelope bore a blue twenty-centime postage stamp, plus an unusual handwritten note: *"Par ballon monté"*—"Via manned balloon." Lhéritier's naturally arched eye-brows rose in surprise.

The owner paused from tweezing through piles of stamps and smiled. "This letter was written in 1870 during the siege of Paris, when the Prussian army surrounded the capital," he told Lhéritier. "It left the city by one of the balloons sent up during the siege. It was part of the first-ever airmail."

To Lhéritier, the story sounded incredible, like something out of a Jules Verne novel. It was the sort of escapade for which he had always yearned. Lhéritier had been born on June 21, 1948, in the village of Void, a quiet burg of a few hundred people located in a rural stretch of northeastern France. Here, a cluster of simple red-tile-roofed homes huddled along a bend in the placid Vidus River, surrounded on all sides by rolling farmland and forests of maple, larch, and beech. It was as far removed from modern city life as one could get, a place where automobiles remained a rare sight well into the 1960s.

The setting made for a pleasant but unexceptional childhood. Lhéritier's parents, industrious and strict, worked long hours; his mother had a job as a tax collector, while his father ran the plumbing business that had been in the family for three generations. The oldest of three brothers, Lhéritier tried his best to stay out of their way. The shaggy-haired boy spent his free time fishing for river trout with his grandfather, also a plumber, perched on the edge of the Vidus armed with bamboo poles and a matchbox filled with long-winged mayflies they'd pick from the leaves of nearby trees. With television an extravagance beyond their reach, Lhéritier and his brothers spent their evenings listening to the scratchy voices of Édith Piaf and Tino Rossi crooning through the static of the family radio.

Among his few escapes were his visits to his aunt in the city of Nice, in the French Riviera. He'd fidget excitedly as his train carriage clattered south through the increasingly arid landscape, the open windows of his compartment letting in pungent, cinder-flecked smoke every time the engine roared through a tunnel. As the train neared its destination, he would glimpse what he'd been waiting for: the endless blue of the Mediterranean. He loved every element of the resort town: the hot, sweet-smelling summer air; the miles of polished-pebble beaches; the bustling waterfront boardwalk of the Promenade des Anglais. From a young age, he swore to himself that he'd one day live in the city by the sea.

It wasn't clear how he'd get there. A headstrong but undistinguished student, especially in math, Lhéritier made a name for himself in school chiefly when he landed in trouble. He developed a strong sense of personal righteousness, refusing to back down in the face of affronts. As a young teenager at a religious boarding school, he organized a hunger strike to protest the institution's maggot-infested food. In response, the headmaster expelled him. Angry and ashamed, Lhéritier ran away, spending most of a night tromping through the woods surrounding the school. Eventually, one of the instructors found him and brought him back, so he could pack his bags to be sent home. Lhéritier soon rebounded from the disgrace, and he never thought very hard about what the incident could have taught him about the dangers of upsetting the status quo.

Eager to prove himself but unable to settle on a career, Lhéritier left school at seventeen and joined the French army. Military life tempered his impetuous tendencies. He was sent to West Germany, becoming part of the French military forces stationed there as the divided nation became a simmering front line of the Cold War. At times he was assigned to West Berlin, catching live symphony performances when he wasn't patrolling the concrete barriers and barbed-wire fences cutting off East Berlin. In 1970, the twenty-two-year-old soldier married his high school sweetheart, a green-eyed brunette named Annie. Together they would soon have two children, a boy named Fabrice and a girl named Valérie.

The following year, Lhéritier's father, René, died in a car accident. Lhéritier would never talk much about how it felt to lose the man whom he had watched work tirelessly for little pay, who'd drilled the moral precepts of the day into him with severe authority. If anything, the loss hammered home a decision the young man had already made: He was going to have to find a way to succeed on his own. The continuation of the family's ninety-year-old business would be left to one of his brothers. Whatever he decided to do with his life, Lhéritier didn't want to be a plumber.

Soon, a more promising option began to take shape. While stationed in Tübingen, a city in southern Germany, Lhéritier discovered a French company that offered far better insurance rates than the local option utilized by his fellow soldiers. He spread the word around his regiment, and in exchange he received a cut of the profits from the grateful insurance dealer. Within a few months, he was making more in commissions than he earned from his soldier's salary. Despite having no formal training, he realized he had a knack for uncovering untapped markets.

In 1974, he left the army and began working for a major French insurance company. Six years later, he opened his own investment company in the city of Strasbourg, in northeastern France. A side venture he launched in precious gemstone investments never took off, and during the diamond market collapse of the early 1980s, the operation went bankrupt in such a spectacular fashion that for several years he was legally barred from running other similar businesses. But in the meantime, his brokerage had done well enough that in 1984 he relocated his insurance operation to Nice. He had made it to the city by the sea, as he'd always dreamed. But he yearned to earn enough money so that his family would never lack anything, to break into the realm of France's elite, where the rich and powerful still operated like the aristocracy of centuries past. At the stamp shop, he felt the stirrings of that splendor and adventure in this mysterious little letter. Here was a piece of history the world had forgotten. He needed to know more.

IN SEPTEMBER 1870, the city of Paris was trapped. The month before, Emperor Napoleon III, nephew of Napoleon Bonaparte, had marched his armies eastward to quell the ambitions of the increasingly powerful Kingdom of Prussia, launching the Franco-Prussian War. But efficient Prussian forces, under the direction of King Wilhelm I and Chancellor Otto von Bismarck, had quickly routed the French military and captured the disgraced Napoleon, then closed in on the French capital.

As refugees from the countryside streamed into the city, the Prussian army encircled Paris, cutting rail lines, severing telegraph wires, bombing bridges, and blocking all escape. Soon residents resorted to eating carriage horses, ducks from local parks, even family pets. Restaurants advertised terrines and stews made from elephants and kangaroos culled from the city zoo. The siege, meanwhile, prevented any form of communication from entering or leaving the city. Within the walls of Paris, two and a half million people were cut off from the world.

That is, until Félix Nadar, an enterprising local photographer, proposed a solution: The city could use hot-air balloons, which had hitherto been used mostly for public spectacles or science experiments, to transport messages out of the city. Nadar offered up his own balloon, the *Neptune,* as the first recruit of what he extravagantly titled the No. 1 Compagnie des Aérostatiers—the Number One Company of Balloonists.

Lhéritier unearthed this story bit by bit from history books and archives, revealing an affair he had never learned about in school. With the regional railways shut down because of the siege, two major Parisian train stations, the Gare d'Orléans and the Gare du Nord, were transformed into balloon factories, where dressmakers varnished and stitched together long strips of calico, which were then strung up and inflated by sailors perched in the rafters. The resulting balloons, loaded with letters and christened with patriotic names like *La Liberté, L'Égalité,* and *La Délivrance,* launched from the city beginning in late September 1870. Powered by coal gas, they sailed high above the Prussian lines, out of range of enemy musket fire, and dropped provocative leaflets signed, "Compliments to Kaiser Wilhelm and Monsieur von Bismarck." Despite traveling by night, braving freezing high-altitude temperatures, and having little control over the direction of their craft, the aeronauts landed safely beyond the Prussians' reach nearly every time.

While there was no way to accurately navigate the balloons back into the city, the aeronauts and their colleagues devised other ways of conveying messages to Paris. Soon carrier pigeons were being released toward the city, transporting collodion microfilms tucked among their tail feathers, with each film negative containing microscopic images of thousands of letters. French forces outside the city also experimented with placing letters in specially designed hollow zinc spheres and dropping them in the Seine upriver from Paris, with the hope that they would roll along the riverbed and be caught in submerged river nets placed beyond the blockade. While none of the spheres ever made it to Paris, in the years to come people would find the balls, still filled with their wartime missives, buried in the Seine.

In early 1871, the Prussians lost their patience and opened up their heavy artillery, shelling the capital and shattering its residents' already weakened morale. On January 28, the city capitulated. During the previous four months, Parisians had sent sixty-seven hot-air balloons over the blockade. Of these, only five fell into enemy hands and three were lost at sea. In total, the aeronauts conveyed out 102 passengers (including French leader Léon Gambetta), five dogs, four hundred pigeons, several boxes of dynamite, thousands of political leaflets, and roughly twelve tons of mail—millions of letters in total. The effort would go down in history as one of the most audacious feats ever accomplished by hot-air balloon.

Lhéritier threw himself into accumulating as many of the associated letters and other materials as he could. He authored four reference books on the subject, mapping the landing sites of the sixty-seven balloons all over France and beyond, compiling the names of every person who took part in the airlift, and cataloging the value of the various letters that penetrated the blockade. He uncovered the correspondence of Alfred Roseleur, a Parisian who fashioned his own version of balloon mail during the siege to communicate with his wife, who had been outside the city when the Prussians closed in. Roseleur had launched a series of letters tied to children's balloons from his balcony. Incredibly, according to Lhéritier's research, many of the missives succeeded in reaching her.

Lhéritier's obsession inspired a creative streak. He launched a jewelry line featuring golden baubles designed to resemble the submersible zinc spheres, each with a hidden compartment that could hold a secret message. And in 1995, he wrote a historical novel about the siege, *Les Ballons de la Liberté*. The account was pure fiction, but in the book, he used a real-life quote from Georges Clemenceau, the French politician who led France to victory during World War I: "In war as in peace, the last word belongs to those who never surrender."

◄ ◄ ◄

LHÉRITIER WAS HOOKED by the world of letter and manuscript collecting. In these documents' unique creases and stains, revisions and deletions, collectors saw a direct connection to the writers, artists, composers, entertainers, scientists, philosophers, explorers, inventors, leaders, rebels, and others who shaped history.

The collection of such texts had existed nearly as long as people had been setting down words. Ancient Sumerians didn't just create one of the world's first written forms of communication when they developed cuneiform writing more than five thousand years ago, in what is now southern Iraq. They also took the time to preserve their clay writing tablets for posterity. It's why modern-day scholars have access to hundreds of thousands of Sumerian texts, including a forty-one-hundred-year-old tablet adorned with the name of a scribe, Gar Ama, on its back—the earliest known writing signed by its author.

In ancient Rome, scholars prided themselves on their letter collections. Naturalist and author Pliny the Elder, an avid collector, complained that Julius Caesar's dispatches had become frustratingly scarce a century after the emperor's demise. The Great Library of Alexandria came into being in part because of the obsessive collecting habits of the Ptolemaic dynasty, which ruled Egypt at the time. Pharaoh Ptolemy II Philadelphus allegedly refused to supply wheat to famine-ravaged Athens until the city lent him the writings of its great thinkers. He then kept the materials for his library, sending forgeries back to Greece. Similarly, along with founding Baghdad in the eighth century to serve as the capital of his Islamic empire, Caliph Abu Ja'far al-Mansur had emissaries gather rare books and poetry collections for his private library, which he housed in a structure he called the House of Wisdom. The effort turned the Middle East into an epicenter of culture and learning, launching the Islamic Golden Age.

After the fall of the Roman Empire and centuries of European cultural decline, the fourteenth-century poet Petrarch reignited interest in historic manuscripts by scouring monasteries across Europe for written treasures and calling on religious orders to establish libraries. While Petrarch insisted that divine mercy had cleansed him of nearly every earthly craving, he admitted that his need to amass such texts was the "one insatiable desire which I so far have been quite unable to control." By the sixteenth century, students and aristocrats in Germany and elsewhere had taken to accumulating notable quotations, written mementos, and salutations from prominent figures; these would be inscribed in a small notebook called an *album amicorum,* or "book of friends," as a way of accruing prestige.

In nineteenth-century Europe, amassing letters and manuscripts developed into a full-fledged mania. In Victorian England, documents attributed to Shakespeare exchanged hands for millions in today's dollars, and an acquaintance of John Keats's cut one of the poet's sonnets into pieces so he could sell each fragment for maximum value. Celebrities of the day became so inundated with collectors' requests for writing samples that some called on Parliament to "take measures for suppressing the troublesome and increasing sect." The writer John Ruskin issued a public notice declaring, "Mr. Ruskin never gives autographs but to his friends, and of late has scarcely, even for them, consented to add in any way to his usual task of daily penmanship."

France became an epicenter of the letter trade. In 1821, the École Nationale des Chartes was founded in Paris, becoming the first school devoted to the study of archives and manuscripts. A year later, Mathieu-Guillaume-Thérèse Villenave, a Parisian lawyer and journalist who'd narrowly avoided the guillotine during the Reign of Terror, put up for sale 550 historic documents that he had saved from destruction during the revolution—the first-ever auction devoted to letters and manuscripts. Not long after, Maison Charavay opened for business in Paris; it was one of the world's first shops dedicated to selling manuscripts. Over the next four decades, nearly one hundred thousand historical documents came up for sale at French auction houses. As Étienne Charavay, son of the founder of Maison Charavay, noted in 1887, "Paris is the center where all the amateurs of the world come to shine. This is where the authenticity, value, and price of manuscripts are determined."

As the pursuit of letters and manuscripts evolved into a small but professional industry, collectors developed different interests. Some focused on the works of specific individuals, such as obtaining materials penned by Leo Tolstoy or the writings of Simón Bolívar. Others assembled their works by subject matter, accruing original texts related to the Canadian fur trade or German Expressionism. Still others aimed to complete a predetermined set of documents, such as letters authored by every Nobel Prize recipient or each First Lady of the United States.

They all came to be known as autograph collectors, but they had little in common with those who sought out celebrity signatures. "They think that I carry about with me a gilt-bound volume and ask luckless magnates to write their names in it," grumbled Adrian Hoffman Joline in his 1902 autobiography *Meditations of an Autograph Collector*. "It jars me to reflect that, in the minds of the multitude, the school-girl with her scrap-book and the fiend with his awful album are all of apiece with *me*!"

For those who traded in historical texts, what counted was the content and context of each document: not just who wrote it but the date it was written, to whom it was directed, and the subject matter at hand. A document authored by John Hancock from the seminal year of 1776 would be considered superior to a similar record from 1769. A missive by Charlotte Brontë would be more precious if it happened to be addressed to her sister Emily. A single signature of Ernest Hemingway's scribbled on a bullfight program might fetch a decent price on the open market, but one of his manuscripts would set off a bidding war. And while locating any Abraham Lincoln dispatch would be considered a remarkable find, unearthing one that touched on slavery could be a career-making discovery.

The type of document also mattered a great deal. Most experts considered isolated signatures the least interesting sort of material, followed by short letters and signed typewritten missives. More precious were lengthy handwritten dispatches, then collections of correspondences, and, after that, detailed notebooks and journals. At the top of the pecking order, most valuable of all, stood original manuscripts of seminal works.

Historical document collectors and dealers liked to boast about the very real value of their acquisitions. In 1988, *Les Autographes,* an influential French book on the pursuit, noted, "It is certain that, for important pieces, the collection of autographs constitutes an excellent investment value." But most authorities insisted that any financial gain collectors achieved should be considered an added bonus; the vast majority frowned on the idea of acquiring letters and manuscripts primarily for profit. The pursuit was too personal, the worth of each text too subjective, to reduce the activity to a series of commercial transactions. As Mary Benjamin, a leading U.S. expert and one of the few women in the field, warned in the 1978 guide *Autographs and Manuscripts: A Collector's Manual,* "Though the records show that prices have zigzagged up and down over the years, with the high always higher than the last high and the low always higher than the last low, the fact remains that though a collector may profit from what he sells, he may also suffer a considerable loss. He who buys primarily to invest and who is not familiar with price fluctuations may find himself obliged to sell unexpectedly, sooner than he had planned." In short: The pursuit of high-end letters and manuscripts was best left to those who had made their fortunes elsewhere.

Lhéritier disagreed. He believed that the insular discipline had masked these historical texts' true worth, allowing the majority of documents to be vastly undervalued compared to items like rare coins or gems. This state of affairs seemed particularly true in his home country. Thanks to the small cadre of dealers who had long controlled the local market and the fact that French institutions weren't in the habit of buying up materials the way university libraries were in the United Kingdom or the United States, in France at the time, letters and manuscripts appeared to be a hidden treasure.

He felt the first inkling of his discovery that day in the Roumet stamp shop, as he examined the letter delivered by balloon. Through his research, he would come to price the missive at hundreds if not thousands of dollars. But the proprietor offered it to him that day for 150 francs—less than $20. As he would later write, "I felt like a gold digger who discovers a vein."

LHÉRITIER STARTED SMALL. The year after he found his first balloon-mail letter, he set up shop in Nice in a two-room office near the city center. On a brass plaque by the entrance, he engraved his company's name: Valeur Philatélique. The firm offered historical letters and stamps not simply as collectors' items but as financial products, marketing the materials as investment vehicles that would quickly generate a profit. Investing in postage stamps wasn't particularly unique; in the 1970s, philatelic investment firms flourished as a surge in stamp prices briefly outstripped inflation rates and yields from stocks and bonds. Adding old letters to the mix was more innovative. By allowing customers to purchase missives from the siege of Paris delivered by hot-air balloons and other means, Lhéritier was offering people a chance to capitalize on what he saw as the country's undervalued cache of historical documents.

Lhéritier's knack for finding novel business opportunities, his interest in historical discoveries, and his relentless ambition all culminated in his new enterprise. In 1986, however, he suffered a major blow: Annie, his wife of seventeen years, fell in love with someone else, leading their marriage to collapse. Devastated, Lhéritier struggled to maintain his confident demeanor as he consoled his children. To distract himself from the pain, he threw himself into his work.

His labors paid off. Customers were interested in his balloon-mail letters and, thanks to his efforts, the value of their purchases grew with mounting demand. Farther down the coast in Cannes, Lhéritier opened a second outpost of his operation. His historical detective work earned laudatory coverage from local newspapers and news broadcasts, major French philatelic magazines championed his materials as promising investments, and he collected awards from the Nice Chamber of Commerce and the Spellman Museum of Stamps and Postal History, in the United States. With money no longer a concern, he rented a luxury sailboat and toured the Mediterranean with his children, recalling the afternoons he spent fishing with his grandfather as he reeled in giant bluefin tuna.

In the fall of 1995, signs of trouble emerged. Local media outlets broke the news that the authorities were closing in on a major financial scam originating from the Principality of Monaco, just east of Nice. The tiny, densely populated city-state huddled on less than a square mile of rocky Mediterranean coast—the second-smallest sovereign state in the world, after Vatican City—was best known for its luxurious Monte Carlo Casino. But law enforcement had long rec-ognized the country as a hotbed of shady financial deals, courtesy of the low tax rates and permissive banking policies instituted by the house of Grimaldi, the princely house that had ruled there since 1297.

The newest scandal to arise from the city-state involved, of all things, philately. According to reports, the Monégasque govern-ment had issued unusually large numbers of commemorative stamps. While the ceremonial stamps couldn't be used for postage, the sheets were being marketed as valuable commodities and sold to consumers at a hefty markup through a series of intermediaries. All in all, more than twelve hundred buyers had allegedly been swindled out of €60 million. As one website that covered philatelic crimes put it, it was "the biggest scandal in the stamp world, ever." While he wasn't men-tioned by name, rumors swirled that authorities had come to believe that the person responsible for selling the stamps to unsuspecting marks was Lhéritier.

Desperate to stem the damage, Lhéritier arranged an informal meeting with the investigating judge assigned to the case, a hotshot magistrate named Jean-Pierre Murciano. Since Lhéritier hadn't yet been charged with any crimes, he hoped the judge could help quash speculation that he had done anything wrong. In December 1995, Murciano welcomed Lhéritier into his office in Grasse, the judicial seat of the region. But before Lhéritier could plead his case, Murci-ano, a balding man with an intense look in his eyes, pointed his finger at him and called him a crook. In France, investigating judges ran major criminal investigations the way prosecutors did in the United States, and Murciano had made a name for himself nabbing safecrack-ers, con artists, and jewel thieves. Now the magistrate had decided to make Lhéritier his next target.

"The Monaco stamps you market are worthless," he told Lhéri-tier. "When the police come looking for you and all the press starts talking about you, you'll see how your customers will react."

Three months later, on March 18, 1996, Lhéritier stood in the early-morning quiet of his kitchen in his villa above Nice and pon-dered the judge's threats. He still hadn't been charged with anything, but the controversy was worrying his clients. To calm his nerves,

Lhéritier sipped his coffee and prepared to let the chickens he kept on his property out of their henhouse. That's when he looked out his window and spotted a convoy of police vehicles descending a ridge toward his home, their lights flashing in the muggy air.

The officers searched his home, then took him into custody. After an interrogation that stretched into the following day, Murciano placed him under investigation for fraud and other crimes. As Lhéritier was led into the sprawling prison complex in Grasse, he couldn't avoid thinking of the 1960s French hit "Le Pénitencier," an adaptation of the American folk song "The House of the Rising Sun": "The penitentiary's doors / Soon will close again / And that's where I'll end my life."

But he was far from defeated. Sitting in the solitude of his cell, prisoner No. 5546 fortified himself by comparing his situation to that of others who had been unfairly locked away: prisoners of war, the Man in the Iron Mask, the Count of Monte Cristo. He didn't include the Marquis de Sade. Leaning over his prison-cell desk, he began arguing his innocence, filling page after notebook page with details of what he saw as a years-long conspiracy that had been building against him. He had never been one to back down from a fight, and he believed he had worked too hard to let interlopers ruin his plans. Through his head ran the words of Georges Clemenceau, the World War I hero he had quoted in *Les Ballons de la Liberté*. He would never surrender. He would have the last word.

Lhéritier's crusade for redemption began once the Aix-en-Provence appeals court reversed one of Murciano's rulings, releasing him after two weeks behind bars. Lhéritier encouraged his business clients to advocate for their investments by refuting critical news reports and lobbying for answers in the legal proceedings. He filed defamation suits against media outlets he felt had unfairly attacked him. When Lhéritier learned that the head of France's stamp dealers' association had questioned his business practices to the media and the police, he fired off an eighteen-page letter to the organization's president suggesting that he might have fallen on his head and gone mad. He sent copies to stamp dealers all over France.

Despite his best efforts, Lhéritier's financial operations couldn't survive the turmoil. His businesses succumbed to bankruptcy, his shops in Nice and Cannes shuttered and liquidated. With his social clout extinguished, he lost his memberships in social clubs and philatelic associations. But finally, in 2000, Lhéritier scored a coup. Six years earlier, the case against him had been set in motion when a local woman had filed a complaint against his business, saying she had been fooled into buying stamps that weren't valuable. Now, through an intermediary, Lhéritier convinced the woman to withdraw her grievance, saying she had been manipulated into criticizing the company.

The following year, the Aix-en-Provence appeals court removed Judge Murciano from the case, noting Murciano's delay in responding to the withdrawn complaint and other matters. Perhaps the magistrate had been too quick to seize on the Monaco stamp affair as his next big case, and now it was all coming apart. In 2002, Marciano's replacement dismissed the main fraud allegations, and three years later, the criminal court in Nice cleared Lhéritier of all remaining charges.

Lhéritier wasn't satisfied. Despite the fact that this was his second business venture to end in shambles, and despite the financial suffering unleashed on his former clients, Lhéritier refused to concede that he had ever done anything wrong. If he was guilty of anything, it was of being too gullible, of trusting people who would end up stabbing him in the back.

He built on the account he had started writing in jail and in 2006 published *Intime Corruption,* a memoir of his ordeal. According to the three-hundred-page book, the ordeal began when a former business colleague made off with some of his company's stamp sheets and customers' money. When Lhéritier sounded the alarm, the aggrieved associate joined forces with Judge Murciano and a police detective to take him down. "It is a demonic assembly involving a crook . . . a corrupt police officer, [and] a vain and media-hungry magistrate," he wrote. Lhéritier went so far as to launch a literary award, the Count of Monte-Cristo Prize, to recognize other French books detailing similar miscarriages of justice.

The Monaco stamp affair, which had triggered headlines across France and beyond, began to fade from public memory. It didn't matter that in response to a legal petition, in 2007 an appeals court would overturn part of the earlier rulings and find Lhéritier guilty of violating consumer law for refusing to reimburse two of his clients, slapping him with a €3,000 fine and a suspended eight-month prison sentence. By that point, Lhéritier had already moved on, with a far more ambitious plan.

CHAPTER THREE

In the Bosom of Luxury and Plenty

OCTOBER 19, 1763

JEANNE TESTARD HAMMERED ON THE DOOR OF PARIS POLICE INSPECTOR Louis Marais's home, shattering the early-morning quiet. She was desperate to report the events of the previous night. As the head of the Département des Femmes Galantes, the police unit that tracked the murky world of the prerevolutionary Parisian sex market, Marais often heard from women like Testard, a fan maker who occasionally worked as a prostitute.

Mid-eighteenth-century Paris, still two and a half decades away from the fall of the Bastille, had become the vice capital of the continent. The century before, to keep the nobles in line, Louis XIV had moved the royal court to Versailles and instituted a byzantine system of ranks and responsibilities his subjects had to follow if they hoped to keep the so-called Sun King's favor. Since then, the country's monarchy and class structure had become ever more centralized and absolute. Bristling under the tedium of the royal court, the upper classes had embraced libertinage—the pursuit of physical pleasure—with a mania verging on religious fervor. Erotic novels evaded royal censors and became underground bestsellers. The procurement of a *petite maison,* or "little house," an apartment where noblemen could engage in extramarital liaisons, had shifted from a surreptitious endeavor to an important public fashion statement. And several decades before, members of all-male sodomy fraternities engaged in their amorous pursuits in the halls of Versailles and the gardens of the Tuileries Palace, just below the window of a young king Louis XV.

Marais had been assigned to keep watch over this world in 1757, after a convict killed the vice squad's founder while being escorted to prison. To keep the activities of the city's thriving sex market within bounds, he cultivated an extensive web of sources among Paris's prostitutes, madams, and their patrons. Aloof and arrogant, Marais wasn't just in charge of regulating these businesses; he was also a patron, and he angered brothel madams by declining to pay for visits and refusing to disguise himself while doing so, since his presence proved bad for business. He compiled thousands of records on *dames entretenues,* or kept women, and their customers, allowing law enforcement to track the intimate personal and financial dealings of France's rich and powerful. Rumors abounded that Marais's reports were also highly prized by King Louis XV and his mistress, who would peruse the accounts to spice up their sex life.

During his tenure, Marais heard all sorts of disturbing stories about the city's *demimonde,* or underworld. But Testard's tale stood out. According to her, the previous night a young nobleman had offered her two gold coins to accompany him to his *petite maison* in the southern part of the city. Once he locked her inside, the man asked if she believed in God. When she replied that she did, he declared he would prove her wrong. He shouted profanities, masturbated over religious effigies, demanded that she trample on a cross, and placed Communion wafers inside her and then had sex with her. All the while he yelled, "If thou art God, avenge thyself!" Taking her into a room filled with flagellation instruments and religious decorations, he had her whip him with a cat-o'-nine-tails that had been heated until its metal strands glowed red. Gesturing to a set of pistols lying nearby and threatening to kill her, he demanded that she whip herself and defecate on a Christ statue, both of which she refused to do.

The next morning, the man made her promise to engage in similar activities the following Sunday, after they attended church together. He also forced her to sign an oath promising she'd never reveal what had transpired. Instead, as soon as he released her, Testard went to the police. Marais and his colleagues soon matched her description of her abuser with the culprit, a young man who had never been in major trouble with the law: Donatien Alphonse François, a twenty-three-year-old aristocrat who went by the name the Marquis de Sade.

Marais knew the family name. As one of the oldest and most distinguished Provençal clans, the house of Sade traced its ancestry back to at least the tenth century, although family legend went further, insisting that the line descended directly from one of the three Magi. The Sades had made their fortune in textiles and had long been associated with the *noblesse d'épée,* or "nobles of the sword," the oldest and most esteemed class of French nobility. In 1177, Louis de Sade, then provost of the Provençal city of Avignon, had financed the construction of the first iteration of the Pont Saint-Bénézet, the city's iconic footbridge over the Rhône River. More famously, the beauty of another family member, Laura de Sade, had allegedly motivated the fourteenth-century Renaissance poet Petrarch to renounce his priesthood and inspired many of his subsequent love poems. The Sade line had gone on to boast many other achievements, its family tree dotted with magistrates, captains, papal chamberlains, governors, knights of Malta, and other dignitaries.

Marais was aware that the Sade title had lost some of its luster, courtesy of its current patriarch, Jean-Baptiste Joseph François, the Comte de Sade and father of the marquis. Jean-Baptiste, as attractive and charming as he was crafty and ambitious, had been the first of his lineage to depart Provence, where the family owned several châteaus, and try his hand at the royal court in Paris. He did well, attaching himself to the house of Condé, a powerful household with direct ties to the royal family, and serving the king on ambassadorial assignments in Holland, Russia, England, and the Electorate of Cologne.

But the Comte de Sade had largely exhausted his family's fortune to keep up appearances and satisfy his luxurious tastes. He was also an unabashed libertine. He wrote poems celebrating his love of sodomy, noting, "Like a resident of Sodom, I play the woman with a man." He confessed in a letter to one of his female acquaintances how much he detested the idea of sexual fidelity: "I have seen faithful lovers on occasion: their sadness, their gloominess, is enough to make one tremble." His behavior attracted attention. When he was twenty-two, the Paris vice squad arrested him for soliciting a young male prostitute in the Tuileries Garden who turned out be a *mouche,* or "fly," a police informer.

This run-in with the law, swept under the rug thanks to Jean-Baptiste's connections, did little to temper the comte's ways. Instead, his dissolute interests went on to shape his marriage. In 1733, at age thirty-one, he became infatuated with Caroline Charlotte of Hesse-Rheinfeld, the young wife of the Prince de Condé, for whom he worked as a trusted adviser. Since the prince kept his spouse under careful watch, the comte came up with a plan. He decided to offer to marry Marie Éléonore de Maillé de Carman, an aristocratic but financially limited relative of the Prince de Condé and the princess's lady-in-waiting. Once firmly established as a member of the Condés' household, he could pursue the true object of his affection.

Jean-Baptiste and Marie Éléonore married on November 13, 1733. That night, the nervous twenty-one-year-old bride begged the Princess de Condé to remain with them in their bedchamber. The comte welcomed the added company. "The presence of the princess heightened my rapture and made me keener and more eager than ever not to be without her," he would later write. Sure enough, thanks to his intimate position in the palace, the comte soon had access to the princess's private quarters, which he used to seduce her.

Now, according to the account of the woman who had appeared at Inspector Marais's door, it seemed that Jean-Baptiste's only son, the Marquis de Sade, was following in his father's footsteps, but with a far more troubling bent. The crimes described by Testard weren't the result of an impulsive fit of debauchery; this was a carefully choreographed attack—and among the victims were the values and customs the nation held dear. Several days after the incident, the police inspector arrested the marquis and locked him in the dungeon of Vincennes. Because of the crime's extreme nature and the perpetrator's noble birth, the order had come from the king.

AS HE'D BEEN led into the prison, with its sixteen-foot-thick walls, iron-reinforced doors, and steep spiral staircases, the Marquis de Sade had been stripped of everything: his lace-lined garments, his powdered and curled wig, his jewelry and pocket watch. The young courtier usually spent his evenings amid the bustle of high-end Paris: its gambling halls, upmarket brothels, and grand venues like the Palais Garnier opera house and the Comédie-Française theater, where the social chatter in the audience often drowned out the drama onstage. But here in his dismal chamber, high up in a castle keep that towered over the countryside, his only company was a meager sleeping pallet, a couple of straw-stuffed chairs, a greasy table, and a chipped chamber pot. He was accustomed to sumptuous foods like pâtés, brochettes, and biscuits smeared with rich Breton butter. Now he had to make do with cold, desiccated mutton and beef accompanied by unseasoned vegetables and served just twice a day.

The prisoner stood five feet, six inches tall, with a healthy figure and a full, handsome face with such a striking combination of delicate features—brilliant blue eyes, curly blond hair framing a prominent forehead, an aquiline beak of a nose, a dainty, disdainful smile—that women on the street were known to stop and stare. The attraction wasn't simply sexual. Ever since Sade was a young boy, those of the opposite sex had felt an innate need to care for him, to mother him. It was as if they could sense his inherent sensitivity, his loneliness, the extreme neediness of a soul that had never known anything but utter indulgence.

Sade had come into the world on June 2, 1740, in one of the largest and most opulent palaces in all of Paris: the Hôtel de Condé. The vast estate, with its elegant white-limestone buildings, magnificent furnishings, and acres of formal gardens, housed the house of Condé and its retinue, including Sade's parents. Soon after the boy's birth, both the Prince and Princess de Condé passed away from natural causes, putting an end to the Comte de Sade's extramarital affair and leaving the Condés' only child, Louis Joseph de Bourbon, lord of the palace. As playmate to the young prince, the infant Sade enjoyed similar royal treatment. The boy adopted a skewed view of reality, an assumption that everyone and everything should bend to his will. As Sade would later note, "Born in Paris in the bosom of luxury and plenty, I believed, from the time I could reason, that nature and fortune had joined together to heap their gifts upon me. . . . It seemed that everything must give in to me, that the whole world must flatter my whims, and that it was up to me alone to conceive and satisfy them."

Once, when the young Prince de Condé had taken one of his toys, the two-year-old Sade attacked the slightly older boy, screaming "you child," the only name he would ever call his patron. It didn't help that the young Sade received little direction from his parents. Such aristocratic marriages were often unions of convenience rather than love, with both parents having little time for children, thanks to their noble responsibilities. Even so, Sade's caregivers proved particularly neglectful. His father's ambassadorial duties meant he lived abroad for much of his son's early childhood, and even when he was home, the comte's profligate ways made him a poor role model. Sade's mother, Marie Éléonore, meanwhile, was by all indications a cold and supercilious woman. Her detachment was likely exacerbated by her husband's rakish behavior and a motherhood beset by tragedies. In 1737, three years before Sade's birth, she had a daughter named Caroline-Laure, but the girl died at age two. In 1746, she had another daughter; this one lived only five days. Not long after the second loss, Marie Éléonore moved to a convent in Paris, while Sade was still young. There she would spend the majority of her remaining years, rarely bothering to bestow affection or guidance on her only child.

With his parents largely out of the picture, Sade looked up to an extremely troubling authority figure at the Hôtel de Condé: the Comte de Charolais, the Prince de Condé's uncle, who had become the young scion's guardian once his parents passed away. In an era when the social elite frequently engaged in degenerate behavior, the Comte de Charolais's conduct stood apart. As a pastime, he supposedly enjoyed shooting peasants. When he became jealous of his favorite prostitute, he assaulted her and everyone else in her vicinity. And according to reports, he poisoned the infant child he had with the woman, declaring, when the baby perished, "That child certainly was not mine if that drink made him die!" Under Charolais's tutelage, Sade began to learn just how far aristocrats could go without the fear of consequences.

◄ ◄ ◄

IN THE SUMMER of 1744, the four-year-old Sade left Paris, watching from his carriage window as it moved south on the long, dusty road to Provence. With his behavior leaving him no longer welcome at the Hôtel de Condé, his parents had decided to send him to the land of his ancestors, to learn the ways of a young nobleman. That task fell to his paternal uncle, the Abbé de Sade, who resided at the Château de Saumane, an ancient family castle outside of Avignon.

Sade found his new home poised on a rocky bluff, the stone citadel looming over the rolling hills and terraced farms of southern France. Within its six-foot-thick medieval walls, Sade discovered elegant apartments adorned with Renaissance frescoes and vaulted ceilings. But through secret passageways and down narrow spiral staircases, he found damp and lonely prison cells buried deep in the rock. He also came across a workshop stocked with instruments for studying plants and animals, a recently planted orangerie, and an extensive library filled with the works of Hobbes, Locke, Molière, Rousseau, Cervantes, Diderot, and other literary greats. This was all the work of his uncle the abbé, Jacques François Paul Aldonse. A witty and esteemed intellectual, the Abbé de Sade counted Voltaire, the preeminent philosopher of the French Enlightenment, among his friends and was in the middle of compiling a three-volume biography of Petrarch, the Renaissance poet who figured prominently in Sade family legend.

The abbé also enjoyed less respectable pursuits. In his library, Sade surely found his uncle's collection of illicit books, including *The Bordello, or Everyman Debauched* and *History of the Flagellants, in Which the Good and Bad Uses of Flagellation Among the Christians Are Pointed Out.* Elsewhere in the château lived a mother and daughter, both of whom were apparently carrying on with the abbé. "Priest though he is, he still has a pair of trollops in his house," Sade would later write. "Is his château a [harem's quarters]? No, better still, it is a bordello."

At age ten, Sade returned to Paris. By that point, his father's career had cratered, and he had committed what was left of his wealth and influence to ensure that his son would assume his rightful place in society. As a first step, he had secured him admission to Louis-le-Grand, among the most prestigious grammar schools in France. There, in between prayers at six A.M. and eighty forty-five P.M., Sade studied literature, languages, and rhetoric alongside the sons of France's greatest families. Every August, he watched as the school's central courtyard was transformed into an outdoor performance space to host the fruits of the institution's celebrated dramatic arts program. Amid the vibrant sets, machine-driven theatrical effects, and stirring performances, the boy developed a lifelong love of theater.

At school he likely experienced his first sexual encounter, but not by choice. A police report late in the marquis's life noted the discovery among Sade's papers of a short personal essay where he described being assaulted by one of Louis-le-Grand's instructors. According to the officer's description, "The author recounts his first experience in debauchery before embarking on the career in which he made such rapid progress. He tells how, after being sodomized from five o'clock in the morning until eight . . . he went to confession and took communion."

Sade's schooling came to an end at fourteen, when his father pressed him into military service, less to achieve martial valor than to accumulate social status. Sade joined the Chevaux-légers, an elite cavalry regiment open only to young men with extensive noble lineage, then moved on to an even more prestigious unit, the Carabineers. He entered the military just in time to serve in the Seven Years' War, the continent-spanning conflict among France, Russia, Austria, Prussia, and England. On the front lines in western Prussia, Sade, astride his ornamented warhorse, in a royal blue uniform and plumed tricorn hat, made use of his tempestuous demeanor. A commanding officer described the young soldier as "deranged, but extremely courageous."

Even as Sade moved through all the necessary steps to attain social standing, he remained incapable of forming lasting relationships. He wrote to his father that he had "few friends, perhaps none, because there is no one who is truly sincere and who would not sacrifice you twenty times for the slightest advantage." As an adolescent, he'd be-

come emotionally overwhelmed when one of his father's many female companions offered him affection, causing him to shift from
tongue-tied paralysis to violent fits of jealousy and longing. By the
time he joined the army, his yearning for affection had morphed into
a growing sexual mania. When he heard from his fellow soldiers that
the best way to learn a new language was to regularly sleep with a
native speaker, he decided to test the theory: "I equipped myself, in
my winter quarters near Cleve, with a nice fat baroness three or four
times my age, who educated me very nicely."

On leave, Sade would immediately head to the nearest brothel,
which soon would plunge him into self-loathing. "Does one ever
really enjoy a happiness one buys?" he wrote in sorrow to his uncle.
But the self-reproach wouldn't last. By the next morning, without
fail, he'd awaken with his conscience clear and hungry for new pleasures.

WHEN SADE'S MILITARY career came to an end in 1763, with the conclusion of the Seven Years' War, his father threw himself into achieving the next social objective for his son: securing a suitable wife. He
settled on Renée-Pélagie de Montreuil, the oldest daughter of a merchant family that had recently acquired a noble title. While the
Montreuils lacked an impressive aristocratic history, they boasted a
considerable personal fortune—not to mention a willingness to over-
look the marquis's and his father's dwindling assets and notoriety in
order to marry into one of France's notable lineages.

Renée-Pélagie wasn't particularly beautiful or graceful. She stood
four feet ten inches tall, with a plain round face marked by gray eyes
and brown hair, looks she rarely bothered to accentuate with stylish
makeup or clothes. Sade had nurtured hopes for a more romantic
union; as he'd written to his father, "I ask your forgiveness if I am
resolved to marry only where my heart leads me." None of that mattered; like the marriage of his parents, the match would be one of
practicality. On May 15, 1763, the dutiful son met Renée-Pélagie for
the first time at her parents' mansion in an upmarket Parisian neighborhood, bearing several dozen artichokes and a bundle of thyme,

which his father had instructed him to bring as a traditional—not to mention frugal—Provençal wedding present. Two days later, the couple recited their wedding vows in the nearby parish church.

In the years to come, Sade would condemn his arranged marriage as "a mercenary and vile pact, a shameful traffic in fortunes and names." He insisted that he felt no passion for his bride, and that he had only managed to subdue "the repugnance that she inspired in me from the first moment I saw her." But the two were a perfect match. Like Sade, Renée-Pélagie had struggled through a neglectful childhood. She confessed to her husband that "my father was not a loving man" and that she often felt overshadowed by her stunning younger sister Anne-Prospére. Like her spouse, this plainspoken, unpretentious young lady had developed a distaste for French high society, calling its denizens "a bunch of riffraff, the most successful of whom are the most fraudulent." And most important for Sade, what Renée-Pélagie lacked in beauty and elegance she made up for in devotion to her new husband. As her mother declared, her daughter "will never scold him. She will love him beyond one's wildest expectations." Here was a woman who could provide the adoration and mothering Sade had craved all his life.

By all appearances, married life suited Sade. With his new bride he toured Paris's fashionable boulevards, taking in the Spanish dancers, circus performers, and exotic beasts like monkeys and bears performing for the crowds. On the Montreuils' country estate, he enjoyed horseback rides and deer hunts with his father-in-law. He so charmed his mother-in-law that she declared him the epitome of "reason, gentleness, and good breeding." Sade now had access to the wealth and influence of one of the capital's most powerful mercantile families, while still being able to enjoy dalliances on the side. "Oh, the rascal! That is what I call my little son-in-law," his mother-in-law wrote to his uncle the Abbé de Sade, not long after the nuptials. "Yes, he's distracted, but marriage is settling him down. Unless I miss my guess, you would already notice the progress if you saw him."

But instead of settling down, Sade, just six months married, now found himself behind bars in the prison of Vincennes for what he had done to the woman named Testard. The authorities were not especially concerned about his victim's claim that Sade had her whip him. As Marais noted in one of his reports, "There is no public house today in which one does not find cane whips in large numbers ready for the 'ceremony,' as the practice of spurring the ardor of jaded debauchees is called." Far graver was the fan maker's account of sacrilegious activities. Three years later, a young aristocrat would be arrested in northern France for vandalizing crosses, singing blasphemous songs, and refusing to kneel and remove his hat when a religious procession passed by. He would be executed and incinerated in the local public square.

Far from denying the accusations, Sade admitted to the conduct, begging forgiveness. He pleaded with the prison warden to let him see a priest: "Through his good lessons and my sincere repentance, I hope before long to achieve those divine feelings whose utter neglect became the primary cause of my ruin." In truth, he was an avowed atheist, so the ploy was simply an attempt to weasel out of his predicament. He begged his captors to let him see his wife, writing that "her conversation, more than anything else, is capable of restoring to the straight and narrow a wretch whose despair at having departed from it has no equal."

Sade's family, meanwhile, worked to have him released. His father traveled to the royal palace in Fontainebleau and begged the king to pardon his son. The maneuver worked: After fifteen days behind bars, Sade earned a royal reprieve. Louis XV had him discharged from Vincennes and transferred to his in-laws' château in Normandy. There he remained under house arrest until the following September.

FOR THE NEXT few years, Sade conducted himself well, at least publicly. He assumed control of a playhouse located on the grounds of his wife's uncle's château, staging plays in which he often starred alongside friends and family. He mourned the death of his father in early 1767—although, perhaps out of either respect or resentment, he never adopted the mantle of "comte," as had long been family tradition when authority passed from one patriarch to the next. Later that year, he celebrated the birth of his first son, Louis-Marie.

But away from his family, Sade continued to indulge himself. He consorted with actresses and dancers who, like many female performers at the time, moonlighted as escorts to supplement their pay. He took up with a distinguished courtesan, bankrolling her lavish lifestyle and at times passing her off as his wife. While not particularly honorable, his behavior wasn't especially scandalous; many aristocrats enjoyed the services of high-class prostitutes. "When he has passed the ebullient age of passion, he will appreciate the value of the wife you have given him," wrote the Abbé de Sade, who frequented his nephew's numerous parties, to Sade's mother-in-law.

But Inspector Marais kept an eye on Sade, and signs were mounting that Sade wasn't simply in the throes of postadolescent reverie. He attacked a coachman for asking to be compensated for delivering women to him. During a traffic dispute on a busy street, he charged out of his carriage and stabbed a horse blocking his way, breaking off his blade in the animal's stomach. And according to local police, at a small one-story villa he'd acquired as a *petite maison* in the upscale town of Arcueil, south of Paris, he received "persons of both sexes with whom he is in debauched commerce." That included a group of four girls whom he beat, then invited to dinner.

Finally, on Easter Sunday 1768, Sade's impulses again spiraled out of control. That morning at the Place des Victoires, a busy public square in central Paris, the twenty-seven-year-old, dressed in a gray frock coat and white lynx muff, approached a widow named Rose Keller who was begging for alms. He told her he wanted to hire her to be his housekeeper and took her to his *petite maison* in Arcueil. There, according to Keller's deposition, he ripped off her clothes and pushed her onto a bed. Lying facedown, she felt him whipping her until she bled, slicing her repeatedly with a knife, and pouring hot sealing wax into her wounds. Afterward, he gave her an ointment to rub on her injuries and locked her in a bedroom.

As soon as Sade left her alone, Keller set about finding an escape. She managed to pry open a window and climbed the short distance to the ground using a rope she'd fashioned from bedsheets, then ran for help.

Once again, authorities arrested Sade and locked him away, in this instance at the Château de Saumur, a medieval castle in western France being used as a prison. This time, officials wanted to make an example of Sade. People were losing patience with the nobility's excesses and demanded a crackdown on such behaviors. "He is, just now, a victim of the public's ferocity," wrote a family friend at the time of Sade's arrest. "For the past ten years court nobles have committed horrors beyond belief, that is for certain. Remonstrances will be made." It didn't help that Sade's father had left him with few useful court connections, or that the marquis himself had never been adept at cultivating his own political power. So several weeks after the incident, the Paris Parlement, one of France's most powerful courts, launched a high-profile criminal investigation into the "horrible crime that took place in Arcueil." This time, Sade's punishment wouldn't be left to the whim of the king.

Sade, however, had an important ally: his mother-in-law, the forty-six-year-old Marie-Madeleine de Montreuil. Known by everyone as "the Présidente," she, not her docile husband, wielded the power in the Montreuil household, asserting political authority that stretched far beyond the norm for a woman of relatively undistinguished lineage. Sade noted she had "the charm of the devil," and an observer later described her as "shrewd as a fox, yet eminently likable and attractive." When she needed to, the Présidente employed all these traits, plus a ruthless diligence, to protect those in her inner circle—or destroy those who stood in her way.

Under the Présidente's direction, Keller received a hefty payment in exchange for dropping her charges, and agents under her direction cleansed the *petite maison* in Arcueil of incriminating evidence. The Présidente also likely spread the word that Keller had been soliciting sex rather than begging for alms. According to Marais, at the public square where Sade found her, "One can be sure of meeting there any number of beauties, who assault you with their charms and are certainly for hire." That wasn't the only part of Keller's story that failed to stand up to scrutiny. A surgeon who examined her not long after the incident testified that Keller's injuries suggested that Sade had only whipped her, not cut her or poured wax into her wounds.

The Présidente's efforts paid off. In June 1768, the king and the Paris Parlement agreed to annul the case against Sade. He spent five more months in captivity before being released, on the condition that he withdraw to his family estate in Provence. "A disreputable deed, which cannot be condoned, could not have turned out more reputably," wrote the Présidente to Sade's uncle with a touch of pride. Still, she'd become disillusioned with her once-adored son-in-law. "For my part, I wash my hands of him," she wrote to the abbé. If Sade wasn't careful, he'd end up with the Présidente as an enemy.

Marais had little doubt the nobleman would strike again. As he noted in one of his reports, "It will not be long before we hear talk of the horrors of M. le comte de Sade."

CHAPTER FOUR

Psychopathia Sexualis

1900

IWAN BLOCH COULD NOT BELIEVE WHAT HE WAS READING. AS HE plunged deeper into *120 Days of Sodom,* his eyes grew wide behind the lenses of the pince-nez perched on the bridge of his nose. Around him, bookshelves displayed his sprawling collection of ancient and modern tomes, a library well on its way to ten thousand volumes, despite the fact that its owner was only in his late twenties. Bloch read them all voraciously, feeding a formidable intellect that had allowed him to master English, French, Greek, Latin, and a good deal of Hebrew and Sanskrit. He loved the escape of books, how they allowed him to amass a deep understanding of the world, free from the personal disappointments and slights that often sent him into depression.

Outside his window, early-twentieth-century Berlin buzzed with energy. A few decades earlier, the city had languished as a sleepy provincial backwater, a place French novelist Honoré de Balzac called the "capital of boredom." That changed in 1871, when Berlin became the capital of the newly unified German nation. Since then, the population had more than doubled and Charlottenburg, the affluent suburban borough where Bloch lived with his wife, Rosa, and their young son, Robert, was well on its way to being subsumed by the metropolis.

Everywhere Bloch looked, Berlin rumbled, honked, and flickered with progress. In the center of the metropolis, steam engines chugged along the brick archways of mainland Europe's first elevated railway. In the ground below, subway lines thundered through the earth alongside a state-of-the-art sewage system. On the asphalt-paved avenues, carriages and horse-drawn omnibuses shared the road with electric streetcars and motor taxis. On the city's outskirts, colossal factories churned out dynamos, lightbulbs, and pharmaceuticals. And at night, under the brilliant arc lamps that had led Berliners to nickname their home "Elektropolis," city dwellers admired the window displays and illuminated billboards of department stores and sat in open-air cafés discussing the strange airships being designed by Count Ferdinand von Zeppelin.

"It is a new city; the newest I have ever seen," reported Mark Twain after passing time in Berlin. He christened the place "the Chicago of Europe."

Within this new city, behind closed doors, other, more intimate transformations were taking place. In the anonymity of Berlin's teeming crowds and in the privacy of its vast apartment complexes, people were exploring their sexuality. Unlike France, which had technically decriminalized same-sex relationships by avoiding mentioning them in its revolutionary and Napoleonic penal codes, Germany still regulated sexual activity; according to Paragraph 175 of its criminal code, sodomy was a crime. But in part to push back against the country's anti-sodomy laws, the country's gay community had become among the most outspoken in Europe. In 1867, Karl Heinrich Ulrichs, a German lawyer who had already come out to his family, stood before the Congress of German Jurists in Munich and argued that people shouldn't be persecuted simply because "nature has planted in them a sexual nature that is opposite of that which is usual." Two years later, an Austrian journalist named Karl-Maria Kertbeny coined the term "homosexuality" in a series of letters and pamphlets demanding the abolition of Paragraph 175.

While the law remained on the books, in Berlin it came to carry very little weight. That was due in part to Leopold von Meerscheidt-Hüllessem, the police commissioner in charge of the city's new "Department of Homosexuals," who in the 1880s decided that the best way to keep his charges in check was to allow them to fraternize in respectable fashion. Under his watch, a vibrant gay nightlife scene blossomed around the city, from blue-collar male gathering spots to lesbian clubs to upscale bars showcasing performers in drag. Same-sex costume balls became a prominent element of Berlin's social season, filling grand venues like the Philharmonie and the Café National with men dancing with men, women dancing with women, and Police Commissioner Meerscheidt-Hüllessem and his colleagues sometimes presiding as guests of honor.

Bloch was intimately familiar with this world. Born in 1872 to a Jewish textile merchant in the rural town of Delmenhorst, in northwestern Germany, he quickly attracted attention for his exceptional mind. When, at a young age, he got his hands on a volume of an old encyclopedia, he promptly read it cover to cover. However, Bloch's sensitive nature, not to mention his Judaism, left him ill-suited for the scrutiny and competition of a university career.

Instead, he settled on dermatology, in 1898 opening a practice specializing in skin and sexual diseases. Located just off Kurfürstendamm, one of the area's most fashionable boulevards, his practice was inundated with the results of his fellow city dwellers' profligate behaviors. He treated rashes and pustules and lesions and other disfiguring conditions. He witnessed the consequences of sexually transmitted diseases: broken marriages, infertility, lives derailed beyond repair. And he came face-to-face with the dreaded scourge of syphilis, the "poison of the darkness," which had the potential to cause blindness, deafness, dementia, and paralysis, before dooming its victims to an early death.

Bloch came to believe that humanity's potential was being curtailed by out-of-control promiscuity and its repercussions. Unlike Ulrichs, the gay-rights activist, Bloch didn't believe nature had implanted unique sexual interests in certain individuals. To the contrary, he was convinced that in most cases, people acquired such proclivities, as if they were diseases. And, like many ostensibly well-meaning medical experts at the time, he aimed to use his expertise to cure them.

"The epitome of sexual hygiene," he argued, "would be to enter into marriage as early as possible." The women's-rights movement, he warned, risked destabilizing gender roles and stirring unnatural feelings between its members. And he believed that the seeds of same-sex attraction lay everywhere, like germs ready to be caught, arguing that homosexuality could arise from drug use, alcoholism, masturbation, celibacy, polygamy, cross-dressing, extreme spirituality, excessive vanity, epilepsy, exposure to balmy climates, ballet performances, and landscape gardening, among many other risky choices. The abolition of Paragraph 175 and the official German sanctioning of homosexuality would be a disaster, he maintained, one that would lead to "a progressive moral and physical degeneration of the human race."

Bloch's efforts, however misguided, placed him at the forefront of the blossoming field of sexual science. As the rise of diverse and crowded urban societies made people's intimate behaviors a matter of growing social and legal concern, doctors and scholars decided it was time to advance the public understanding of sexuality, which was still in large part based on antiquated sex manuals such as *Aristotle's Masterpiece,* which argued that many creatures, like flies and mosquitoes, weren't conceived through procreation but, instead, were born spontaneously from inanimate objects such as rotting materials. Like Bloch, many emerging sex researchers were Jewish, largely because the marginalized field of human sexuality was one of the few scientific realms where they had an opportunity to thrive.

The nascent field of study, however, suffered from a distinct lack of empirical evidence. Most people had no interest in offering up their sex lives for analysis, much less submitting themselves to invasive experiments. And matters like physical attraction and sex drive couldn't be parsed inside test tubes, within cadavers, or through standard medical examinations. To remedy the situation, many enterprising sex researchers turned to materials that had been probing the intricacies of human desire for ages: romantic literature, philosophical discourses, and, to a large degree, erotica.

In France, the psychologist Alfred Binet explored the writings of Alexandre Dumas and Jean-Jacques Rousseau to develop the concept of erotic fetishism. In Britain, physician Havelock Ellis pondered the potential sexual perversions of Walt Whitman, Christopher Marlowe, and William Shakespeare in the first English-language textbook on homosexuality. In Austria, Sigmund Freud looked to Greek mythology to formulate his concept of the Oedipus complex, narcissism, and other psychoanalytic theories. And in 1886, Austro-German psychiatrist Richard von Krafft-Ebing peppered *Psychopathia Sexualis,* his groundbreaking taxonomy of sexual pathologies, with numerous examples from the world of literature. That included, most famously, the story of the Marquis de Sade. According to Krafft-Ebing's analysis of Sade, "Coitus only excited him when he could prick the object of his desire until the blood came." Krafft-Ebing coined the term "sadism" to define the phenomenon of deriving pleasure from cruelty and violence—thereby introducing Sade into the global lexicon.

Like Krafft-Ebing, Bloch became fascinated by Sade. He began his publishing career with the 1899 work *The Marquis de Sade and His Time,* which argued that the marquis was an exemplification of the depravity and lawlessness of the French Revolution. As he noted in the book, "The main characteristics of [the eighteenth century] of injustice, egoism, and sexual immorality are to be observed at their highest in the life and works of the Marquis de Sade." He had taken it upon himself to shed light on that debauchery, to ensure that modern society did not stray down the same path.

Amid preparations for his book, Bloch became acquainted with Henry Spencer Ashbee, the famed British erotica collector. The two grew close, trading cordial letters until Ashbee's death in July 1900. In their correspondence, Ashbee, in the strictest of confidence, revealed his secret identity as Pisanus Fraxi, author of *Index Librorum Prohibitorum* and its two follow-ups. Bloch, touched by the gesture, would later describe his departed colleague as a beacon of "goodness, frankness, and generosity" and "the greatest bibliographer and bibliophile of erotica that has ever lived."

In all likelihood, Ashbee shared something else with Bloch: the details of how he had been offered *120 Days of Sodom* by the erotica illustrator Chauvet. Struck by the story, Bloch tracked down the manuscript, most likely finding it in the custody of a relative or representative of its last rightful owner, the recently deceased Marquis de Villeneuve-Trans. He acquired and transported it back to Germany, likely by train, and now in Berlin, he gazed upon the lost scroll of the Marquis de Sade.

But this was not the novel he had anticipated. The delicate text scratched across the yellowed paper, in spindly strokes that reminded him of a thousand tiny knife points, was not, as he saw it, the rantings of a degenerate aristocrat caught up in the revolutionary turmoil. This was something else, an effort far more radical than anything he'd yet seen produced by Sade. The more he read, the more the work came to feel astonishingly prescient. The very nature of the novel, its depictions of sexuality, seemed to be anticipating the concerns that now consumed Bloch and his colleagues. It was as if Sade were reaching through the centuries and speaking directly to him.

IN 1904, 119 years after its prison-cell conception, the first published edition of *120 Days of Sodom* emerged from the presses. Designed to be distributed exclusively via subscription for physicians, lawyers, anthropologists, and other scientific experts, the two hundred copies of the novel were priced from 150 to 350 francs each, depending on the quality of their paper. All were luxury items, destined for an elite audience; at the time, the average Paris construction worker earned just 216 francs a month.

Nearly everything about the book's publication was a lie. While the work remained in its original French and its ornamented title page noted that it was published in Paris by the "Club des Bibliophiles," like many books with illicit subject matter, its publication details had been intentionally obscured. In reality, the book was published by Max Harrwitz, a rare-book dealer and publisher in Berlin. Similarly, while the title page declared that the book was published and annotated by "Dr. Eugène Dühren," the name was a pseudonym. Bloch, after confirming the scroll's authenticity with Sade scholars and hiring a language expert to produce an enlarged, readable version of the text, had spearheaded the effort himself.

According to Bloch's lengthy introduction, which he had written under his alias, an unnamed German bibliophile had, with his help, located and purchased the manuscript in France for a considerable sum. But this, too, was most likely a falsehood, one designed to protect Bloch's reputation from associations with the scandalous novel.

In the years to come, there would never be any indication that anyone else in Germany would ever possess the scroll. Bloch had always been a deeply covetous collector; as a colleague would later put it, "It was difficult for him to reconcile himself to the thought that someone else might possess a book for which he had searched for years in vain." In all likelihood, Bloch had purchased the scroll, complete with Villeneuve-Trans's custom-made phallic container, then kept it for himself.

There was one matter in the introduction that Bloch wrote about with honesty. He noted that his discovery of the scroll had demolished his previous theory that Sade, through his writing, had been channeling the revolutionary mayhem of his era. Instead, he had come to believe that Sade had designed *120 Days of Sodom* as a catalog of human sexuality. As he put it, Sade "gathered all his observations and ideas on the sexual life of man," composing the book "according to a systematic plan, with the aim of a scientific grouping of the examples cited." Why else would Sade have so methodically ordered the six hundred perversions of his novel, dividing them by month into "simple passions," "dual passions," "criminal passions," and "murderous passions"? Why else would he have written, in the midst of his narrative, "The man who could identify and describe these depravities would perhaps produce one of the finest works on customs one could ever hope to see"?

Bloch was convinced that Sade shouldn't be relegated to a case study in Richard von Krafft-Ebing's classification of sexual pathologies. Sade, he believed, had blazed a trail for Krafft-Ebing more than a century before the psychiatrist published his influential treatise. From his perspective, *120 Days of Sodom* was the first and most thorough example of a *psychopathia sexualis,* making Sade the forefather of sexual science.

In the following years, Bloch followed in Sade's footsteps, throwing himself into the investigation of erotic desire. Looking ever more professorial with his thinning hair, well-groomed mustache, and high-collared shirts and ties, he traded insights with colleagues on religious prostitution and sex cults amid the crystal chandeliers and mirrored columns of downtown Berlin's bustling Kempinski restaurant. Between 1901 and 1912, in a burst of productivity, he published ten additional books, covering everything from the origins of syphilis and the intricacies of British sex life to the history of prostitution and the science of erotic odors. Many became international sensations, likely due as much to their salacious subject matter as to their scientific insights, cementing Bloch's position at the forefront of sex research.

He further established his reputation by using the 1906 publication of *The Sexual Life of Our Time,* his 850-page encyclopedia of sexual knowledge, to give his chosen field its name. Within its pages, he used the term "sexology" to define the interdisciplinary approach needed to study human sexuality, arguing that the only way to unlock the secrets of human desire was through a fusion of medicine, psychology, philosophy, biology, anthropology, ethnology, and, as he knew firsthand, the study of literature.

But as his stature grew, doubts began to gnaw at him about the views he had espoused on his way to prominence. The seeds of those misgivings arose from, of all places, *120 Days of Sodom.* Sade's recounting of myriad sexual activities at all levels of French society seemed to suggest that sex wasn't just a matter of right or wrong, moral or depraved, but existed on a wide spectrum. And Bloch's long-held belief that sexual orientations arose from outside influences seemed to be directly refuted by one of the novel's protagonists when he declared, "There is no need for me to restrain my tastes in order to please [God], since it is from Nature that I receive these tastes." The very same idea, albeit with less salaciousness, had been voiced by gay-rights pioneer Karl Heinrich Ulrichs.

But if sexual deviations came about naturally, what could Bloch do to help those who developed them? To solve this new conundrum, Bloch began venturing beyond his books, and started meeting regularly with members of Berlin's gay community. He witnessed their habits, their attitudes, and their relationships with one another. He realized that homosexuality was far more common than he had imagined. And he saw with his own eyes that these men and women were no more likely than anyone else to be unhealthy, degenerate, or in any way abnormal. Maybe, he started to realize, there was nothing to cure.

Bloch's investigations brought him into close contact with Magnus Hirschfeld, a wealthy Jewish physician who was quickly becoming Berlin's most prominent gay activist. Hirschfeld had been forever transformed in 1896, when one of his patients killed himself on the eve of his wedding, admitting in a suicide note that he couldn't live with the shame he felt over his secret homosexual desires. The death spurred Hirschfeld into action, and he founded the Scientific-Humanitarian Committee, history's first gay-rights organization, dedicated to eradicating Paragraph 175. He mounted an ambitious study, whose results, he said, proved that 2 percent of his country-men identified as strictly homosexual. He convinced German offi-cials to issue passes allowing men and women to dress in the clothes of the opposite gender without risk of arrest. And he and his col-leagues pondered launching direct actions like a far-reaching "self-outing" that would involve so many prominent figures revealing their homosexuality that the authorities would have no choice but to condone their behavior.

Bloch began taking regular walks with Hirschfeld along the ram-bling tree-lined pathways of Berlin's Tiergarten Park. While just a few years apart in age, the two made an odd pairing: Bloch slight and reserved, Hirschfeld stout and gregarious. But they recognized that they had two important traits in common: a thirst for knowledge and a hunger to make things right.

Bloch would take to heart Hirschfeld's deeply held belief that sex-uality existed on a natural spectrum, with every permutation of human desire as normal as any other. The insight would lead Bloch to an utter reversal of his thoughts on sex and gender, and he no longer deemed an early and lifelong marriage the pinnacle of sexual hy-giene; he and Rosa had divorced in 1905. Instead, he came to believe that free, unfettered love would discourage unhealthy promiscuity far more successfully than traditional marriages ever had.

Now, rather than dreading the effects of the women's-rights move-ment, he called for "the complete equality of man and woman." But his most radical shift concerned sexual orientation. After everything he had seen, everything he had experienced, he declared, "For me there is no longer any doubt that homosexuality is compatible with complete mental and physical health." Paragraph 175, he insisted, should be abolished.

Hirschfeld, too, found his friendship with Bloch transformational. For years he had been casting about, trying to find a way to elevate his advocacy above rhetoric and polemics. Thanks to Bloch and the insights he'd gleaned from his trove of books, Hirschfeld hit upon a solution. With the help of sexology, Hirschfeld realized, he could change the world.

ON A WARM July evening in 1919, a song of celebration drifted through the trees of Tiergarten Park. At the edge of the municipal gardens, a grand brick villa bustled with the city's elite—doctors, literati, and politicians. As the Jewish cantor in attendance concluded his hymn, Magnus Hirschfeld moved forward to address the crowd, welcoming his guests to the grand opening of the Institute for Sexual Science, the first establishment in the world dedicated to the study of human sexuality. In this mansion, he had taken Bloch's multidisciplinary concept of sexology and built an institution that would apply the approach for the good of the world. The organization would be the embodiment of Hirschfeld's maxim: "Through science to justice."

Visitors that night toured the elegantly appointed facilities. They took in the consultation rooms, where institute staff would treat venereal diseases, dispense birth control information, and counsel gay men and women that they had no reason to be ashamed. They passed through gathering spaces that would host political strategy meetings and afternoon teas frequented by dapper cross-dressers. And they toured the onsite museum, which would draw thousands of visitors a year with its collection of fetish objects from all over the world and its photo exhibits on the lives of "transvestites"; Hirschfeld had coined that term from the Latin words *trans,* or "across," and *vestitus,* or "dressed." Soon the complex would also include cutting-edge medical facilities, where staff would zap away unwanted body hair

with X-ray equipment, inject patients with nascent hormone thera-
pies, and even undertake some of the world's first sex-reassignment
surgeries.

Hirschfeld had chosen the perfect moment to launch his institute.
After their recent defeat in the Great War and the founding of the
progressive yet beleaguered Weimar Republic from the rubble of
Kaiser Wilhelm II's empire, Germans had thrown themselves into indulgence with all the abandon of a people with nothing left to lose
and no one around to stop them. Berlin's sexual decadence thrived
like never before, giving rise to a Babylon of boy bars and drag caba-
rets and lesbian social clubs and homosexual periodicals and even an
overtly homosexual feature film, titled *Different from the Others* and
co-starring Hirschfeld himself. "Here was the seething brew of history in the making," declared the novelist Christopher Isherwood in
his memoir of living in the city at the time. Spurred on by that brew,
Hirschfeld would take his message worldwide. He used the institute
to host the First International Congress on Sexual Science, attended
by three thousand scientists from all over the globe, then helped organize the World League for Sexual Reform. Dazzled by his activities, the American press would christen him "the Einstein of Sex."

Over the years, Bloch had worked closely with Hirschfeld, col-
laborating with him to launch the *Journal of Sexology* and partnering
with him on a planned handbook for the field of sexual science. And
while he still preferred the solace of his books, he no longer had any
qualms about the kinds of people Hirschfeld drew to his new venture. But he wasn't a major part of the Institute for Sexual Science—
because by this point, he was a shell of his former self.

In 1915, Bloch, like so many of his medical colleagues, had been
drafted into the Great War. Because of his expertise, he was assigned
to do battle with his old nemesis syphilis, treating soldiers afflicted by
the disease and conducting weekly medical examinations of the state-
sanctioned prostitutes authorized to do business with the army. Although stationed at reserve hospitals far from the front lines, he
witnessed firsthand the devastation of the global war. He wasn't made
for such work; the forty-three-year-old looked lost and haunted in
his gray officer's tunic and peaked cap.

Near the end of the war, Bloch found himself and his publication of *120 Days of Sodom* the targets of attack. In 1918, Louis Morin, a French illustrator and journalist, published a propaganda pamphlet titled *How Doctor Boche, to Justify in Advance the German Infamies, Accused the French in General and the Parisians in Particular of Bloody Sadism.* The name "Boche," the French word for "Hun," a derogatory term for Germans, was clearly meant to refer to Bloch. The leaflet, decorated with vivid illustrations of pillaging German soldiers and a bearded academic reveling in sex and torture, accused Boche of conspiring to convince the world that Sade's degeneracy exemplified French literature and customs, in order to "rob French civilization of its unparalleled graces." Furthermore, Morin argued that Boche was using his research on Sade to advise the kaiser and his army on how to "rape, kidnap, murder, torture, and engage in all the other diabolical practices which would have delighted the ferocity of the Marquis." As someone who counted the Paris bookstalls along the Seine among his favorite places in the world, Bloch considered the Frenchman's condemnation nearly too mortifying to bear.

Bloch emerged broken from the war, sapped of all productivity. In November 1921, two years after the opening of the Institute for Sexual Science, he endured another blow, falling ill to a devastating bout of influenza that left his body racked by sepsis. Confined to a hospital bed for months, he had no choice but to let doctors amputate one leg, then the other. During his lengthy recovery, he got married again, to a woman named Lisbeth, and celebrated his fiftieth birthday. Early in the autumn of 1922, he left the hospital, eager to finally get back to work. He would not get a chance to do so. Weeks later, after completing a short treatise on an important eighteenth-century letter he had uncovered, he suffered a major stroke, from which he would never recover. On November 19, 1922, he passed away. Bloch's colleagues lamented his early death. Sigmund Freud wrote to an associate, "Science has lost a great deal." But in hindsight, some would come to see his passing as a gift. He never had to witness what happened next.

▲ ▲ ▲

IN 1929, THE Scientific-Humanitarian Committee came tantalizingly close to its chief political goal. That year, a government committee voted to abolish Paragraph 175, which would have legalized homosexuality nationwide. But before the matter could be finalized, the government ground to a halt amid financial collapse and political strife. From the upheaval arose a new power: the National Socialist German Workers' Party, or the Nazis. As a Jew, a homosexual, and a vocal advocate for lifestyles that ran counter to the Nazi ideals of sexual discipline and procreation for the good of the fatherland, Hirschfeld became a prime target of attack. Nazi thugs distributed flyers condemning his activities. They derailed one of his lectures by setting off fireworks in the auditorium in the middle of his speech. They even assaulted him in the street, leaving him so bruised and bloody that newspapers reported he had died of his injuries.

While Hirschfeld recovered, the social crusade he'd helped launch was foundering. Plagued by infighting over strategies and objectives, Germany's gay community stood little chance of thriving once Nazi leader Adolf Hitler assumed absolute power. As shopkeepers unfurled swastika flags up and down Berlin's streets and loudspeakers blared, "Germany is awake," same-sex nightspots closed, gay periodicals shut down, and homosexual advocacy organizations obliterated their membership records.

Just after nine A.M. on May 6, 1933, the sound of music once again echoed through the park near the Institute for Sexual Science, as a convoy of black trucks rumbled to a stop in front of the building. From one emerged a brass band engaged in a triumphant anthem. Others disgorged a throng of students, one hundred in all. Moving into formation on the street, the young men turned and faced the institute, their shoulders swept back, their bearing resolute and menacing. Above the left elbows of their crisp white shirts, they wore crimson armbands emblazoned with Nazi swastikas.

The students kicked in the locked doors and stormed through the mansion. Finding Hirschfeld and most of his staff absent, they turned their fury on the facility. Smashing furniture, shattering glass, and splattering inkwells wherever they went, they wrecked examination rooms, demolished museum displays, and ransacked the library. They tossed anatomical models out windows, chucked the contents of bookshelves and cabinets into jumbled heaps all across the floor, and tore apart exhibits on sexual diversity. Later that afternoon, a squad of paramilitary officers arrived and carted away thousands of books and records—possibly, it would be said, to ensure that evidence about the sexual activities of certain Nazi Party members would never come to light.

Four days later, the institute's extensive collection of books and journals was deposited in the wide public square in front of the Berlin opera house, where they were gathered into a pile amid thousands of other volumes. That evening, as a sea of onlookers raised their right hands in the Nazi salute, students set the materials alight. Gazing upon the flames, Propaganda Minister Joseph Goebbels addressed the crowd. "The future German man will not just be a man of books," he declared over the roar of a million burning pages, "but a man of character."

The destruction that night marked the end of Germany's grand experiment in sexual diversity. Hirschfeld, abroad on a world speaking tour, would never return to Germany. He would die of a heart attack in the French city of Nice two years later, before he had time to rebuild his organization. In the coming years, thanks to an expansion of Paragraph 175, the Nazis would arrest tens of thousands of individuals for suspected homosexual acts. Thousands of those convicted would be sent to concentration camps, and most would never return.

The Nazis had done their job well: The legacy of Germany's gay-rights pioneers was almost completely wiped away. In East and West Germany, same-sex relations would not be fully decriminalized until the late 1960s, and remnants of Paragraph 175 would remain in the criminal code until 1994—nearly a century after the Scientific-Humanitarian Committee had been launched to abolish it. None of the major figures of Germany's groundbreaking exploration of sex disappeared more completely than the founder of sexology. Without a university or private institute to safeguard his legacy, Bloch's work would be largely overshadowed by the efforts of his protégé, Hirschfeld, and, to a larger extent, the innovations of his colleague Sigmund Freud. In 1972, on the centennial of his birth, a New Zealand psychology professor would write a short tribute to Bloch, noting, "His writings have suffered—more than any other psychologist's—at the hands of literary pirates, unscrupulous publishers, [and] Nazi book burners."

Sure enough, many editions of Bloch's works were undoubtedly consigned to the bonfires that night in 1933, including his books on Sade. But the basis of his trailblazing research on the marquis, the scroll that helped change the way he viewed the world, was not lost to the conflagration. As the Third Reich tightened its grip on much of Europe, *120 Days of Sodom* had already slipped away.

CHAPTER FIVE

Rise of an Empire

2007

JEAN-CLAUDE LE COUSTUMER LISTENED CAREFULLY TO THE DETAILS OF an opportunity that sounded almost too good to be true. The sixty-one-year-old sat in his small living room, paying close attention to the financial adviser who sat across from him. Le Coustumer had invited the adviser to his half-timbered farmhouse on the outskirts of Reims, a city of 180,000 people a two-hour drive east of Paris, after he'd heard that the broker had arranged some interesting investments for a friend of his wife's.

Le Coustumer had recently sold the four hair salons he owned to a larger company for a considerable sum. He had always been careful with his money, tracking every cent he earned and never splurging on luxuries like new cars, so he was nervous about what to do with his nest egg. He wasn't interested in things he couldn't easily understand, and so he didn't want to pursue options like real estate or stocks, a decision that would soon prove prescient as the Great Recession took hold. The adviser, however, was telling him about a financial option that sounded appealingly simple: A company called Aristophil would allow him to invest in letters and manuscripts.

Le Coustumer wasn't particularly erudite. He hadn't been especially supportive when his two sons wanted to take up tennis, preferring they focus their energies on their careers, as he had done. But he appreciated the value of writing; everyone in France did. If Italy was known for its painters and Germany for its composers, France was celebrated for its writers. It boasted the densest concentration of bookstores of any nation in the world; the country set book prices nationwide and developed interest-free loan programs for the benefit of its booksellers. This was a society that gathered every Wednesday evening to watch *La Grande Librairie,* a ninety-minute prime-time TV show devoted to the written word. For the French, literature possessed a sacred status, playing as large a role in the country's all-important *patrimoine,* its deep-rooted cultural heritage, as Notre-Dame, the Louvre, and the Eiffel Tower. And now, according to the financial adviser's sales pitch, Le Coustumer could own a piece of that *patrimoine* himself.

The adviser explained how the system worked. He explained that Le Coustumer could purchase joint-ownership shares of various collections of letters and manuscripts, such as an autographed manuscript of Jean Cocteau's or letters penned by the painter Eugène Delacroix. The collections would be insured by Lloyd's of London and safeguarded in Aristophil's Paris facilities, much the same way a bank maintains its customers' funds. As an added bonus, Le Coustumer wouldn't be taxed on the assets, since works of art, including letters and manuscripts, weren't subject to France's wealth tax.

According to the contracts the adviser showed him, at the end of five years, Le Coustumer would offer to sell his shares back to Aristophil. By that point, he could expect the texts to have surged in value. And why would they do so? For starters, the company would heavily publicize the materials, boosting their profile. More important—and this was key—the documents would have skyrocketed in worth for a simple but compelling reason: There were more and more people on earth, but less and less writing by hand. Thanks to emails and word processors, text messages and dictation software, handwritten documents were becoming a thing of the past.

While most people hadn't been paying attention to the shift, those with a stake in the matter had been tracking the transformation for several decades. In 1984, the Association of American Publishers reported that nearly 50 percent of all U.S. literary authors had turned to word processing. "Writers of all descriptions are stampeding to buy word processors," noted Thomas Pynchon in *The New York*

Times. "Machines have already become so user-friendly that even the most unreconstructed of Luddites can be charmed into laying down the old sledgehammer and stroking a few keys instead."

A century earlier, Mark Twain had been all too happy to apply new technologies to his writing, composing his memoir *Life on the Mississippi* in a way that had never before been attempted. "I was the first person in the world to apply the type machine to literature," he declared in ads designed to promote the first commercial typewriter. But at the dawn of the computer age, many writers and lovers of literature found something ominous in the idea of processing rather than inscribing words. It was as if the act of setting down and rearranging thoughts and ideas was becoming so easy, so instantaneous, that something vital about the writing process was in danger of being lost. "What is to become of that written language which was for two millennia wisdom's only mold?" bemoaned Gore Vidal in *The New York Review of Books*. "What is to become of the priests of literature, as their temples are abandoned?"

By the time Le Coustumer was sitting in his living room listening to the financial adviser's sales pitch, such objections were ancient history. The Luddites had lost the battle; pens and pencils had largely been replaced by digital 1's and 0's. The handwritten documents Aristophil was amassing would indeed be among the last of their kind. History was littered with examples of dwindling resources and scarce materials leading to sky-high prices, from the 1970s oil crisis to gold rates rising as the mines dried up. Surely it would be the same for letters and manuscripts.

The prospects were so promising that everyone involved was certain to reap the rewards, explained the adviser, who was not an employee of Aristophil, but was clearly keen on the company. Aristophil would take the documents it bought back from Le Coustumer and other shareholders and sell them at a profit to other investors. Le Coustumer, meanwhile, would walk away with a substantial yield on his investment: 40 percent returns after five years, promised the broker—not as lucrative as a good stock market run, but less prone to market fluctuations.

All over France and beyond, others were hearing independent financial advisers make similar sales pitches about Aristophil—and they liked what they heard. In Avignon, Robert Cipollina, a motorcycle racer turned small-business owner, invested €35,000 in documents related to scientific engineering, planning to use the resulting revenue to buy a hybrid car. In a suburb of Paris, Geoffroy, a sweet-faced actor and father of five, bought €150,000 worth of shares of materials tied to Impressionism and Surrealism, figuring the earnings would help his family through the lean times between roles. Jean-Marie Leconte, a retired Parisian telecommunications manager, spent €250,000 on letters written by famous figures like Charles de Gaulle, Napoleon, and Baudelaire, while his brother-in-law used proceeds from selling his restaurant to obtain €550,000 worth of shares of medieval manuscripts and other materials, with the hope that the eventual payout would supplement his pension. They joined priests, police officers, merchants, business executives, lawyers, army sergeants, dentists, bankers, real estate agents, veterinarians, journalists, doctors, judges, air traffic controllers, and thousands of others who decided to invest in Aristophil.

The list included Le Coustumer. Not long after he learned about Aristophil, he invested in a series of love letters the company had acquired by Antoine de Saint-Exupéry, the author of *The Little Prince*. Le Coustumer later purchased joint-ownership shares of several other Aristophil collections. In total, he sank roughly €1.7 million into Aristophil, nearly his entire savings.

GÉRARD LHÉRITIER HAD founded Aristophil in 1990, several years before his businesses in Nice and Cannes succumbed to scandal. He came up with the name by fusing the words for art, history, and philology (the study of language), and designed a regal logo featuring heraldic lions, a ship at sea, and a hot-air balloon in midflight. At first, the company focused on buying and selling letters and documents related to the 1870 siege of Paris; then it expanded to other historical texts, including books.

The venture remained relatively modest until Lhéritier's masterstroke in October 2002. Bidding over the phone during a Christie's

New York auction of scientific papers, he acquired a collection of correspondence between Albert Einstein and his collaborator Michele Besso written in 1913. The pages, covered in intricate equations, helped lead to Einstein's general theory of relativity. After consulting with experts, Lhéritier became convinced the manuscript was worth millions, far more than the $559,500 he'd paid for it. But since there were very few collectors around with that sort of money, he didn't know how he would be able to sell it. That's when he came up with the idea of selling joint-ownership shares of the manuscript to multiple people, a common practice in real estate but not in manuscripts or art. That way, even those with modest means could own a piece of a costly document like the Einstein letters. Within two weeks, Lhéritier had found nearly four hundred people willing to buy shares of the text, for a total price of €12 million.

Thanks to Lhéritier's innovation, financial advisers all over France were soon encouraging customers to invest in Aristophil's materials, which the company sold through a distributor called Finestim as well as its subsidiary, called Art Courtage. While the advisers weren't on Aristophil's payroll, the operation trained them to promote its offerings. Many of the brokers were so taken by the innovative opportunity, they bought joint-ownership shares themselves. They also appreciated the substantial commissions: On each sale, agents received a cut of 5 to 11 percent, significantly more than they usually made from selling stocks or real estate.

Offering rare documents to the masses wasn't a completely novel idea. The tactic had been tried before in the United States. In the 1980s and '90s, an enterprising autograph dealer named Todd Axelrod opened a series of letter and manuscript stores in upscale shopping malls across the country under the moniker Gallery of History. But the pricey materials had never caught on with American consumers. Eventually the operation contracted to a single gallery in Las Vegas and an online store at historyforsale.com. Lhéritier's approach, however, boasted several improvements. For one thing, the company's unique shareholder arrangement meant people could claim ownership, albeit partial, of incredibly valuable and seminal texts. For another, Aristophil wasn't targeting U.S. mall-goers on their way to

Sharper Image or Banana Republic. The operation directed its offerings toward the French, among the most literary and document-
obsessed people in the world.

Aristophil's system was a hit. Some investors, especially those who
were well-off, signed up for Aristophil's "Amadeus" contracts, meaning they purchased particular letters or manuscripts outright. Far
more opted for "Coraly's" contracts, the joint-ownership option
whose unnecessary apostrophe echoed the names of the iconic auction houses Christie's and Sotheby's. To ensure that everything about
the process was legitimate, Lhéritier had contractual terms and conditions reviewed by a prominent law professor at the Sorbonne. And
he made the operation a family affair, hiring his daughter, Valérie, to
work as the company's director of purchases.

Flush with capital, Lhéritier set up shop on the Champs-Élysées in
Paris and went about making Aristophil a major player in the letters
and manuscript market. At auctions, the appearance of company
agents soon sent bids skyrocketing, fueling a bull market in historic
documents and drawing out texts that had long been hidden away in
château libraries. As *Le Figaro* declared, France was enjoying "the
heyday of the manuscript."

At the Fontainebleau Auction House south of Paris, the company
outbid Russia's State Hermitage Museum, one of the largest art museums in the world, for an 1812 letter by Napoleon detailing in a secret code his plans to blow up the Kremlin. Aristophil spent €150,000
on the missive, ten times the pre-sale estimate. At Sotheby's in London, the firm bought a miniature manuscript written by fourteen-
year-old Charlotte Brontë for €800,000, more than double the
anticipated price tag, dashing the hopes of the Brontë Parsonage Museum to acquire the work and return it to the Brontë sisters' home in
West Yorkshire. And in 2008, when Sotheby's Paris auctioned off the
seminal manifestos of Surrealist leader André Breton and supplemen-
tary manuscripts, company representatives waited quietly while each
piece sold individually. Then they set off an ovation in the auction
room by announcing that Aristophil would purchase the whole lot
for €3.2 million, outbidding the total of the nine sales and quadru-
pling the collection's expected selling price.

The company's treasure trove would eventually swell to 135,000 items. While there was no official ranking of manuscript libraries, since most major collectors remained tight-lipped on the extent of their efforts, Aristophil was clearly well on its way to amassing one of the largest private collections of letters and manuscripts in the world.

The upstart company's achievements were a direct challenge to a literary scene that, like many elite French institutions, had long been fueled by entrenched traditions and exclusive social circles. Jurors for most of the country's top literary prizes enjoyed lifetime appointments, and many in this predominantly white, nearly all-male group thought nothing of casting votes for colleagues and friends. And for seventy years, Paris's rare-book market had been dominated by a single powerful dealer: Pierre Berès, who, until his retirement in 2005, ruled the auction halls and boasted an unrivaled inventory, thanks to friendships with Pablo Picasso, Henri Matisse, and Simone de Beauvoir. The world of French letters was due for a shake-up, and the self-made son of a plumber found himself perfectly positioned to take up the challenge.

IN JUNE 2004, an institution unlike any other opened its doors in a modern gallery space in the heart of Paris. Amid exposed wooden beams and red marble floors, one-of-a-kind documents rested within glass displays. In one case, yellowed sheets of paper bore the blotchy, disheveled scrawl of Napoleon Bonaparte. In another, a handwritten musical score featured the hurried, swooping notes of Ludwig van Beethoven. Elsewhere, a letter displayed the elegant cursive of Leon Trotsky in suitably red ink, while a signature from Joan Miró, with its haughty accent mark, was exhibited like a work of art. Under the glow of soft lighting, these pages offered up stirring moments in time: A pre–World War II Charles de Gaulle wondered about the relevance of armored military vehicles. Claude Monet cast about for financial backers, desperate to stop an Édouard Manet painting from being shipped out of the country. In the center of it all, a special exhibit showcased the relic that had led to the gallery's creation: the Einstein text purchased by Lhéritier.

Lhéritier had been amazed when he'd learned that Paris had never boasted a museum dedicated to its beloved written words. So with the inauguration of the Museum of Letters and Manuscripts, he opened one himself. Six years later, he expanded the private institution, moving it to a ten-thousand-square-foot mansion right on the city's tony, tree-lined Boulevard Saint-Germain. There, for the admission price of a few euros, twenty thousand students, researchers, and tourists a year browsed professionally curated displays of materials owned by Aristophil's clients. If the museum doubled as a showroom for potential new Aristophil clients, all the better.

Lhéritier, splitting his time between Nice and Aristophil's headquarters in Paris, wasn't simply interested in building his company. Orchestrating ambitious marketing efforts and philanthropic ventures, he worked to propel himself into the upper echelons of French society. Under his guidance, Aristophil began putting out *Plume,* a magazine dedicated to written heritage, and published dozens of glossy hardcover books on various selections from its holdings. It lent documents to institutions all over the world, from the National Art Museum of China in Beijing, to the Museum of Modern Art in New York. It hosted symposiums staffed with experts and journalists, who were well compensated for their time, and threw opulent galas frequented by Lhéritier's growing cadre of celebrity friends, like Patrick Poivre d'Arvor, one of the country's most famous newscasters, and the award-winning novelist Didier van Cauwelaert. When Lhéritier, through his company, acquired the original manuscript of Charles de Gaulle's 1945 speech announcing the liberation of Nice from its Nazi occupiers, he bequeathed it to the city that had become his adopted home, free of charge. And when the Bibliothèque Nationale de France, the country's national library, needed funds to acquire a fifteenth-century illuminated manuscript and, later, the archives of the French philosopher Michel Foucault, Aristophil donated more than €4 million to the library. The media started calling Lhéritier "the king of manuscripts" and "the text hunter," claiming he was a cross between Indiana Jones and Hercule Poirot, a man who had the ability to turn old documents into gold.

Lhéritier's ambitions extended beyond France. In 2005, he opened an Aristophil subsidiary in Brussels, followed by a Belgium annex of his Museum of Letters and Manuscripts. He made plans for similar expansions in Switzerland, Austria, Luxembourg, and Hong Kong. Through his efforts to acquire texts from all over the globe, Lhéritier became acquainted with Kenneth Rendell, a major U.S. letter and manuscript dealer who had been in business since the 1950s, along the way running document galleries in New York, Beverly Hills, and Tokyo. One of the most respected historical manuscript experts in the world, Rendell had a track record of exposing dirty dealings in the business. In 1983, he proved that the "Hitler diaries" that had recently been uncovered to international acclaim were hoaxes. A few years later, he helped reveal that a Utah rare-book dealer named Mark Hofmann had forged numerous texts he'd sold to the Mormon Church and other buyers for millions of dollars, a case that ended with Hofmann trying to cover his tracks by detonating several home-made bombs and killing two people.

Rendell was as adept as anyone in the business at spotting suspicious behavior. But, for him, Lhéritier didn't set off any alarms. The Frenchman seemed driven by the excitement and passion of a real collector. Once, when Rendell congratulated him on a multimillion-euro acquisition, Lhéritier replied, "I would have paid twice as much to get it!" Plus, there was no question that Aristophil's holdings, sourced from the world's most respected auction houses and dealers, were genuine.

So Rendell was happy to do business with Lhéritier, especially since the arrangement benefited both of them considerably. In 2008, Rendell sold him a collection of five hundred letters by Napoleon for several million dollars, leading Lhéritier to organize a flashy exhibit of the materials at the Dôme des Invalides, the grand Paris church housing Napoleon's tomb. The following year, Lhéritier paid Rendell handsomely for the sixteen-page farewell letter King Louis XVI wrote to his subjects before attempting to flee the country during the revolution, an acquisition hailed by the press as a patriotic triumph.

Still, Rendell was struck by Lhéritier's increasingly grandiose behavior. He dined at the poshest restaurants, drank the finest wines, and had taken to commuting from Nice to Paris in a private jet. Rendell had never known anyone in the business to adopt such an extravagant lifestyle. During one of Rendell's visits to France, Lhéritier invited him to his lavish new business offices. "This isn't your office, this is a throne room," Rendell told him. Then he warned, with a playful smile, "Remember what happened to Napoleon."

CHAPTER SIX

The Tyranny of Lust

JUNE 27, 1772

AS THE CHURCH BELLS STRUCK EIGHT IN THE MORNING, A LONG-HAIRED young man named Latour made his way through the narrow streets of the old port district of Marseille. Quietly, so as to not attract attention, he knocked on the doors of various local prostitutes, looking for volunteers for a very particular arrangement. At the time, in prerevolutionary France, the fact that the young man was working on behalf of a nobleman lent authority to his negotiations. Eventually he convinced four women to gather at a small third-floor flat nearby.

The young women assembled at the apartment, awaiting their client. At noon, he arrived: the thirty-two-year-old Marquis de Sade, his blond hair and delicate features as striking as ever. He wore a silk vest and breeches a brilliant shade of marigold yellow, and in his hand he brandished a gold-knobbed cane. At his side stood Latour, his personal valet, attired in a striped sailor's outfit. "There will be money for everybody!" Sade announced—provided they successfully amused him. He pulled from his pocket a handful of coins and asked each woman to guess the number of *écus* in his hand. Once each had done so, he declared the youngest of the group, eighteen-year-old Marianne Laverne, the winner. Telling the others to wait outside, Sade escorted Marianne into the bedroom along with his manservant, then locked the door behind them. As her prize, he would have his way with her first.

For the previous four years, Sade had resided far away from the commotion of Paris at the Château de La Coste, a Sade family castle perched high on a hill in a mountainous stretch of Provence, as had been required by the terms of his prison release in the wake of his assault on the beggar Rose Keller. His wife had given birth to their second son, Donatien-Claude-Armand, in 1769, and the two had a daughter, Madeleine-Laure, two years later. As a result, Sade seemed willing to leave his frenzied past behind. Prior to the arrival of Donatien-Claude, Sade had written a letter to his wife noting his excitement about the impending birth and "the hopes it gives him and of the docility with which he awaits its effects on him."

As part of his rehabilitation, Sade turned to his long-standing love of theater. At La Coste, he furnished an auditorium he'd built there several years earlier with elaborate backdrops, scenery, and lighting equipment. He oversaw similar renovations of a playhouse at another family château, in the Provençal town of Mazan. The fact that he was in such dire financial straits from bankrolling his libertine indulgences and paying off his late father's debts that he had been briefly incarcerated in a debtors' prison did not stop him. He'd become determined to make a name for himself in the world of dramatic arts, and in early 1772, he began organizing a theater festival that would transpire at his properties at La Coste and Mazan for much of the year.

That June, in the middle of the performance season, Sade traveled to Marseille to obtain funds for his festival. But once he was there, his predilections got the better of him. After Sade departed, the four young prostitutes his valet had recruited for him came forward alleging that the marquis had subjected them to a series of sexual tortures. They said Sade had whipped them and demanded they do the same to him. At the same time, he'd engaged in sodomy with Latour. The women, as well as a fifth prostitute Sade had visited later that night, reported that he'd forced them to consume large quantities of anise-flavored pastilles, saying he wanted to savor the gastric aromas the sweets would cause them to produce. But several of the women became so sick after eating the candies that authorities grew convinced that the marquis had poisoned them with excessive amounts of Spanish fly, a powder made from beetles that had long been used as an aphrodisiac but could prove toxic in large doses. After hearing the women's story, the prosecutor in Marseille promptly issued arrest warrants for Sade and Latour.

Sade waved away his mistreatment of the women in Marseille as simply "a party with some girls, which happens eighty times a day every day in Paris!" As for the vomiting, pains, and fever that afflicted several of his victims, that was just a common local ailment; as Sade would later write, "A mild disturbance of the entrails is a considerable malady in Marseilles." After a lifetime of entitlement, he believed himself above the law. He noted in a letter, "A man can commit every possible abuse and every conceivable infamy provided he takes care with the whore's ass. The reason for this is quite simple: the whores pay, and we don't."

Sade even developed his own philosophy to justify his crimes, elevating his selfishness to a form of virtue. Calling his way of thought "isolism," he argued that everyone was utterly alone, so there was no need to care about the well-being of anyone else. "My neighbor is nothing to me: there is not the slightest connection between him and me," he declared. From such a perspective, the pain and suffering to which he subjected others meant nothing compared to the joy he experienced from achieving whatever his heart desired.

Sade's uninhibited approach to desire borrowed from bold new ideas spreading across Europe in what would become known as the Age of Enlightenment. As the eighteenth century progressed, economists explored novel concepts like free enterprise, while France's leading thinkers labored to compile all of human knowledge into the wildly ambitious *Encyclopédie*. Most important, philosophers like Voltaire and Rousseau were arguing for a new approach to society, one that would be governed by laws derived from nature and human reason, rather than edicts passed down from the church or the king. The movement gave the well-read marquis justification for his behavior: Since he received his appetites from nature, he figured ignoring them would be downright irrational.

As he noted, "Let us give ourselves indiscriminately to everything our passions suggest, and we will always be happy. . . . Conscience is not the voice of Nature; do not be fooled by it, for it is only the voice of prejudice." But Sade never embraced the Enlightenment's central tenet of a better world for all. His conviction that people should give themselves over to their passions applied only to himself, not to those he considered beneath him, and certainly not to those he abused.

Sade's obsession with debauchery led to his willingness to sacrifice everything—his social standing, his financial well-being, the support of his family, his freedom—to engage in violent, abusive sex. As he would write, "Lust's passion will be served; it demands, it militates, it tyrannizes, it must therefore be appeased, and to its satisfaction all other conditions are totally irrelevant." He told his wife he had a sexual defect, comparing his libido to a "taut and well-drawn" bow: "I want it to shoot, but the arrow will not fly." The condition would leave him so frustrated that he'd be seized with what he called "the vapors," a term that at the time referred to psychological states such as mania and hysteria. When he would finally achieve sexual relief, he'd experience a seizure-like orgasm with convulsions and cries of pain. One of Sade's accusers testified that when he climaxed in the middle of whipping her, he let out "very loud and very terrifying shrieks."

But Sade wasn't simply seeking out sexual release through his transgressions. He had come to yearn, consciously or not, for the response that would come after. He would note years later, "It made no difference whether one behaved well or badly, and that it was only those who cause a racket, make a fuss, who get anything." As a long-pampered and theatrical only child who found himself in an arranged marriage and constrained by the conventions of his class, he sought the high drama that came from breaking all the rules.

ON SEPTEMBER 12, 1772, residents of Aix-en-Provence gathered in the Place des Prêcheurs, a busy public square near the heart of the Provençal city. The picturesque plaza, dotted with trees and a fountain topped with a soaring obelisk, served as a social center for the community, hosting open-air markets and lively religious festivals. But today, the crowd gathered there to witness an execution: that of the Marquis de Sade and his manservant Latour for crimes they had committed three months before in Marseille.

Ten days earlier, the royal prosecutor in Marseille had convicted the two of sodomy; Sade had also been found guilty of poisoning the group of prostitutes. The men were sentenced to confess their sins while on their knees, wearing simple smocks and ropes around their necks and holding lighted torches of yellow wax. Once they had sought the pardon of God and their king, the two would be put to death.

As they were led up to the scaffold, the crowd was largely silent, even reverential. Here and there, witnesses whispered songs and prayers. What had transpired in Marseille had been a crime against the community. More than a demonstration of the king's justice or a quenching of public bloodlust, the executions would be a rite of civic redemption.

As the crowd watched, the executioner went about his task. Latour was hanged, his body swaying in the breeze. And Sade, for his more serious crimes, was beheaded. Both were then incinerated, their ashes scattered in the wind.

In reality, however, Sade and Latour were still very much alive, taking in the marvels of Venice, hundreds of miles away. Two months earlier, the two had fled France to avoid arrest. Unable to locate them, the court had sentenced the two to death in absentia. The crowd had gathered that day to witness the punishment carried out on straw-filled mannequins of the men, a not uncommon practice. Over the previous two centuries, roughly a third of all executions in the country had been performed on effigies, when the authorities hadn't been able to apprehend those condemned to death. Along with satisfying the populace's need for justice and closure, the enactment that day in Aix signified the civil death of the Marquis de Sade. He was thereby stripped of the rights and benefits of his nobility.

Sade wasn't especially troubled by news of his mock execution, and he would write years later: "Everyone knows the story of the Marquis de . . . , who, as soon as he learned he'd been sentenced to burn in effigy, pulled out his prick from his breeches and cried out, 'Holy fuck! Here I am just where I wanted to be, here I am covered in opprobrium and infamy—leave me be, leave me be, I need to come!' "

Sade had another reason to be joyful: He was traveling through Italy accompanied by his paramour, Anne-Prospére de Launay, his beautiful twenty-year-old sister-in-law. Normally, Anne-Prospére lived in an upper-class convent, where as a secular canoness she was expected to lead a pious life but was free to eventually marry. But several times she had taken a leave from the monastery for health reasons and lodged at La Coste. During her stay at the château three years earlier, in the summer of 1769, Sade had become obsessed with her delicate features and dark, piercing eyes framed in her black-and-white habit. He was pleased to discover that she yearned for him as well. "I swear to the Marquis de Sade, my lover, that I will be only his, that I will never marry or give myself to others, and that I will be faithful to him, as long as the blood I use to seal this oath runs in my veins," Anne-Prospére later wrote to her brother-in-law from her convent, signing the missive with her blood.

Sade's wife had caught wind of the affair but lacked the resolve to stop it. So when Sade had fled from the turmoil in Marseille, she'd remained at La Coste, watching as her younger sister absconded to Italy with her husband.

It wouldn't take long for Sade's lack of self-restraint to derail his romantic Italian getaway. Anne-Prospére soon discovered that he had cheated on her. Devastated, she returned to France and swore to spend the rest of her life in religious celibacy. "An austere life will bring me closer to the end of my desires," she wrote Sade in a letter, begging him to help her put her wayward conduct behind her.

Sade, too, departed Italy. Calling himself "the Comte de Mazan," he took up residence with Latour in Chambéry, the alpine capital of the Duchy of Savoy, an independent state east of France. But the loss of Anne-Prospére had left him despondent, wounding him more deeply than any of his legal calamities. For the first and only time in his life, he felt the pain of unattainable love. "I see only too well . . .

that I must give up the happiness of having you," he wrote to his sister-in-law. "And with this cruel certainty, is it astonishing that I seek only death?"

On November 20, 1772, Sade attempted to take his own life. There were no indications that he tried to shoot himself, hang himself, or cut his own throat, among the most common methods of suicide at the time. Most likely he turned to poison; in the Marseille affair, he had shown an interest in toxins. Whatever form of self-destruction he chose, it nearly worked. For ten days, Sade hovered between life and death. A local surgeon tended to him quietly, keeping the true cause of his malady under wraps. If he returned to France, the royal punishment for attempting suicide, though rarely enforced, was death.

Sade recovered, but he would not have long to enjoy his salvation. A few days later, he found his villa surrounded by local police. They came armed with a *lettre de cachet,* a royal arrest warrant signed by the king of France in response to his crimes in Marseille.

The operation had been set in motion by a new and fearsome adversary: Sade's mother-in-law. The marquis had gone too far by corrupting her second daughter and making a mockery of his marriage to her first. From that point forward, the Présidente would use her political power to condemn him.

The officers took Sade and Latour to the fortress of Miolans, a remote prison perched on a mountainous outcrop in the Alps that had become known as the "Bastille of the Dukes of Savoy." Sade struggled against his captivity—attempting to bribe his guards, begging for mercy from the governor of Savoy, spewing invectives at his mother-in-law in his various appeals. But as the months passed, Sade appeared to resign himself to his fate. In mid-April 1773, the prison warden wrote to the Présidente that Sade had spent the recent Easter Sunday making amends to fortress guards for his ill-mannered behavior. "This change for the better seems to be a clear effect of the grace of the sacrament," declared the warden. "I see no plans that he plans to attempt an escape."

Two weeks later, after being alerted that something was amiss, the warden entered Sade's cell in the middle of the night to find it empty.

The marquis, Latour, and another prisoner had absconded by climb-
ing through a latrine window and scrambling down a ladder set up
for them by an accomplice. In Sade's now-vacant chamber, the prison
warden found a letter addressed to him. Do not attempt to apprehend us, warned the note: "Fifteen well-armed men with good horses
are waiting for me below the château, and all are resolved to sacrifice
their lives rather than allow me to be recaptured." Gone were all
traces of the hopeless man who had tried to kill himself a few months
before. It was signed, with a flourish: the Marquis de Sade.

IN THE DIM light of a waning moon, troops made their way up the
steep Provençal hillside, armed with pistols and dueling blades. As
their horses clattered along the rocky path, mist from their breath
lingered in the January evening. Soon their torches illuminated the
walls of the Château de La Coste. Inside, they knew from surveillance, hid the fugitive Sade. Among the ranks were enough constables
and deputies to wage a full-scale battle. This time, for the marquis,
there would be no escape.

The previous autumn, after spending several months on the run in
France and Spain, Sade had rejoined his wife at La Coste. In his growing paranoia, he saw this secluded redoubt as his only safe harbor. To
recapture her son-in-law and seize incriminating materials that could
besmirch her family's name, the Présidente had set a massive police
operation in motion, placing spies disguised as peasants in the nearby
village and hiring archers to protect her home in Paris in case Sade
returned to the city.

Now, on the night of January 6, 1774, the moment had arrived.
Positioning ladders against the ramparts, several officers scaled the
château walls, while others forced open the castle gates. They spread
out through the estate, some taking position on the battlements to
watch for counterattacks from the countryside, the rest ransacking
the property. They shredded family portraits, rifled through desks
and cabinets, and snatched up heaps of documents for confiscation
while throwing others into bonfires lit in the courtyards. But their
main order was simple: to put three bullets in the Marquis de Sade

and deliver his corpse to his mother-in-law. Their commander found Renée-Pélagie amid the mayhem, cowering in terror, and demanded that she turn over her husband. "I must have him," he cried, "dead or alive." Sade was gone, she replied. Tipped off a half hour earlier, the marquis had fled into the countryside, escaping into the darkness of the Provençal night.

Shaken by his near capture, Sade fled the country, once again taking refuge in Italy. He remained there until the following autumn, when he returned to France and in Lyon once again received a warm welcome by his wife, Renée-Pélagie. The Marquise de Sade, having failed to inherit her mother's iron will, had never possessed the mettle to put a stop to her husband's misconduct or refuse to be a part of it. Renée-Pélagie "is only made of strands or filaments woven or webbed by spiders," noted one of her female companions. "I am no longer so surprised that the unfortunate man committed so many follies; he would have required a woman who had some nerve." From the moment of her wedding, she had vowed to adore and support her husband, no matter his failings, and with the Présidente no longer acting as Sade's protector, Renée-Pélagie took up the job—managing his mounting debts, working to silence his accusers. Whatever transgressions he dreamed up, she felt duty-bound to go along, then clean up the mess.

But Renée-Pélagie wasn't simply Sade's stooge. The twelve years she had spent with the marquis had left their mark. No longer the "excessively chilly and devout" woman Sade had complained about early in their marriage, she had come to accept his tastes in the bedroom. "Here's to a good screw up the ass, and may the devil take me if I don't give myself a hand job in honor of your buttocks!" Sade would later write to her. And, like Sade, she had come to view the outside world with contempt. "I know my world better, and this knowledge makes the human race odious to me," she told him. "I see very little, very little indeed, in every sense of the term, of your intelligence and spirit in the world." For years, Sade and the Présidente had labored to keep the details of his debauchery from Renée-Pélagie; now, with her three children living with her mother in Paris, she found herself directly involved. While he was incarcerated, she sent him letters with secret messages scrawled in lemon juice. When she was barred from visiting his Alpine prison in Miolans, she disguised herself as a man to try to evade the restriction. Most strikingly, after years of acquiescing to her mother, Renée-Pélagie had begun to rail against the Présidente in the same zealous tones as her husband. "Once out of her grip," she wrote, "I would rather till the earth than fall into her clutches again."

Renée-Pélagie remained the one enduring constant in the life of the increasingly isolated and besieged marquis. "I shall never be able to stop adoring you, even if you heap insults upon my head," she would write to him. No matter the calamities he brought upon himself and his family, she insisted in another letter, "I still adore you with the same violence." So she dutifully went along as he began to organize his most elaborate offense yet.

The seasons were beginning to turn when Sade and his wife arrived at the outskirts of their Provençal estate—accompanied by a sizable new household staff of six girls and one boy, nearly all still in their teens. As the retinue made its way up the narrow cobblestoned streets that switchbacked through the ancient hamlet of La Coste, there were few friendly greetings or curious stares from within the shuttered windows of the stone dwellings. The villagers knew to avert their eyes from the odd pursuits of their noble landlord. As Sade once noted with relish, "I pass for the werewolf of these parts."

Reaching the top of the arid plateau, the procession came upon the Château de La Coste. Crossing the castle bridge and passing through the central gate, the group found themselves in what felt more like a dismal stone fortress than a grand country estate. But within its tall stone towers and apartments, the marquis had installed an oasis of luxury: salons furnished with thickly upholstered armchairs and ornate card tables, bathrooms outfitted with copper water heaters and portable toilets, bedrooms endowed with gold-trimmed bedspreads and canopies. The château's theater was ready to host whatever sorts of performances suited the marquis's whims. In the library, an extensive collection of erotic literature stood ready to be perused. Through a hidden door, a secret room displayed an assortment of sexual devices and pornographic curios. And down dark staircases, deep within the rocky plateau, lay the remnants of a medieval dungeon, for which Sade possessed the only key.

As the young charges took stock of their new home, they heard an ominous sound behind them: Sade closing and fastening the gate. "We have decided, for a myriad of reasons, to see very few people this winter," the marquis soon wrote to Gaspar François Xavier Gaufridy, a childhood friend who had become his family's lawyer and notary. "Come nightfall," he added, "the château is locked up tight, the lights are extinguished." No one would be allowed to leave.

Outsiders would never learn exactly what transpired within the walls of his château that winter. Most likely he elaborated on his past transgressions, building ever more extravagant scenes of violence, debauchery, and sacrilege. Here, far removed from the morals of society and the laws of the crown, he had complete control over an entire household of innocent youths. And this time, there would be no police or outraged relatives. This time, there would be no limits.

By the following January, troubling rumors had begun to spread. According to reports, a visitor to the château had found human bones buried in the garden. Concerned, several of the servants' families filed charges of abduction against Sade. Rather than release the girls, Sade dispersed them to various locations, including convents and the home of his uncle, to keep them from going public with what they'd endured and, most likely, to allow any incriminating wounds to heal. When Sade's uncle considered releasing the servant they had dispatched to him, Renée-Pélagie threatened him with blackmail. The following spring, when one of the girls gave birth to a daughter and appeared ready to reveal what had happened at La Coste, Renée-Pélagie had her arrested for allegedly stealing silver plates and money. Her infant, left behind at La Coste, died of starvation.

"I take them with me; I use them," Sade would write of his young wards. "After six months, some parents appear to ask for these girls, assuring me that they are their children, I return them, and suddenly there appears against me a charge of kidnapping and rape!" Yes, he admitted, someone had uncovered a collection of bones: "It was a joke, in good or bad taste (I leave it to you), to decorate a study with them."

To escape the new turmoil, Sade absconded to Italy for the third time, where, again under the guise of "the Comte de Mazan," he toured Florence, Rome, Naples, and other destinations, collecting notes for what would become his first literary venture, a travelogue titled *Voyage d' Italie*. Unbeknownst to him, his endeavors were tracked by a network of paid informants—dancers, actors, the son of a chimney sweep—who sent details of his activities to Inspector Marais, head of the vice squad in Paris.

Once the latest uproar had subsided, Sade returned to La Coste and attempted to repeat the activities of the previous winter by hiring a new crop of young servants. But when the father of one of them, a twenty-two-year-old scullery maid Sade had taken to calling Justine, heard that the marquis was soliciting sexual favors from his staff, the man rushed to La Coste to reclaim his daughter. In January 1777, he arrived at the château and fell into a heated dispute with the marquis. In the altercation, the man pulled out a pistol and fired point-blank at Sade's chest. The muzzle flashed, but Sade felt nothing. Somehow, only the primer had gone off. Panicking, Sade's attacker fled. A commoner attempting to take the life of a nobleman, even one as disgraced as Sade, was still considered far worse than anything the marquis had done within the bounds of his château.

NOT LONG AFTER his brush with death at La Coste, Sade and his wife hurried to Paris through fearsome winter storms. He'd received news that his mother, still living in a convent, had become gravely ill. But when he arrived at the capital on February 8, it was too late. His mother had died three weeks earlier, on January 14, 1777, without anyone informing him. Those who knew Sade suspected he'd fallen into a trap. The Présidente, in response to a menacing letter she'd received from her daughter, had recently noted, "If they attack me as they threaten to, I have the means to respond, and I have no fear of anything in the world."

Five days after Sade arrived in Paris, Inspector Marais tracked him down in an apartment on Rue Jacob and arrested him. Once again, Sade found himself locked in a dimly lit tower cell in Vincennes, the fortress outside of Paris where he had first been imprisoned fourteen years earlier. Even Sade's uncle, who'd once argued that his nephew's behavior was simply due to "the ebullient age of passion," rejoiced at the news. "Now I am at peace, and I believe that everyone will be happy," noted the Abbé de Sade, who would pass away later that year.

"When will I get out?" the marquis wrote to his wife, who had stayed in Paris. "Tell me, tell me, or I will smash my head against the walls that contain me!" In a letter written in blood, he begged the Présidente to release him. But his supplications accomplished nothing, and he spent more than a year in Vincennes—passing much of that time "in solitude, weeping," as he put it—before Marais transported him to Aix-en-Provence in the summer of 1778. There, he stood before the regional court as he was cleared of all charges relating to his treatment of the prostitutes in Marseille that had led to his mock execution years earlier. Several of the women, paid handsomely by Sade's wife, had recanted their testimony; plus, investigators had never conclusively proven that the marquis had fed them Spanish fly.

That didn't mean Sade would be freed. Thanks to the court decision, the Présidente's family name had been cleared of dishonor. But because the royal *lettre de cachet* on which Sade had been detained in Savoy was still in effect, she could keep her unmanageable son-in-law locked away indefinitely, without embarrassing public trials. That was exactly what she planned to do.

Sade wouldn't accept the arrangement willingly. On the way back to Paris from Aix, he escaped from Marais and his men while they stopped for the night at an inn. He made his way back to La Coste, where he celebrated his getaway with his remaining servants, since Renée-Pélagie remained in Paris.

Marais, however, refused to give up the chase. The inspector soon had agents disguised as silk merchants keeping the château under surveillance, and early on the morning of August 26, he and a squad of officers burst into La Coste and seized the marquis, still dressed in his nightshirt. After years of tracking Sade only to have him slip from his grasp, Marais lost control. He hurled vulgar curses at the marquis, demanding to know how he'd escaped from his clutches five weeks earlier. "Speak, speak, little man," he yelled, as his men held Sade at bay with drawn swords and pistols. "You who're about to be locked up for the rest of your days."

Marais had gone too far in speaking like that to a nobleman. "It is inexcusable to use such language in such a fashion," declared the Présidente when she learned of the inspector's behavior, and she promptly lodged a complaint against him. In response, Marais's superiors docked his salary and refused to reimburse his expenses from tracking down the marquis. The inspector would die two years later, disgrace hanging over him. Like Sade, he had crossed the wrong woman.

For the time being, however, Marais savored his triumph. He and his officers hauled Sade, his hands and feet bound, into a police wagon and made their way out of La Coste. As the convoy headed north, hundreds gathered along the road. They hoped to catch a glimpse of the man who the broadsheets said had sliced up a beggar to try out a new healing balm; the scoundrel who, according to rumors, had used doctored pastilles to turn a costume ball into an orgy where "women were unable to resist the uterine rage that stirred within them"; the lunatic who, it was whispered, had poisoned his own wife in order to bed his sister-in-law.

As the bystanders watched, the procession slowly made its way to Paris, then proceeded to Vincennes. There, in the early-evening darkness of September 7, 1778, the officers conveyed their prisoner across the drawbridge and into the towering fortress, then locked the gate.

CHAPTER SEVEN

Reign of the Red Vicomtesse

JUNE 19, 1929

WITH ELECTRIC LIGHTS BLAZING IN EVERY WINDOW, THE MANSION AT 11 Place des États-Unis shone like a beacon in the night, summoning all of Paris high society for the soirée of the 1929 season. As police officers in flat-topped kepi caps directed traffic with illuminated batons, Rolls-Royce limousines and Mercedes convertibles jockeyed for spots beneath the chestnut trees fronting the entrance of the spacious nineteenth-century mansion. From the vehicles stepped patricians with brilliantined hair and women in bobbed coiffures, but instead of tuxedos and ball gowns, they wore dresses of feathers and reeds, jackets of cardboard and upholstery. "We are requesting that you do not come in the usual clothing," warned the invitations to what its hosts called the "Bal des Matières." The status quo would not be tolerated.

Inside, through the glass double doors that opened into an expansive entrance hall and up a marble staircase surrounded by Corinthian columns and rock-crystal chandeliers, many of the city's most provocative artists mingled among the crowd. In the grand salon, where the works of old masters like Goya and Rubens hung incongruously along modernist parchment-clad walls, author Paul Morand made the rounds in a coat of book jackets, while artist Valentine Hugo modeled a dress fashioned from paper placemats. In the garden, where guests enjoyed a magic-lantern show accompanied by a live orchestra, writer Maurice Sachs banged about in a suit of pebbles and stones.

Amid the revelry stood the hostess of the evening: Marie-Laure de

Noailles, better known as the Vicomtesse de Noailles. Clothed in a gown of plastic holly leaves and a matching headdress, the twenty-six-year-old surveyed the gala with the satisfied look of a woman who had become one of the city's most influential patrons of the arts. Noailles was a facilitator, not a creator; the tools of her trade were her taste, her connections, and, above all, her fortune. While she was not beautiful, her features had become famous, thanks to the well-compensated artists who had captured their likeness: her long, youthful face sketched by Pablo Picasso, and the dark, plaintive eyes photographed by Man Ray.

She relished parties like this, and not just because they burnished her already formidable reputation. The carousing allowed her to flee the boredom of never having to want for anything. Her eccentric costume allowed her to conceal her own shyness. And amid the festivities, she could break free of the gilded bounds of her upbringing. Marie-Laure was born on October 31, 1902, the only child of Maurice Bischoffsheim, the scion of a powerful Jewish banking family. When her father and grandfather died while she was a child, the young girl became one of the richest heiresses in all of France. Fearing that she harbored the same physical frailties that had struck down her father, her mother ensconced her in a quiet villa in the south of France, where the young girl fantasized about fairy kingdoms and evil magicians. She lost herself in literature, including Dante and Edgar Allan Poe. She was infatuated with a friend of the family's, the writer Jean Cocteau, and she admired her maternal grandmother, the Comtesse de Chevigné, an imperious Parisian personality who inspired a major character in Marcel Proust's famous novel *In Search of Lost Time,* and was said to be the first lady of high society to ever utter the word *merde.* From the comtesse, the girl inherited a scandalous legacy: They were both direct descendants of the Marquis de Sade.

At twenty-one, Marie-Laure married Charles de Noailles, a mustache-clad aristocrat eleven years her senior. The two were well matched. Like his young wife, Charles boasted immense wealth and an illustrious family. With her marriage, Marie-Laure received the noble title "vicomtesse," placing her just a couple steps down the social hierarchy from "marquise." The new husband and wife might not have been consumed by passion for each other—during their cruise-ship honeymoon, he cultivated his tan while she hid in her cabin reading Freud's *Introduction to Psychoanalysis*—but they got along well. And together they decided to use their fortune, influence, and abundant free time to nurture the cultural movement that was diametrically opposed to every element of their upbringing: the French avant-garde.

During the Bal des Matières, a celebration of all that was radical, the Vicomtesse de Noailles pulled guests aside to show off the couple's latest acquisition: the scroll of *120 Days of Sodom*. Earlier that year, on January 29, 1929, a French writer named Maurice Heine had arrived in Berlin and, acting on the Noailleses' behalf, spent ten thousand reichsmarks to purchase the manuscript from Max Harrwitz, the publisher and bookseller responsible for putting out the books on Sade authored by Bloch, who had died earlier that decade. Now, five months later, it resided as a curio among the mansion's esoterica, alongside bejeweled snuffboxes and Byzantine statuary. This was a fitting new home for the manuscript, considering that it now lay in the hands of Sade's great-great-great-granddaughter.

But the scroll was destined to become much more than a fascinating trinket. Soon it would help the Noailleses create a work of such staggering transgression that it would scandalize Paris, threaten everything the couple held dear, and allow the Vicomtesse of Noailles to follow in the footsteps of her infamous ancestor. In the years to come, she would often ask people, "At what age did you become yourself?" For her, the answer was easy: 1929, the year she obtained *120 Days of Sodom*.

IN THE DARKENED auditorium of Studio 28, a small cinema halfway up a steep cobblestoned street near the Paris hilltop of Montmartre, the audience settled into their seats for the feature film of the evening: *L'Age d'Or*. The name, French for "The Golden Age," brought to mind a time of harmony and splendor. But when the show began, on the evening of December 3, 1930, nothing about the film seemed to suggest a celebration of human achievement—or, for that matter, to make much sense at all.

The black-and-white images that flashed across the screen appeared to have little relation to one another. A science documentary depicting an enraged scorpion striking down a rat segued into a vignette of bedraggled outlaws. Four Catholic bishops withered into skeletons on a rocky Spanish coast, leading to the founding of imperial Rome on the site of their remains in the year 1930. The soundtrack, piped through a speaker system that had just been installed to accommodate the new cinematic invention, seemed to be designed for another film entirely: During a shot of bubbling lava, the noise of a flushing toilet reverberated through the auditorium. The longer the film went on, the more it seemed to slip the bounds of reality. A man kicked a violin down a street. A cow lounged in a woman's bed. A father gunned down his own son. A giraffe tumbled out a window. A woman sucked lovingly on the toes of a statue. It was as if the logic of the audience's dreams had been extracted from their minds and projected directly onto the screen.

The film was a work of Surrealism, the philosophical and artistic movement that had spread like a bout of delirium through Paris's cultural milieu. Emerging from the devastation of the Great War, Surrealism aimed to replace society's restrictive customs with the power of the unconscious, the epiphany of chance coincidences, and the energy of unbound human desire. The movement was spearheaded by André Breton, a French writer and poet who had developed his philosophies while working in wartime neurological wards. He now held court amid rounds of mandarin curaçao cocktails at select Parisian cafés, imparting the tenets of the crusade to his devotees with all the dogmatism of the age-old social structures he aimed to obliterate.

Decrying the pretentiousness of modern literature, Breton and his colleagues generated nonsensical poetry through automatic-writing sessions and published a magazine, *La Revolution Surrealiste,* that reported on members' dreams and replaced the typical birth and marriage notices with a column titled "Suicides." Surrealist artists like René Magritte and Man Ray captured the uncanny realm of hallucinations by painting lovers kissing through veils and fastening an image of an eye to a ticking metronome. In their performances, Surrealists reveled in blasphemy, nudity, and bizarre stunts—performers screaming bestial cries, ballerinas pirouetting to the sound of silence. The efforts often devolved into physical fracases, and emerging bruised and battered from such events, audiences would declare the evening a success.

Surrealists found a perfect medium for shock when they turned to film. While the thirty-year-old film industry was mostly known for lighthearted mass entertainment, Breton's followers had realized they could utilize cinema's hyperrealism to reimagine modern life. The most startling example was the seventeen-minute silent Surrealist film *Un Chien Andalou,* which stunned all of Paris when it appeared to capture a man slicing open a woman's eye.

The Noailleses had attended a screening of the film in June 1929, just before their Materials Ball. The couple had already decorated their properties with works by Max Ernst, Francis Picabia, Man Ray, Yves Tanguy, and other Surrealist artists. They helped bankroll Surrealist periodicals and other efforts, overlooking the fact that Breton and his colleagues viewed their wealth with disdain. And they had been among the first to recognize the potential of an eccentric young Catalonian with dandyish tastes and a nervous laugh named Salvador Dalí, providing him with the funds to turn a fisherman's house on the Catalan coast into his home and studio. With *Un Chien Andalou,* they had witnessed Dalí's first cinematic effort, which he had co-created with a Spanish filmmaker named Luis Buñuel. They came away exhilarated, and offered to underwrite the duo's next venture.

The Noailleses would end up spending nearly a million francs on the project, which would be among the first French films with synchronized sound. After Dalí and Buñuel suffered a falling-out, the latter took charge. In January 1930, the brawny, heavy-browed director, who displayed the graces of his affluent upbringing but the rebelliousness of an iconoclast, moved into the Noailleses' villa in southern France to work on the script. Each evening, Buñuel would read aloud the latest passages to his patrons. In exchange, they offered up creative inspiration: *120 Days of Sodom.*

By that point, the Surrealists had come to know Sade well. Guillaume Apollinaire, an experimental poet and early champion of the avant-garde art scene, had inspired that fascination by uncovering many of Sade's handwritten manuscripts while digging into the off-limits section of the Bibliothèque Nationale de France; that department of the library was called Enfer, after the French word for "hell." In *L'Oeuvre du Marquis de Sade,* a short but influential anthology of Sade's writing that he published in 1909, Apollinaire argued that Sade wasn't simply the pioneering sexual scientist imagined by Bloch but the ultimate artistic rebel, a man who aspired to demolish the moral, political, and religious hypocrisies of his day. "The Divine Marquis," as he called Sade, was the "freest spirit who ever lived," one whose ideas deserved to "dominate the twentieth century."

In Sade's frenzied thirty-seven-day composition of *120 Days of Sodom,* the Surrealists saw the precursors of their own automatic-writing experiments, and in his pornographic obsessions, they perceived the origins of their celebration of erotic desire. Surrealists generated explicit artworks inspired by his life and penned esoteric essays on his theories, mounted excursions to his Provençal childhood home, and planned a masked orgy in an abandoned mansion, à la the saturnalia in Silling Castle. And like the marquis, the predominantly male group treated female bodies as objects they could freely prod and probe, dissecting and reassembling them in sculptures, photography, and paintings. Breton, in his pivotal first Surrealist Manifesto, announced that "Sade is Surrealist in sadism"—welcoming the long-dead writer into his elite inner circle.

The year before, Buñuel had been lent a copy of *120 Days of Sodom* that had once belonged to Proust. Buñuel found the novel a revelation. "I find next to Sade, all other masterpieces paled," he would write. Now, thanks to the Noailleses, he had unfettered access to the original version of the manuscript.

The novel permeated Buñuel's resulting creation, *L'Age d'Or*. The central plot of the sixty-three-minute film, as much as it has one, revolves around a couple's frustrated attempts to consummate their passion, a story line dripping with Sadean undertones. For its conclusion, the film shifts to the Château de Selliny, a castle perched high in the mountains. According to an intertitle, four scoundrels are about to emerge from the stronghold after passing 120 days in the throes of a criminal orgy, starting with the main organizer of the debauchery. From the fortress steps a long-haired, bearded man, radiating benevolence as he strides across the drawbridge in billowing robes. With *L'Age d'Or*, Buñuel had brought *120 Days of Sodom* to the silver screen, and turned its central villain into Jesus Christ.

The Noailleses debuted the film in the summer of 1930 with screenings at the private theater installed in their mansion, followed by a grand premiere at the Cinéma du Panthéon, next to the Sorbonne. Buñuel considered the events a triumph, while Dalí proclaimed that the final film looked like a Hollywood movie, meaning it as a compliment. But not everyone appreciated the work. When, after the screenings, the Noailleses took their places at the exit to bid their guests adieu, many of the city's privileged set left without saying a word. At a post-show reception in their grand salon, a Surrealist activist made a scene, spewing insults, shoving waiters, and smashing apart the buffet, incensed at the unholy alliance he had witnessed of revolutionary art and aristocratic largesse.

Undeterred, the film's organizers carried on. They decorated the lobby of Studio 28, the Montmartre theater where it was scheduled for an extended run, with artwork by Dalí, Ernst, Tanguy, and Man Ray. They produced a gilded forty-eight-page film program in which Breton and other Surrealist writers tied the work to the theories of Lenin, Freud, and Hegel. Finally, on November 28, the film opened, accompanied by several shorts and a cartoon, possibly a Walt Disney "Silly Symphony." The show that night and the subsequent four evenings proceeded without incident.

But now, in the middle of the screening on December 3, cries erupted in the auditorium: "Death to Jews!" and "This will teach you there are some Christians left in France!" The shouts came from fifty members of the far-right League of Patriots and the Anti-Semitic League, who had stormed the building and proceeded to set off smoke bombs in the aisles and fling purple ink on the screen. As the theater devolved into chaos, protesters pummeled the staff with cudgels and slashed up the paintings in the lobby on their way out the door.

The show resumed, with paper patches tacked over the ink stains on the screen. But in the city beyond, the backlash carried on. Newspapers began to condemn the film as a Bolshevik spectacle, and critics called the work *"L'Age d'Ordure,"* French for "The Age of Garbage." Italian diplomats decried the depiction of imperial Rome and other perceived offenses against Benito Mussolini's Fascist regime. A week after the riot, state censors revoked the film's authorization, and police confiscated every copy of *L'Age d'Or* they could find. The movie would remain out of circulation for the next fifty years.

Members of the Surrealists delighted in the fiasco, penning a treatise that speculated, "Isn't the use of provocation to legitimize subsequent police intervention a sign of fascism?" But those targeted by the attacks weren't so pleased. Buñuel, telegraphing from Hollywood, where he had taken what would prove to be a short-lived job at MGM, took full responsibility for the uproar. Dalí wondered if he would be deported back to Spain. Charles Noailles was forced to resign from the Jockey Club, the city's most exclusive association, and rumors made the rounds that his mother met with Pope Pius XI in Rome to save her son from excommunication.

To escape the turmoil, the Noailleses fled to the south of France, where they settled in for an uncharacteristically quiet Christmas holiday with their two young daughters, Laure and Nathalie. Charles in particular emerged shaken from the controversy. He reined in his experimental patronage and would never again dabble in filmmaking. As he would reportedly say to a colleague the following year, "I think we will have fewer problems with music."

His wife felt differently. Amid the scandal and upheaval unleashed by *L'Age d'Or,* Noailles experienced an epiphany as unexpected as it was liberating: She realized she was having fun.

NOAILLES STEPPED FROM her bedroom, dressed in a long white negligee, and padded down the hallway of her Mediterranean villa. The thirty-one-year-old and her husband had received this hilly stretch of land in the French Riviera as a wedding present years before, and on it they had built a sprawling Cubist complex of fifteen bedrooms, a hairdressing salon, a squash court, and a state-of-the-art indoor pool. Now the light of a full moon cast strange, disorienting shadows across its modernist expanses and tubular rubber-coated furniture.

She paused at another bedroom door, then quietly slipped inside. Here in bed lay one of the many distinguished guests the Noailleses invited for extended stays in their seaside retreat. The visitor's name was Edward James, and he was a British poet and wealthy art patron, but his identity wasn't particularly important. In the years to come, there would be many others like him, many more moments just like this. Without saying a word, she climbed into his bed. Noailles's personal escape had begun with the *L'Age d'Or* affair, but her transformation was helped along by another incident not long afterward: She found her husband in bed with the villa's in-house calisthenics trainer. Rather than end their marriage, the encounter clarified their relationship. The two would remain close, writing each other every day when they were apart, but in their pursuits they would go their separate ways. Charles turned to horticulture, immersing himself in the simple pleasures of camellias, boxwoods, and lilies. His wife opted to cultivate something more exotic: rebellion.

Now, rather than facilitating from the wings, she came to star in her own drama. Starting with James, she collected a series of lovers: The youthful Russian composer Igor Markevitch. The boisterous Spanish painter Óscar Domínguez. A bull breeder named Jean Lafont, a fraction of her age. She became a fashion icon, modeling the designs of Coco Chanel and Elsa Schiaparelli in the pages of *Vogue* and *Harper's Bazaar*. She published a collection of whimsical short stories titled *Ten Years on Earth,* launching a publishing career that would span eleven books and numerous articles. She eventually took up painting, producing phantasmagoric landscapes populated by strange animals and ghostly figures. And she reigned as a rabble-rousing queen of Paris's high society: causing scandals by spreading false rumors of love affairs, and acting on what she read about in sexology books by Magnus Hirschfeld. As one colleague would describe her behavior: "Marie-Laure is first of all a child, second an artist, third a vicomtesse. . . . Fourth, she's a saint, fifth, a masochist . . . and sixth, a bitch. . . . Above all, she is generous, not to mention crazy."

Among her favorite props was *120 Days of Sodom*. At gatherings, she would bring out the scroll and read prurient passages aloud. "Marie-Laure was a descendant of the Marquis de Sade," her husband would later explain. "So you know, she was very violent."

Noailles's notorious ancestor had also begun to acquire a new reputation, courtesy of Maurice Heine, the man who had retrieved *120 Days of Sodom* from Germany for the Noailleses. A doctor turned ultra-left firebrand and devoted Surrealist, Heine had been a member of the French Communist Party until the organization expelled him in 1923, not long after the avowed pacifist reportedly pulled out a revolver at a meeting and in a bout of passion fired it in the air, injuring his wife. In the years that followed, Heine dedicated himself to the one individual he believed could match his ardor for liberty: the Marquis de Sade. After tracking down *120 Days of Sodom* for the Noailleses, he was granted access to the scroll by its new owners in order to produce a new published edition of the novel, correcting the numerous mistakes he'd found in Bloch's version.

His results appeared in 1931 and 1935: a three-volume "critical edition" of *120 Days of Sodom*. The print run of 396 copies was distributed via subscription by the "Société du Roman Philosophique," a private organization Heine had founded to celebrate the life of the marquis, including through sumptuous banquets of crayfish bisque, mimosa salad, and truffled foie gras held every year on Sade's birthday. Rather than the scientific catalog described by Bloch, Heine saw *120 Days of Sodom* as a work of artistic liberation. He wrote in his introduction that the work should be directed "not to the public, but to the elites prepared by their culture to receive the ultimate expression of rational thought." He envisioned Sade, like himself, as a provocateur unfairly persecuted for his beliefs. As he noted in one of his many Surrealist articles on Sade, the marquis was "the tamer of nature," "the aggressor of the gods," "the contemptor of the laws," and "the liberator of sex." Before dying of illness in 1940, Heine would devote nearly all his time and money to unearthing and publicizing the writings of his patron saint. Thanks to his work, Sade would come to be known far beyond the domain of the Surrealists as an icon of artistic freedom.

Sade's Surrealist aficionados, meanwhile, found themselves floundering. Breton, ever the petty tyrant, had excommunicated or alienated many of his group's early members, and the movement was plagued with deep divisions over whether and how to translate their ideas into politics. At a time when more and more people were calling for societal change, the Surrealists suddenly seemed incapable of spreading their promised revolution beyond the bounds of their artistic creations.

Noailles, on the other hand, became a revolutionary. She took up with a left-wing radical named Michel Petitjean, marched in street protests, threw her support behind the progressive Front Populaire coalition when it took control of the French government in 1936, and even reportedly helped procure munitions for leftist brigades battling Francisco Franco in the Spanish Civil War. Her social peers took to sneeringly calling her "the Red Vicomtesse." It was a name she more likely than not appreciated.

But on June 14, 1940, the Red Vicomtesse kept quiet as she watched Nazi soldiers goose-step into Paris along the Champs-Élysées. She had attempted to flee the city when it became clear that the French forces would prove no match for the German invasion begun the month before, but had turned back her limousine amid the hopeless congestion of overloaded carts, honking automobiles, and ashen-faced Parisians trudging along on foot.

While Charles stayed in the south of France, she settled into occupied Paris, trying her best to resume the lifestyle she had always enjoyed. She dined with the remnants of her social circle at the Café de Flore, while the majority of city dwellers saw their intake of bread, meat, and cheese rationed to a few daily scraps and their coffee replaced with brewed chickpeas and acorns. Thanks to well-placed contacts and the fact that only her father was Jewish, which meant that under Nazi law she wasn't unduly tainted, she remained largely unmolested in her mansion on the Place des États-Unis—even as tens of thousands of French Jews began to be shipped to concentration camps. And either out of self-preservation, boredom, or simply her inability to tear herself away from scandal, the heiress of Sade ended up engaging in what some would see as the ultimate betrayal of her radical roots.

On November 21, 1940, a car careened off the road in the dark of a Paris night. Amid the wreckage lay Noailles and her companion: a Nazi officer. Her nose was badly injured in the crash, leaving her plagued by a telltale wheeze. She would attempt to have it repaired, but the damage had been done, and the scar would linger on. For the vicomtesse, the party had come to an end.

CHANTS OF "POWER is in the streets!" echoed through the twisting alleyways around the Théâtre de l'Odéon, in central Paris. It was May 17, 1968, and the calls that spring day resonated with the force of truth: In the span of a few weeks, the Parisian neighborhood had wrested itself free of the French authorities.

The revolt had begun several weeks earlier. Inspired by left-wing movements taking root across Europe and the United States, university students in and around the capital had come together in mass demonstrations over restrictive campus regulations and rising youth unemployment. Soon the avenues of Paris's Latin Quarter had been filled with clouds of tear gas as helmeted troops squared off against angry youths shielded by barricades of uprooted trees and overturned cars and armed with paving stones pried up from the streets. The upheaval had spread as workers, weary of the long, repressive presidency of World War II hero Charles de Gaulle, walked out of factories, department stores, and medical facilities. Now half of the country's labor force had stopped working, the largest general strike in French history.

Emboldened, students stormed the Sorbonne, turning its lecture halls into a "citadel of the revolution," where passersby could walk in and debate the particulars of the coming new world order. Then, two days before, with the declaration that "all bourgeois theaters should be turned into national assemblies," the protesters had seized control of the Odéon, transforming the theater into a public forum where anyone could take the stage and proclaim whatever came to mind.

At the time, most people considered the official permutation of Surrealism long since dead. The horrors of World War II and the looming threat of nuclear annihilation had left the group's giddy celebrations of nihilism looking both naïve and frighteningly accurate. Breton had passed away in 1966, a few years after welcoming an excommunicated Surrealist painter back into the fold for having had the audacity to brand the Sade family coat of arms into his chest on the anniversary of the marquis's death. But here, in this newly liberated section of Paris, the ideals of the movement were bursting forth. Amid the red velvet seats and gilded pilasters of the Odéon, revelers donned old theatrical costumes and engaged in freewheeling spectacles that one actor declared to be "the great surrealist event of the century." In the streets beyond, lithograph posters proclaimed, "Be realistic, ask for the impossible" and "Bibliotheque Nationale, set the books free." Nearby, graffiti scrawled on building walls declared, "Down with the toad of Nazareth" and "Ejaculate your desires." It was as if Sade himself, armed with silk screens and spray paint, was happily running amok.

That afternoon, in the midst of the disorder, the young radicals milling about the Odéon beheld an unexpected sight: a sleek black Citroën DS pulling up in front of the theater, a stately chauffeur behind the wheel. From the back seat lumbered Marie-Laure de Noailles, aged sixty-five. She looked like an oddly dressed gypsy, with her baggy Chanel tweed suit, dyed-brown hair, and garish sunglasses. While the years had robbed her of her thin figure and her "Gauloises Bleu" cigarette habit had left her voice a gravelly rasp, her eyes still blazed with the fervor of the Red Vicomtesse. She was here to impart the wisdom of her years to a new generation of troublemakers.

She likely didn't know that the Théâtre de l'Odéon and its environs had been built on the site of the Hôtel de Condé, the palatial home of the powerful house of Condé, demolished shortly before the revolution. That meant that she was taking her revolutionary stand at the birthplace of her notorious ancestor, the Marquis de Sade.

But her exploits, subversive as they were, had never served much of a purpose other than to shock, and the performance had run its course. The students who had paralyzed the nation had no need for the carefully organized provocations of her beloved Surrealists, no interest in her money and influence, tainted as they were by her elitism. As one of the nearby street posters declared, "Culture: The favorite weapon of the bourgeoisie." Noailles had become little more than a fascinating artifact, one more curio filling the mansion on the Place des États-Unis. So, respectfully but firmly, the protesters disregarded her opinions that day, allowing the vicomtesse to hold forth in vain until she returned to her town car and directed her chauffeur to take her away.

The following month, shaken French authorities managed to regain control of the Odéon and the Sorbonne. The events of May '68 hadn't led to revolution, but France would never be the same. The following year, de Gaulle announced his resignation after losing a vote on a relatively minor governmental issue. When asked why he was leaving, he replied, "Because of the absurdity."

The protests would mark one of the last adventures of the Red Vicomtesse. Two years later, on January 29, 1970, terrified screams filled the mansion on the Place des États-Unis: "I don't want to die! I don't want to die!" Noailles had suffered a stroke the night before, and now the sixty-seven-year-old lay in her bed, struggling to breathe. As usual, she refused to accept the status quo. She grabbed desperately at her longtime live-in maid, leaving deep scratches along her arms. But this time, her antics would fail: Later that morning, Noailles passed away.

She left behind Charles, who remained a dear friend, if not her lover, to the end. He would live another eleven years, so committed to his gardening that a variety of his cherished camellias would be named "Vicomte de Noailles." She also left behind two daughters and four grandchildren, who always saw her as more of a living myth than an intimate family member, since she was usually too busy making a spectacle of herself to devote much energy to familial affection. And she left behind something else: the scroll of *120 Days of Sodom*.

The manuscript went to her younger daughter, Nathalie. A professional equestrian, she had never had much interest in the high jinks of her mother, but she, too, became enchanted by the scroll. The phallic container designed by the Marquis de Villeneuve-Trans the century before had been lost to time, so she kept the manuscript in a leather box stored in a cabinet in her home. And, like her mother before her, Nathalie would remove it and roll it out on a table for perusal when illustrious guests stopped by, such as the Italian writer Italo Calvino and the onetime Surrealist Louis Aragon. Eventually, however, she showed it to the wrong person. In November 1982, Nathalie's son Carlo Perrone received a panicked call from his mother: The scroll was gone.

120 Days of Sodom, she told him, had been stolen.

CHAPTER EIGHT
Trouble in Bibliopolis

2007

LHÉRITIER TOOK A SIP OF HIS WINE AND BEAMED AT HIS LUNCH GUEST. On the other side of the dining table sat Frédéric Castaing, a Parisian manuscript dealer and president of the Syndicat National de la Librairie Ancienne et Moderne, the country's auspicious association of rare-book sellers. Lhéritier had given Castaing a tour of his operation, then taken him to lunch at Fouquet's Paris, one of the flashiest brasseries in the city. The point of the meeting was to impress. Everything about Castaing—his elegant suit, his slicked-back pompadour, his sophisticated demeanor—exuded old-world authority. He was just the sort of person Lhéritier could use to provide Aristophil with clout.

Lhéritier, nearly sixty, had lost so much hair and added enough heft to his short frame that he resembled Alfred Hitchcock. His most salient feature was his sly, roguish smile, which he now flashed as he got down to business. The world of letters and manuscripts was insular, he explained to Castaing. The French market for such materials was becoming more irrelevant by the day. It was time to leverage the end of handwriting and take the business to heights the country had never seen. With Castaing's expertise and Lhéritier's financial acumen, the operation could be unstoppable. In short, Lhéritier concluded, "You should work with us."

Castaing remained graciously noncommittal throughout the meal. He thanked Lhéritier for his time, then made his way back to his manuscript shop on Rue Jacob, a narrow street lined with art galleries and designer boutiques not far from the Seine. Castaing glanced around his small but elegant workspace: On the eggshell-blue walls hung framed missives from D. H. Lawrence, Oscar Wilde, and Jack London. Statuettes of James Joyce and Victor Hugo kept watch over the shop's orderly shelves of reference books and leather-bound tomes. In the back stood a well-worn cabinet that had been used to store precious texts for more than a century. This was where Castaing helped patrons determine the relevance and worth of documents that had been passed down for generations, and where he offered up to a select clientele letters and manuscripts valued from €500 to more than a thousand times that. As he stood in his quiet gallery, a bastion of all that Lhéritier considered old-fashioned and stale, Castaing made a silent vow: He would never work with Aristophil.

Castaing had been born into the business. His paternal grandmother, Madeleine Castaing, had been one of the most important French antiques dealers and decorators of the twentieth century, while his father, Michel, had been the final proprietor of Maison Charavay, the first and longest-running French manuscript shop, before it closed in 2006. Castaing had spent his childhood exploring his grandmother's eclectic Parisian design boutique, where overstuffed Russian armchairs mingled with leopard-spotted carpets and fake ivy vines. Around the corner at Maison Charavay, the young boy perused the ancient letter archives stored in the cabinet now located in his shop, finding handwritten manuscripts by Marcel Proust, Auguste Rodin, and Gustave Flaubert. And he spent his summers in northern France, playing at the family country house, where his grandmother entertained friends like Jean Cocteau, Chaïm Soutine, and Pablo Picasso.

Growing up, Castaing didn't always get along with his father, since the two clashed over politics. Michel Castaing would go to his grave believing that his son had been responsible for a paving stone thrown through Madeleine Castaing's store window during the May '68 riots. At first, Castaing opted to forsake the family business, becoming a history teacher. But one day, he showed his class original letters written by French revolutionaries Maximilien Robespierre and Georges Danton that he'd borrowed from Maison Charavay's collections. When he saw the excitement in his students' eyes, he decided to follow in his father's footsteps.

Some whispered that Castaing had simply ridden on his family's coattails, taking advantage of Maison Charavay's fame and clientele, and opening his shop in what had once been part of his grandmother's furniture gallery on Rue Jacob. But Castaing had forged his own path, receiving little help from his father. Inspired by Hollywood westerns and other Americana he'd loved as a kid, he focused on materials penned by F. Scott Fitzgerald, William Faulkner, and Alfred Hitchcock long before most French dealers discovered the appeal of American celebrities. As president of France's rare-book sellers' association, he orchestrated the relocation of the organization's yearly book fair to the Grand Palais, the iconic glass-ceilinged exhibition hall not far from the Eiffel Tower, turning the event into a major annual spectacle.

By studying Maison Charavay's extensive archives, Castaing had become a skilled document specialist, eventually taking on the role of president of the Compagnie Nationale des Experts, a private organization of book, art, and antiquities specialists often called to serve as court experts. He learned how to use paper composition, watermark patterns, manufacturing imprints, and ink-absorption rates to pinpoint the exact age of a document. He knew how to identify the microscopic differences between writing from quill pens and that from more modern steel nibs. And he became adept at spotting the effortlessly consistent, hasty, and even careless handwriting associated with authentic materials. In historic documents, as in life, anything that appeared too perfect was bound to raise suspicions.

Castaing had reached a point where he was considered one of the biggest names in the French letters market—until the arrival of Lhéritier. To Castaing, the idea of turning precious documents into investment vehicles was a perversion of everything his field held dear. The fact that Aristophil was located just down the street from him, in this particular neighborhood, made the affront even worse.

At last count, the International League of Antiquarian Booksellers, the global trade group for rare-book dealers, listed 138 member booksellers in Paris, more than the total number in New York, London, and Rome combined. The majority of these shops, including Castaing's, were located in and around the Saint-Germain-des-Prés and Odéon neighborhoods in the Sixth Arrondissement, a history-rich stretch of the Left Bank situated around the Sorbonne. Booksellers and publishers had first begun congregating in the district in the sixteenth century to be close to the university, and now the small area boasted roughly a third of all the bookstores in Paris. While the open-air bookstalls, or *bouquinistes,* that ran along the river captured most of the tourist attention, the major deals took place in the medieval alleys that snaked away from the Seine. Here, through doors emblazoned with LIVRES ANCIENS and AUTOGRAPHES, one could find tiny, cluttered bookshops boasting autographed first editions from Victor Hugo; love letters by Marie-Antoinette; mammoth incunabula, the rudimentary fifteenth-century tomes that emerged during the dawn of printing; and miniature books a few centimeters tall. It was a world composed of leather bindings and gilt-edged pages, smelling of dust and decomposing paper, where the exact position of a title-page illustration could mean a difference of thousands of euros.

This was where, in the 1920s, a struggling young writer named Ernest Hemingway had browsed the bookstalls on the riverside quays, learning from a seller how to judge the value of a French book: "If a book is good, the owner will have it bound properly," she told him. "All books in English are bound, but bound badly. There is no way of judging them."

The area had another writerly claim to fame: It was home to Rue de l'Odéon, a stately one-block street between the Boulevard Saint-Germain and the Luxembourg Gardens that boasted more literary accomplishments per foot than possibly any other thoroughfare in the world. In one of the row houses along the street, Thomas Paine wrote *Rights of Man,* and in another, author and publisher Robert McAlmon worked to publish Hemingway's first book, *Three Stories and Ten Poems.* Halfway up the lane, at 7 Rue de l'Odéon, Adrienne Monnier had opened La Maison des Amis des Livres ("A House of the Friends of Books"), one of the country's first woman-owned bookshops, which became a gathering place for such members of the French literary avant-garde as Paul Valéry, André Gide, and Paul Claudel, not to mention a young André Breton and his colleagues as they planned their Surrealist revolution.

Inspired by the shop's success, Monnier's companion, American-born Sylvia Beach, opened an English-language bookstore and lending library called Shakespeare and Company across the street at 12 Rue de l'Odéon. Beach's operation became a favorite haunt for Hemingway, F. Scott Fitzgerald, Ezra Pound, Gertrude Stein, and other literary expats of the Lost Generation. The street also produced the first edition of James Joyce's *Ulysses;* Beach, with Monnier's help, became the novel's ad hoc publisher when no one else would do so, ignoring warnings from George Bernard Shaw that the book was "a revolting record of a disgusting phase of civilization."

Before all of this, "Odéonia"—as Monnier and Beach were known to call this tiny pocket of the city—bore witness to a lesser known but no less pivotal literary event. The avenue ran directly through the former grounds of the Hôtel de Condé palace before ending at the Théâtre de l'Odéon. That meant that Rue de l'Odéon lay within a hundred feet or so of the birthplace of the Marquis de Sade.

Booksellers and manuscript dealers in this neighborhood were treasure hunters, cultivating networks of expert informers, scouring death notices for hints of notable collections, and employing "runners" to scour flea markets and estate sales for rare finds. They spoke in esoteric jargon, throwing around terms like "foxed pages," "paraph marks," "gauffered edges," and "remboîtage bindings." At public auctions, they were known to conspire among themselves to outbid outsiders and amateurs, to ensure that prominent materials didn't slip beyond their purview. Dealers could be reluctant to part with their most prized discoveries, no matter the offered price, especially if the interested buyer didn't strike them as particularly worthy of their spoils. They weren't acting out of pompousness or greed. They understood that they weren't simply buying and selling interesting texts; they were dealing in works of art.

Castaing fit in perfectly. If anything, the handful of Parisian dealers like him who specialized in manuscripts and letters catered to an especially intense type of collector of the written word: those who sought to acquire documents written by the author's own hands.

Castaing avoided buying items at the Paris auction houses. Like his grandmother, who would require potential clients to visit her gallery several times before she deemed them worthy of her services, Castaing preferred to do business in the quiet of his shop, where he could read people. There he could judge customers' reactions to seeing one of the few remaining scripts from Orson Welles's 1938 sci-fi radio drama *The War of the Worlds* that hadn't been destroyed during the ensuing public panic and police raid of the recording studio. Sitting with clients over a cup of tea at his tidy worktable, he could gauge their response to hearing his tale of acquiring a copy of *For Whom the Bell Tolls* that, at the end of World War II, Hemingway had signed and handed to a doorman on his way to "liberating" the bar at the Hôtel Ritz.

But Castaing's world had already changed, since the rise of the internet made the hunt for rare books and letters a far less specialized skill. Now, thanks to Aristophil, the entire field had been flipped on its head. For as long as anyone could remember, the tiny French industry had been fueled by the passion of a handful of dealers and the fervor of a few thousand clients. Now texts were being traded and locked away in coffers, owned by people all over France and beyond, often by those who never saw their acquisitions, never ran their hands across the paper. A book or manuscript's price had long been known to rise or plummet based on collectors' shifting whims or impassioned bids at the auction houses. Now texts were being treated like investment vehicles with steady rates of return. Castaing worried that if Lhéritier wasn't stopped, everything about the world he knew and loved could be destroyed.

THE RARE-BOOK SALE in Hall Five of Paris's Hôtel Drouot auction house was about to begin, and if it proceeded like the vast majority of book auctions, it would prove to be a somber affair. Most dealers considered the auction halls hallowed ground, a place of firm rules of etiquette forged over generations of sales. Bidders, for the most part, remained seated and silent. Rather than call out bids, they would flash the subtlest of gestures to the auctioneer. The noise from the spectators rarely rose above a round of polite applause. Everyone understood that this was a place of decorum and restraint.

A man in a black fedora named Jean-Claude Vrain then walked in and proceeded to break all the rules. Within a few minutes of the start of the auction, Vrain's raspy voice broke the silence of his fellow bidders, calling out the winning offer—roughly €71,000—for the original manuscript of one of the Marquis de Sade's lesser novels, *Histoire Secrète d'Isabelle de Bavière, Reine de France.* Then he stood up and removed his overcoat, revealing a hefty figure clad in a cobalt suit that seemed to glow amid the subdued grays and browns of his colleagues. Strolling about the room, Vrain continued his performance. He prevailed in a bidding war for a political treatise by Karl Marx by offering up €76,000, more than five times the estimated price. "Marx is worth it!" he called to the crowd. "He's the best economist in the world." He engaged in another skirmish for an original luxury edition of Gustave Flaubert's *Madame Bovary,* only to lose interest once the price ascended higher than €155,000. "That was the right price," he declared with indifference as others continued to bid.

"You're the best!" cried an onlooker, not being able to restrain himself as Vrain continued to win lot after lot. Women approached and congratulated him, while others rushed to take his photo. At the end of the sale, news crews crowded about the man who had become the star of the show. "I am happy with how I did," Vrain said into a microphone, relishing the attention. "Not too shabby for an old working-class guy like me."

Vrain had come from blue-collar roots, having worked on automobile assembly lines before entering the rare-book business in his thirties. But since then, operating from his cluttered shop just around the corner from Rue de l'Odéon, he had used his aggressive drive and brutal honesty to become one of the biggest rare-book dealers in all of France. He did business with fashion designer Yves Saint Laurent, English couturier Alexander McQueen, and billionaire François Pinault. He supplied materials to former prime minister Dominique de Villepin. And when Hollywood actor Johnny Depp was looking to acquire a few literary relics, the bookseller provided him with first editions of Arthur Rimbaud's *A Season in Hell* and Albert Camus's *The Stranger,* in exchange for a quarter of a million euros.

Vrain had also become known for something else: his fierce, deep-seated rivalry with Frédéric Castaing.

In a hermetic letters market where arguments could last a century, the enmity between Castaing and Vrain was legendary. Some said the discord began with disagreements stemming from their different Communist ideologies. Others said Vrain, with his gaudy attire and arrogant behavior, simply clashed with the prim and fastidious way that Castaing did business. Now Castaing had another reason to hate his rival: Vrain had joined forces with Lhéritier.

Vrain had become one of Aristophil's top document experts, ap-praising its acquisitions before they were sold to investors. He oper-ated as a company spokesperson, appearing in Aristophil videos extolling the company's approach and declaring to reporters that the operation "has taken the place left open by public institutions and the National Library, which do not have a penny to invest in our heri-tage."

Castaing found the partnership galling. In 2005, before becoming familiar with Aristophil, he had published *Rouge Cendres,* a crime novel in which he modeled one of the main villains, Augustin, on Vrain. "In the [auctions], he never sat down like you and me, in a si-lence of good taste," Castaing wrote of Augustin. "No, he'd stay on his feet at the back of the room, he'd speak harshly at everyone and he'd bid like one orders a café crème." In the book, Augustin, thirst-ing for wealth and power, partners with a shady tycoon to try to corner the Parisian letters market. Now the story appeared to be coming true.

Meeting among themselves, Parisian booksellers and manuscript dealers had been quietly voicing concerns about Lhéritier and his business model. France's antiquarian booksellers' association, after all, had long condemned using books and historical documents for financial speculation. But in public, most dealers kept their opinions to themselves. Many of them were making good money from Aristophil's spending and the resulting market boom. Some even received company stipends for providing tips on promising finds. Castaing, however, refused to keep quiet. In his position as president of the booksellers' association, he began to openly condemn Aristophil. When a reporter for the consumer-rights magazine *Que Choisir* approached him about Aristophil's collections in 2011, Castaing didn't mince words. "These papers are not investment vehicles," he told the journalist. "The demand exists, but it comes from a relatively small circle of collectors and public libraries. To suggest that a letter from Victor Hugo or Mallarmé will automatically increase in value each year is not honest."

The resulting stories coincided with the first signs of public unease about Aristophil. The company's success seemed too meteoric, too inexplicable, to be wholly legit. In November 2012, the Belgian public prosecutor's office launched an investigation into Aristophil's Brussels offshoot, on suspicion of fraudulent activity. The following month, France's stock market regulator issued a warning to consumers about "atypical investments" such as letters and manuscripts, noting that the buying and selling of these sorts of materials weren't thoroughly regulated. While Aristophil's contracts were structured as private deals, so the state couldn't technically regulate them, the warning was clearly referring to the company.

Soon, the alert would seem prescient. Aristophil had always provided lucrative offers to its clients when the firm bought their manuscripts back at the end of their five-year terms, allowing shareholders to recoup their investments with their anticipated 40 percent profits. But now the company began to founder. For the first time ever, it struggled to repurchase all of its investors' manuscripts at their expected rates of return.

Castaing continued to voice his concerns, even as his crusade cost him friendships. He had long been friendly with Alain Nicolas, a major Paris manuscript dealer and the author of the French historical document guide *Les Autographes*. Nicolas had spoken at the funeral of Castaing's father, and Castaing had gifted Nicolas a bas-relief of the Goncourt brothers, the inveterate chroniclers of nineteenth-century literary Paris, that had hung in Maison Charavay. But when Castaing learned that Nicolas was doing business with Lhéritier, he severed all ties.

Castaing didn't care that behind his back, Nicolas and others who had aligned with Lhéritier were sneeringly calling him "Don Quixote," and "the White Knight." Nor was he afraid of repercussions that might come his way. He had been in tough spots before.

In 1985, Castaing had traveled to Communist Warsaw to secretly meet with the members of Solidarność, a Polish trade union advocating for workers' rights, to help them disseminate their views. There he was spotted and apprehended by the local police. After taking him to an interrogation room and burning him with cigarette butts, the officers held up a paper they had found on him and yelled, "Who is Victor Hugo?! Who is Baudelaire?!" While searching him they had discovered one of his business inventories, and they thought the items were code names for spies.

Having concluded that Castaing wasn't a threat, the officers eventually released him, and he returned, bruised and shaken, to France. A photo taken after the incident showed a young Castaing with his hands bandaged, his eyes sunken and haunted. If he could survive that experience, surely he could brave Aristophil.

IN 2013, THE sound of drums echoed through a warm April evening, announcing the grand opening of Aristophil's new headquarters, the Institute of Letters and Manuscripts. In this ritzy corner of central Paris, well-dressed politicians and celebrities made their way through the property's wrought-iron gate and down a red carpet, flanked on both sides by Napoleonic guards in full regalia tapping out military tattoos. Stepping through the entrance of the nearly four-hundred-year-old white-limestone mansion, they found themselves surrounded by magnificence: room after opulent room embellished with gold-paneled walls, frescoed ceilings, and crystal chandeliers. As attendees sipped champagne and admired illuminated displays of letters and manuscripts, waiters strolled about in breeches and powdered wigs. Here and there stood "living tabletops"—female attendants clad in eighteenth-century dresses with tables of hors d'oeuvres fastened around their waists, looking like something out of *Alice in Wonderland*.

In the middle of it all stood Lhéritier. The year before, he had spent €34 million to purchase the Hôtel de La Salle, one of the grandest private mansions in all of Paris and the former home to dukes and duchesses and Jean-Jacques-Régis de Cambacérès, the author of France's code of civil law. Lhéritier moved his headquarters into the building and installed salons for special exhibits and events. The resulting testament to his achievements stood directly across the street from Éditions Gallimard, France's most prestigious publishing house. It was just the sort of stunt in which the company specialized. Now Lhéritier, beaming in a crisp black suit beneath a giant portrait of Napoleon, had truly become the king of manuscripts, and this was his palace.

As Paris's well-to-do moved through the crowd to greet their host, they didn't know they were speaking to one of the richest people in the country. Five months earlier, Lhéritier had become obscenely rich—and in a way that had nothing to do with Aristophil.

Thanks to his working-class roots, Lhéritier had always played the lottery. So when he heard in November 2012 that the EuroMillions jackpot had reached into the nine figures, he bought numerous tickets. He played various combinations of the dates of his birthday and those of his children. On November 13, when he learned from his daughter that the winning ticket had been purchased in the area, he checked the results online. He discovered that all seven winning numbers—1, 16, 21, 24, 29, 2, and 6—perfectly matched one of his vouchers. He won €169 million, at the time the largest EuroMillions jackpot in French history.

Lhéritier didn't go public about his windfall, but his lifestyle reached new heights. After giving millions to his children and his ex-wife, he purchased a villa in the hills of Nice, complete with a fishpond and indoor and outdoor pools. He acquired a Mercedes-Benz, a sixty-foot yacht named *Narval II,* a team of racehorses, and two hot-air balloons emblazoned with the Aristophil logo. He had more than enough left over to inject €41 million into his company, shoring up its financial standing.

Now, at the Institute of Letters and Manuscripts' opening, Lhéritier stepped to a glass podium and, flashing his roguish grin, welcomed those gathered to his "Pantheon of letters and manuscripts." He talked about the history of Aristophil and his accomplishments over the past twenty years. Near the end of his speech, he told the crowd that his opponents were madmen and cowards, driven by jealousy of his success. He issued a warning to all who dared cross him: "You can count on me to fight relentlessly against all those individuals who try to destabilize and attack us." Lhéritier, in fact, had already launched the battle.

To derail the Belgian investigation, the company's legal team had uncovered evidence suggesting that the judge running the operation had improperly shared information about the case, forcing the magistrate to recuse himself. Closer to home, the president of a Paris-based wealth-management trade group who had been critical of Lhéritier's operation found himself the target of legal threats and public attacks. Bloggers who questioned the company's business model received threatening letters, and one online critic found himself on the other end of an anonymous phone call suggesting that he could end up with broken kneecaps if he didn't delete his posts.

In response to *Que Choisir*'s critical coverage of the operation, the company filed a libel lawsuit against the consumer-rights magazine. The publication went to court to fight the charge, but ultimately lost on a technicality. For failing to properly disclose that Lhéritier had been cleared of most of the charges related to the Monaco stamp affair, the magazine had to issue a correction and pay €1 in damages, plus €1,500 to cover Lhéritier's legal fees.

That left Castaing. For his most vocal critic, Lhéritier orchestrated special retribution. Payback arrived on November 14, 2012, during an auction of French literary manuscripts at Hôtel Drouot that Castaing had been chosen to preside over as the auction expert. The position was an acknowledgment of Castaing's reputation, as well as a public demonstration of his status and skill. But as soon as the auction began, Castaing knew something was wrong. Sitting at the front of the auction hall, he watched with dismay as the room remained quiet for one lot after another. Handwritten novels, original theater scripts, drafts of unpublished books all failed to garner interest. Of the sixty-five items up for bid, an assortment valued at over €1 million, only sixteen lots ended up finding buyers, bringing in just €146,000.

Only later did Castaing learn the reason for the debacle. Lhéritier had told his staff not to buy anything from the sale. His words carried enough authority that many others in the industry likely snubbed the auction, too.

A few months later, the manuscript dealer arrived at his shop one morning to find a catalog from the failed auction resting on his doorstep. A new catalog appeared the next morning and the morning after that. The warnings continued, every day for a week.

CHAPTER NINE

Citizen Sade

APRIL 2, 1790

AS THE RESIDENTS OF PARIS OBSERVED GOOD FRIDAY, SADE WALKED FREE after thirteen years behind bars. The revolution that had begun with the storming of the Bastille the year before had now delivered him his freedom, albeit following a maddening delay. While imprisoned in the Bastille the previous summer, Sade had been informed that his daily stroll along the battlements had been revoked as a security precaution, since riots had broken out nearby. Incensed, the marquis had grabbed the long metal funnel used for emptying his chamber pot into the prison moat and, employing it as a megaphone, began shouting from his window that prison guards were slitting prisoners' throats.

Sade had gone too far. The following night, at the urging of the prison warden, six armed guards hauled the marquis from his cell and, without giving him time to dress or collect any belongings, bundled him in a carriage to Charenton, a mental asylum outside Paris. There, Sade found himself in a more dire form of captivity than ever before. He described Charenton at the time as "a horrid place arranged in such a way that the air can never reach the interior and the sobs and screams of the prisoners cannot be heard by anyone," a facility filled with "wretches in full possession of their reason but forgotten for centuries in this asylum of woe."

Most pressingly, Sade had been forced to leave his writings at the Bastille. Desperate to retrieve them, the marquis signed a power of attorney allowing his wife to collect his furniture, books, and manuscripts. On the morning of July 14, eleven days after he'd been dragged from his cell, Renée-Pélagie met with a police official assigned to accompany her to the prison. But just then a disturbance broke out in a nearby street, causing the officer to delay the undertaking until later that day. By that point, it would be too late. That afternoon, angry Parisians stormed the Bastille, releasing its remaining prisoners and finding Sade's cell exactly as he had been forced to leave it the week before. The French Revolution had begun.

The marquis would spend the rest of his life believing that *120 Days of Sodom* had been destroyed, lost forever in the sacking and demolition of the Bastille. "Every day," he would write of the loss, "I shed tears of blood."

But on this Good Friday, Sade was in high spirits. The National Constituent Assembly, France's newly formed governing body, had abolished the king's ability to arbitrarily arrest and detain people. The authorities had been forced to liberate Sade and all others incarcerated under royal *lettres de cachet,* leading to his release from Charenton after eight months. "Good day, good works!" the forty-nine-year-old Sade declared in a celebratory letter to his lawyer, Gaufridy. He vowed that from this point forward, he would be a changed man: "I shall resolve to mend my ways, and I shall keep my word!"

Sade emerged into a Paris that had been radically transformed. Throughout the capital, "liberty trees"—an emblem borrowed from the American Revolution—had been draped with garlands in the colors of the revolution: blue, white, and red, which would come to symbolize liberty, equality, and fraternity. Plastered across city walls, posters for new political groups proclaimed radical views that would have been forbidden less than a year before. All over the city, churches were coming down, their bells melted to produce gun barrels. And the Bastille, having been dismantled, now existed only as a fashion statement. Street peddlers hawked baubles shaped like the fortress for Parisians to wear on their otherwise simple attire, the flamboyant garb and powdered wigs of prerevolutionary France very much out of style.

In a series of sweeping decrees, the new government had done away with many of the age-old bulwarks of French society, including the feudal privileges of the aristocracy and the power of the church. King Louis XVI, living under guard in Paris, had been helpless to stop them. Suddenly butchers, merchants, and schoolteachers were being elected to positions of power by their male peers. Gone was the patchwork of medieval parishes that had stretched across the French landscape, replaced by a uniform administration of cantons, districts, and departments.

Even the quantification of space and time would be transformed. Within a few years, the country would replace its byzantine arrangement of weights and measures with the far more orderly metric system. In a more radical move, the nation would revolutionize its calendar system, instituting ten-day weeks and declaring that moving forward, year one of recorded time would begin with the founding of the new French Republic, rather than the birth of Christ.

The shock of such changes left Sade estranged from the outside world for which he'd yearned for so long. "I have lost my taste for everything," he wrote. "At times I am seized by a desire to join the Trappists, and I cannot be sure that one fine day I may not disappear, never to be heard of again."

With only a single gold coin in the pocket of his black ratteen coat, the newly released inmate made his way to the convent of Sainte-Aure, where his wife had been living in a meager apartment in order to afford Sade's expensive prison upkeep and keep his irrational suspicions of her behavior at bay. But Renée-Pélagie wanted nothing more to do with him. For some time, she had been drifting away. Pummeled by her mother's criticisms and steeped in the piety of her religious accommodations, she had tired of Sade's demanding letters and profane manuscripts. Her children had been raised by her parents, and now that she was nearing fifty, her years of flouting the law and covering up her husband's misdeeds were behind her. Suddenly, with her husband's freedom restored, she risked being sucked back into the maelstrom. Her physical safety was on the line; at times during her prison visits, Sade had grown so agitated that prison guards had been forced to restrain him. What's more, the revolution had reinstated all of the civil and financial rights the monarchy had stripped from the marquis. Renée-Pélagie knew her spouse well enough to dread how he'd manage the family's social and monetary affairs.

Renée-Pélagie made up her mind: Her life with Sade was over. But she was too fearful to say that to his face. Refusing to see him at the convent, she passed along a terse note demanding an end to their marriage. Doing so wouldn't be easy; the French authorities had never condoned divorce. Likely the best Renée-Pélagie could hope for was a *séparation de biens,* or separation of property, a legal procedure that resulted in the division of a couple's marital possessions, usually to protect the wife's property from her husband's mishandling. But if Sade refused to go along with such proceedings, Renée-Pélagie could opt for a more uncommon and extreme option: She could petition for a *séparation de corps et d'habitation,* or separation of person and domicile, in which the courts allowed a husband and wife to live apart after finding that one of the two, usually the husband, was guilty of debauchery, bigamy, extreme violence, attempted murder, or other intolerable crimes.

Renée-Pélagie surely considered the latter a last resort, since it would require subjecting herself and her family to legal scrutiny. Still, if Sade forced her to go that route, they both knew she had enough incriminating material to prevail, along the way further wrecking the marquis's already shoddy reputation and likely putting a quick end to his newfound freedom. As she wrote to the family lawyer about her decision to separate, "M. de Sade, if he probes his conscience, is bound to see justice in my motives and acknowledge that it could not be otherwise. As for scandal, he's a master at it. I'll only say what he forces me to say, to justify myself. *But I'll say it if he forces me to.*"

Sure enough, after at first denouncing his wife's initial separation petition as "a monument of lies and foolishness, as crude and obscure as it is flatly and stupidly written," in the end Sade acquiesced to her demands. That September, the two signed a separation agreement in which Renée-Pélagie agreed to not insist on reimbursement of her substantial dowry in exchange for an alimony of four thousand livres a year. Her onetime husband never paid her a cent.

If Renée-Pélagie had waited a bit longer, she would have found an easier way to terminate her marriage. Two years later, the revolutionary government would pass the most radical divorce law anywhere, allowing both men and women the ability to end their marriages for a variety of reasons, ranging from mistreatment to incompatibility. The law would only be on the books for eleven years before a new government regime reversed it. But during that period, Paris would witness more than twelve thousand divorces, or roughly one for every four new marriages. In the vast majority of the cases, women instigated the proceedings. In one of the only instances in her life, the timid Renée-Pélagie had been ahead of her time.

IN THE MONTHS leading up to the legal cessation of his marriage, Sade used a loan from his mother-in-law, of all people, to settle outstanding debts and obtain a series of accommodations, eventually renting a small house with a courtyard in a fashionable part of the city. He also took up with a new acquaintance: Marie-Constance Quesnet, a thirty-three-year-old actress and single mother, who moved into Sade's house with her six-year-old son, Charles. While Sade took to calling Marie-Constance "sensible," meaning "sensitive," he insisted their relationship was strictly platonic. "Nothing is more virtuous than my little household," he wrote in a letter to Gaufridy, one of his few remaining correspondents. "To begin with, not a word of love."

Whether or not his claims of chastity were true, Sade's obsession with libertinage had been largely replaced by a new mania: money. He suffered from a distinct lack of it, especially since there was no easy way for him to derive adequate revenues from his family lands in Provence. Devastated by years of poor harvests and terrified of rumors that nobles were sending brigands across the country to wrest back political control, peasants and townspeople across rural France were rising up in revolt—ransacking châteaus, destroying records of their feudal obligations, even attacking aristocrats. Considering the turmoil, Sade refused to risk a trip to the south of France to set his financial affairs in order.

Sade was right to stay away. The following year, the long-docile residents of the village of La Coste armed themselves with cudgels and pikes and, caught up in the fervor of the moment, stormed the château on the hilltop above. Within an hour, Sade's beloved hideout was reduced to a shambles: the wine cellar pillaged, windows shattered, furniture demolished, valuables carted away.

For immediate income, Sade had little choice but to turn to writing. Identifying himself as a man of letters in his correspondence, he began submitting his plays to theaters around Paris. Several companies rejected his submissions, with one theater director noting that his work was "not compatible with the rules of propriety," even though his dramatic efforts mostly avoided lewdness and blasphemy.

Eventually, he found companies willing to produce selections of his work. In November 1791, the Théâtre Molière, a new operation dedicated to provocative and revolutionary plays, performed his drama *Le Comte Oxtiern, ou les Effets du Libertinage.* But the condescendingly aristocratic tone of one of its characters caused audience members to demand that the house drop the curtain during its premiere, and the company never performed the play again. A few months later, the Théâtre-Italien debuted his one-act play *Le Suborneur* as a curtain-raiser before a comic opera. During the fourth scene, however, a group of revolutionary activists called Jacobins stormed the theater wearing red liberty caps and declared, "In all theaters, the friends of liberty will combat plays by aristocrats!"

"This past month the Jacobite faction closed down a play of mine at the Théâtre-Italien solely because it was written by [a former noble]," Sade grumbled to Gaufridy. "It was reserved for me to be the first victim. I am born for these things."

Sade also tried his luck as an author. In the summer of 1791, the Paris-based publisher and bookseller Jacques Girouard released an anonymous version of his novel *Justine, or the Woes of Virtue,* an expansion of a short novella he had written in the Bastille. Since the book was nearly as obscene as *120 Days of Sodom,* Sade and his publisher hoped it would capitalize on the demand for radical pornographic fiction sweeping revolutionary France. Sade wrote off most of these competing efforts as "miserable brochures" penned by hacks who knew nothing about real lust. Considering himself an expert in such matters, he subjected his protagonist, the pious and good-hearted Justine, to every form of degradation imaginable, courtesy of maniacal doctors, debauched monks, and murderous aristocrats.

In the end, Justine is saved by her sister Juliette, only to be struck dead by a bolt of lightning.

Scandalized, critics denounced the book. A writer for a local broadsheet declared the work "very dangerous" and warned that its title might "lead inexperienced young people astray." Another article counseled only "mature men" to read it, "to see how far one can go in derangement of the human imagination. But throw it into the fire immediately thereafter."

Lurid accounts like these stoked public interest, and *Justine* became an underground success. Over the next ten years, publishers would put out five more editions of the novel. "It is asked for, sought out, it is spreading," an essayist wrote at the time. "The most cruel poison circulates with the most fatal abundance." While Sade never officially revealed himself to be the author of this book or his later pornographic works, the truth of its origins began to spread. Sade started to develop a reputation, one based on the transgressions he committed on the page, rather than those he'd committed elsewhere. It was the first and crucial step toward cementing his place in history.

Still, the novel didn't sell well enough to radically change Sade's fortunes. It's why he had already begun directing his talents to a new effort: the revolution.

ON JUNE 24, 1791, three hundred thousand Parisians took to the streets. They crowded along the avenues, packed rooftops, scaled trees and city gates, all to witness the return of their disgraced king. Four days earlier, Louis XVI and his family had been caught in what appeared to be an attempt to flee the country. The monarch, it seemed, had hoped to arrange an alliance of foreign nations to wrest back control of France. As soldiers and armed citizens escorted the king's carriage toward the Tuileries Palace to be put under house arrest, the crowd watched in silence. Warnings had been scrawled in chalk on the walls of the capital: "Anyone who applauds the king will be bludgeoned. Anyone who insults him will be hanged."

As the coach clattered across the newly rechristened Place de la

Révolution, a man broke from the bystanders and rushed to the carriage, tossing a letter at the king before turning and revealing himself to the crowd. It was Sade.

Or so went the story that spread across Paris. Whether or not the overweight and enfeebled Sade would have risked such a direct provocation of the sovereign, much less have been physically able to manage such a feat, he did write a letter to Louis XVI that his publisher Girouard soon brought out as an eight-page pamphlet titled *Address of a French Citizen to the King of the French*. In the missive, Sade attacked Louis XVI for trying to reestablish his feudal power, noting, "There isn't a single Frenchman . . . who wouldn't prefer death to the restoration of your abusive despotism." Speaking from experience, he mourned for "those sad individuals whom you, with a single signature . . . tore from a tearful family and thrust for life into the cells of those dreadful bastilles which are spread throughout your kingdom." And he railed against the queen, the Austrian-born Marie-Antoinette, telling the king to "dispatch her back to her country, which sent her here only to distill more thoroughly the destructive and venomous hatred it's had for us throughout history."

By the time of the king's attempted getaway, most of the nobility had fled the country, a number that eventually included Sade's two sons, then soldiers in their twenties. Sade, however, not only refused to emigrate but, as he put it in a letter to Gaufridy, was "up to my neck in the Revolution, heart and mind."

Adopting proletarian titles such as "Louis Sade" and "Citizen Sade," he became an active member of his revolutionary Parisian district. His involvement never wavered, even as militant activists and an increasingly powerful Jacobin, Maximilien Robespierre, assumed control of the district and transformed the neighborhood into one of the most radical of the city. The extremists changed the name of the district to the Section des Piques, in reference to the bloody pikes of the September 1792 massacres, which claimed the lives of more than a thousand prisoners, priests, and suspected royalist sympathizers.

Sade made himself indispensable to his fellow revolutionaries. He volunteered for twenty-four-hour guard duty at his district's headquarters, an abandoned church. He served as his section's commissioner of hospitals, orphanages, and other charitable institutions. He took charge of renaming his district's streets, coming up with patriotic designations like "Rue des Citoyennes Françaises," "Rue des Hommes Libres," and "Rue Spartacus." He composed essays that advocated for replacing military forces with an army of citizen draftees, and called for the country's proposed new constitution to be ratified not by elected representatives but directly by people, a radical idea at the time.

Impressed, his colleagues appointed him secretary of his district and chose him to serve on a jury to investigate counterfeiting. "I am a *judge,* yes, a *judge!* . . . Who would have predicted that?" he wrote to Gaufridy in disbelief. "But congratulate me, and above all do not fail to send money to *monsieur le juge,* or I'll be damned if I don't *sentence you to death!*"

On the surface, Sade's revolutionary fervor made sense. As an atheist who'd long been repulsed by the stodgy customs of court life, Sade had much in common with his comrades in arms. He was intimately connected to the fall of the Bastille and the launch of the revolution. But deep down, he remained a nobleman. As he'd written in the Bastille in 1788, just two years before he'd drape himself in the trappings of liberty, equality, and fraternity, the idea of a commoner moving beyond his station reminded him of "a filthy, disgusting toad that briefly attempts to escape from the muck, only to fall back in and disappear."

In reality, he'd taken up the role of revolutionary in name only. As an act of self-preservation, Sade had thrown himself into his most ambitious performance, a farce where one misstep could prove fatal. While he went through the motions of being a model citizen of his section, he quietly worked to ensure that his estate titles and family archives weren't obliterated amid the nationwide effort to destroy genealogical records. He also met discreetly with several financial administrators who would later be put to death for helping aristocrats protect their property from state confiscation.

After having his prison-cell letters scrutinized by police censors for years, Sade knew the value of curating his paper trail. As he noted to an acquaintance, "You must be prudent in your letters, [since] never did despotism unseal as many as liberty is opening now." He composed a missive to his sons lambasting them for fleeing the country, but it was likely only for show, since he never actually sent it. He edited prison-cell compositions that he'd managed to preserve, removing damning portions, such as deleting a passage where he'd noted, "I do [not] want [the nobility] to be given laws by the first [upstart] commoner that the king is pleased to raise up." After the mass slaughters of September 1792, he wrote in a letter, "There is nothing to equal the horror of the massacres that were committed"; then he caught himself, adding between the lines, "but they were just."

And when Marie-Antoinette went to the gallows in October 1793, nine months after her husband the king lost his life to the guillotine, Sade made sure to note in an official report that "the punishment of the Austrian was just." But he composed a very different response to the killing in his personal notebook. There, he imagined the words of the queen as she awaited her sentence: "The ferocious beasts that surround me daily invent some humiliation which makes my fate all the more horrible. . . . They count my sighs with bliss, and quench their thirst with my tears."

At times, Sade felt safe enough to disclose his true feelings in his letters, revealing far more nuance than he provided to the characters of his fiction. As he noted in a missive to Gaufridy in 1791,

> I am anti-Jacobin. I hate them to death. I adore the king but I detest the old abuses. I love any number of articles of the Constitution; others revolt me. I want the luster of the nobility restored, because taking it away solved nothing. I want the king to be the nation's leader. I do not want a National Assembly, but two chambers as in England, which would give the king a tempered authority, balanced by the concord of a nation necessarily divided into two orders; the third [the clergy] is useless, I want no part of it. That is my profession of faith. What am I at present? Aristocrat or democrat? You will tell me if you please, attorney, because I for one have no idea.

◄ ◄ ◄

ONE APRIL EVENING in 1793, Sade received an unexpected guest at the office where he worked as secretary of his district: the seventy-eight-year-old Claude-René de Montreuil, his former father-in-law, whom he hadn't seen in fifteen years. Outside, the darkened streets were plastered with tricolor notices declaring, "Unity, indivisibility, liberty, equality, fraternity, or death." The newly established French Republic had formed the Revolutionary Tribunal to eradicate enemies of the state. The Montreuils, aristocrats who'd seen most of their children and grandchildren flee the country, feared they would be targets. They turned to the one person they knew who had influence in their district, the Section des Piques.

"It went as pleasantly as could be," Sade wrote of the encounter later that night. "I expected him at any moment to invite me to come visit him." But he hadn't forgotten what this family had done to him. "The Montreuils are my greatest enemies," he'd noted to Gaufridy the year before. "They are also acknowledged scoundrels, criminals whom I could ruin with a word if I chose."

He would soon get the chance to do so. In late July 1793, members of the Section des Piques appointed Sade president of their section. While members rotated in and out of the symbolic post on a short-term basis, the position briefly provided Sade with important administrative duties—including the ability to condemn the Montreuils as political offenders, a charge that would have sent them to the guillotine. But instead of doing so, Sade had their names added to a list of citizens to be spared. "If I had said a word, they would have been treated severely," he told Gaufridy. "I kept quiet: that is how I avenge myself." Sade hadn't simply been acting out of self-righteous revenge. In reality, he had never been able to stomach the wide-scale butchery that populated his fiction. That included the murder of the grandparents of his children.

On August 2, 1793, President Sade, with a red liberty cap perched atop his balding head, resigned from his post during a section meeting. "They wanted me to put a horrible, inhumane measure to a vote," he wrote, without noting what the measure entailed. "I did not wish to do so." Maybe the matter had to do with the fate of the Montreuils, who ultimately survived the revolution and passed away the following decade. Maybe he'd been asked to condemn some other suspected traitor. Whatever the subject, the terror that had become the order of the day had proven too much for the notorious marquis.

That didn't mean Sade abandoned the role of ardent revolutionary. In truth, he had gotten caught up in his own charade. Just as two decades earlier he had been unable to resist engaging in ever more debauchery even with the police on his tail, now he strove to attain greater heights in the revolutionary regime, caution be damned. In November 1793, he stood before the National Convention, the legislative body of the new French Republic, and recited a petition renouncing all religions save for the cult of liberty. Calling Jesus "a Jewish slave of the Romans" and Mary "the whore of Galilee," the lifelong atheist urged the citizens of France to discard the "frivolous toys of an absurd religion."

For once, Citizen Sade had expressed what he truly believed to his revolutionary comrades. But he had committed a grievous error. Robespierre, well on his way to amassing dictator-like powers, had grown concerned about the anti-Christian fervor sweeping the country. Religious sites were being desecrated; street posters were going up that declared, "Death is but an eternal sleep"; and Notre-Dame had been transformed into into the "Temple of Reason," complete with decorative busts of Rousseau, Voltaire, and Benjamin Franklin. Such blatant religious provocations ran the risk of sowing national discord and alienating potential European allies. Unabashed atheism could no longer be tolerated.

A week after Sade's speech, Robespierre took the podium at the Paris headquarters of the Jacobins and made his opinion on the matter known. "Atheism," he declared, "is aristocratic."

EIGHT MONTHS LATER, on July 25, 1794, or 9 Thermidor, as it was known according to the new French Republican calendar, the bailiff for the Revolutionary Tribunal made his way across Paris, gathering the latest round of suspected enemies of the people scheduled that day for summary trial by the revolutionary court. He moved through a city awash in fear and bloodshed. The Great Terror had reached its climax, with makeshift prisons all over Paris overflowing with inmates, and more than fifteen hundred citizens put to death in less than two months. The arrival of the bailiff usually meant death for whomever he collected. In nearly all cases, the accused's trial was nothing more than a brief stop on the way to the guillotine. The bailiff's list that day included a former priest, a chemist, a carpenter, a florist, a lemonade vendor, and "Aldonze Sade, ex-noble and count, man of letters and cavalry officer, accused of conspiracy against the Republicans."

Sade awaited his fate at Maison Coignard, a former monastery turned prison hospital near the outskirts of the city. He'd been arrested at his home three weeks after he'd given his speech denouncing Christianity. The resulting indictment had charged him with feigning his patriotism while retaining royalist sympathies, as well as being "in all respects a most immoral man, highly suspect and unworthy of society." He'd been unmasked as the anonymous author of the novel *Justine,* a dangerous revelation at a time when the authorities were cracking down on prostitution and pornography following Robespierre's declaration that "immorality is the basis of despotism."

After his arrest, the authorities had moved Sade through a variety of detention centers: a onetime convent where more than a hundred priests had been massacred, a retrofitted leprosarium, and an asylum for reformed prostitutes so crowded that Sade had to sleep in a filthy latrine. Thanks to the efforts of Sade's devoted companion Marie-Constance Quesnet, he was eventually transferred to Maison Coignard, where well-off prisoners paid to convalesce from fraudulent illnesses in relative comfort. But soon after he arrived, the city moved the guillotine from the center of Paris to a few hundred yards from the prison hospital, because of the stench of the mass killings. The sprawling grave dug in the prison's garden, filled with more than a thousand guillotined bodies putrefying in the summer heat, became a constant reminder to Sade that he would likely join their number.

On July 25, the bailiff completed his rounds of the city's prisons and delivered the inmates to the Revolutionary Tribunal, where the judges quickly sentenced all to death save two, neither of which was Sade. At three in the afternoon, gendarmes herded the convicts into an open cart and the procession made its way toward the guillotine. When they were halfway there, a crowd of angry citizens, sick of the killings, stopped the procession and began to unhitch the wagon's horses. The prisoners had nearly obtained their freedom when the commander in chief of the national guard arrived, quashing the agitation. The tumbrel resumed its journey to the gallows.

One by one, the convicts were led up the scaffold, to the machine that had been lauded for the efficient and humane way it dispatched the condemned. Each in turn was laid facedown on a bench, with a wooden collar slotted around their neck to hold them in place. From where they lay, they couldn't see the eighty-eight-pound weighted blade, which hovered at an angle fourteen feet above them, or the release lever positioned near their left ear, upon which the executioner, dressed in a blood-red smock, now placed his hand. In an instant, there was the howl of iron scraping against wood, a flash of metal in the sunlight, a dull thud as the blade struck home. Finally, a somber thump in the basket below.

That evening, as the gravediggers unloaded the bodies into the nearby mass grave, Sade was there—but he was not among the dead. He remained in his cell above the garden.

As the bailiff had collected the accused from the prisons that day, he'd marked Sade absent. Maybe he'd made a mistake in the chaos of the moment. Or possibly Marie-Constance had succeeded in petitioning or bribing the right officials to ensure that Sade would be skipped. Sade would later come to believe she had delivered his salvation, and in his will he'd leave her everything, noting that "she plucked me from the revolutionary scythe most certainly suspended over my head."

Whatever the reason, the Revolutionary Tribunal would not get a chance to remedy the error. The following day, the authorities escorted a discredited Robespierre to the guillotine, bringing an end to his Reign of Terror. A few months later, Sade once again left prison a free man—but more shaken from his time behind bars than ever before. As he wrote to Gaufridy, "*The guillotine under my eyes* did me a hundred times more harm than all the imaginable bastilles ever did."

◂ ◂ ◂

SADE FOUND HIMSELF in a city beset by upheaval. The turmoil had led to runaway currency deflation, plunging many into extreme poverty—including Sade. His Provençal properties had been confiscated during his imprisonment, and officials were loath to release them because his name had incorrectly appeared on a list of nobles who'd fled the country. For the first time in his life, he tried to get a job, writing to government officials that he was "well-traveled in parts of Europe, possibly useful to the composition or editing of a literary work, to the direction or the maintenance of a library, a government office or a museum."

His appeals went nowhere. Sade decided to sell what remained of Château de La Coste and another family property, proceeds from which allowed him to purchase a small but comfortable country home in a town north of Paris in 1796. But his funds eventually ran out, and two years later, Sade's dire financial situation forced him and Marie-Constance to abandon the home and split up, having decided that it would be easier to get by if they lived independently. In the months to come, Sade struggled through a series of progressively dismal accommodations. He lived in the house of a farmer who owed him money, then subsisted on food scraps in the back of an attic, and finally he moved into a public hospice, where he lived among vagrants so as not "to die on a street corner," as he put it in a letter.

He continued to write. In 1795, the widow of the publisher Girouard, who had been executed during the revolution, released anonymous versions of two of Sade's books: *Aline and Valcour,* a fairly chaste epistolary novel he had written in the Bastille, and *Philosophy in the Boudoir,* a more licentious work in the form of a dramatic dialogue. In the latter, one of the protagonists reads aloud a philosophical pamphlet, *Frenchmen, One More Effort If You Want to Be Republicans,* which argues that the laws of nature not only justify the abolition of the death penalty, the freedom to obtain abortions, and the decriminalization of homosexuality but also permit incest, rape, theft, and murder. The treatise was pure satire; Sade had become as disillusioned with the cult of liberty as he'd always been with Christianity.

Over the next several years, Sade anonymously released a far more ambitious series: a ten-volume, graphically illustrated work of extreme pornography that included both *The New Justine, or the Woes of Virtue,* an expansion of his earlier book *Justine,* and *The History of Juliette, or the Prosperities of the Vice,* the story of Justine's sister Juliette. In the latter tale, Juliette, as depraved as her sister is virtuous, joins a secret evil organization titled the Society of the Friends of Crime and embarks on a tour of Europe, leaving behind a trail of theft, rape, and murder. Among other real-life public figures she encounters, Juliette consorts with Pope Pius VI, in truth famously virtuous but in Sade's telling a crazed pervert who engages in a group orgy during a Black Mass at the Vatican.

The work made an impression at a time when reopened dance halls all over Paris echoed with songs lampooning the revolutionary extremes, and trendsetters sported revealing outfits fashioned after ancient Greek and Roman attire. According to the police, perverts overran the gardens of the Palais-Royal, a popular shopping arcade, acting out scenes from Sade's tale: "The lessons of the execrable novel *Justine* are put into practice with unprecedented audacity."

With the profits from the sales of these books, in April 1800 Sade and Marie-Constance returned to the home they'd shared north of Paris. But their serenity would not last. Eleven months later, on March 6, 1801, Sade was in his publisher's office discussing business matters when officers stormed the building and announced that he was under arrest. Sade had made himself a new enemy: Napoleon Bonaparte.

CHAPTER TEN

The Purloined Scroll

1983

THE POLICE MOVED THROUGH THE CLUTTERED APARTMENT, LOOKING for stolen goods. The flat belonged to Jean Grouet, a French publisher who had a history of putting out controversial political treatises and supporting anti-government causes. But the authorities were less interested in Grouet's radical leanings than his friendship with Nathalie de Noailles, daughter of Marie-Laure de Noailles, the infamous Red Vicomtesse. The year before, in September 1982, Nathalie had loaned Grouet the manuscript of *120 Days of Sodom*. When she'd asked him to return it, Grouet had handed over the scroll's leather container, but when she'd later opened it, she'd found it empty. Now the police were on the hunt for the missing scroll. Combing through Grouet's apartment, officers found another manuscript he had taken from Noailles—an original Igor Stravinsky ballet score—but not *120 Days of Sodom*.

Grouet admitted to having taken the scroll, but he told the authorities it was no longer in his possession—or in France. He had smuggled it to Switzerland, where he had sold it to a man named Gérard Nordmann. In response, Noailles's son Carlo Perrone traveled to Geneva from his home in Italy. Perrone was just twenty-seven, but he held himself with the maturity of someone who shouldered considerable responsibilities. Perrone's father, Alessandro, had been born into one of Italy's most powerful families and had used his means to expand the clan's media empire. When Alessandro had died two years earlier, control of the businesses—the newspapers *Il Messaggero* and *Il*

Secolo XIX and the television stations Tivuesse Telesecolo and RTI Rete Televisiva Italiana—had fallen to his son, hardly out of college. As the family's newly designated patriarch, Perrone had been the one his mother turned to for help to retrieve the stolen manuscript.

Perrone had the long, regal face of his grandmother the Red Vicomtesse, but he acted more like his grandfather Charles: poised, courteous, and genteel. After his parents divorced when he was ten, Perrone spent most of his time in Italy. He had never been particularly close with his maternal grandmother; he remembered her as an affectionate yet distant woman who would spend a few hours holding court at his mother's manor house before being driven away in her Citroën DS. Nor did he have much connection to the odd little scroll the vicomtesse had passed down to his mother. He had once tried to read a bit of it, only to find it boring. But he understood the importance of the manuscript—what it meant for his family and for France.

It's why Perrone now sat in Nordmann's office on the top floor of a six-story building in downtown Geneva. Through the office windows, Perrone could see much of the city: the sprawl of modern structures; Lake Geneva, with its Jet d'Eau fountain spouting water hundreds of feet into the sky; the snowy peak of Mont Blanc in the distance. On the floors below lay the bustling grocery aisles, clothing racks, and cosmetics counters of La Placette, the largest department store in Switzerland. This was the flagship store for Maus Frères, a corporate group that oversaw hundreds of department stores, supermarkets, hardware stores, and restaurants across the world. All of it was co-owned by Nordmann, then in his early fifties. The retail kingdom, launched by the Nordmanns and another Swiss family in the early 1900s, had flourished as Switzerland emerged largely unscathed from World War II and settled into a sustained economic boom.

Nordmann, with his neatly combed gray hair and plastic glasses, smiled at his young guest, displaying the genial attentiveness for which he was known among his employees. Like many prominent Swiss capitalists, he maintained a discreet profile. He exhibited little of the authority and drive that in a few short years would lead *Fortune* magazine to report that he and his Maus Frères co-owners had amassed a $3.6 billion fortune, making him among the one hundred richest people in the world.

Perrone explained how his mother had lost *120 Days of Sodom,* and how the authorities had learned that the scroll now lay in Nordmann's possession. He was here to retrieve it, and in exchange he would reimburse Nordmann for the amount he'd paid for it. Since they were both business executives, Perrone believed, they operated in a world of upright conduct and lawful obligations. Surely they could come to an agreement over a centuries-old manuscript.

At the mention of relinquishing the scroll, Nordmann's face fell, like a velvet curtain dropping away to reveal a brick wall. When he spoke, his words were marked with finality.

"It is my dream to have this manuscript," he told Perrone. "I will keep it the rest of my life."

AT THAT MOMENT, the scroll lay in Nordmann's villa on the outskirts of Geneva, in a prominent part of the house with stirring views of the mountains. Here, bookshelves rising to the ceiling held what many considered the greatest private collection of erotica in the world.

Nordmann had begun collecting erotic books as a teenager. During his first meeting with the woman who would become his wife, he offered her a book on eighteenth-century courtesans. He scoured Parisian bookshops and combed through book-auction catalogs, hunting for editions rarer than the tomes stored in the British Museum's Private Case or the Enfer section of the Bibliothèque Nationale de France. His discoveries included the only known edition of Pietro Aretino's sixteenth-century "Lust Sonnets," considered to be the first example of modern European pornography. He obtained the series of school-exercise books that contained the original version of the blockbuster 1950s erotic novel *The Story of O,* whose author had long been a mystery. Only late in life would the French writer Anne Desclos reveal that she had penned the tale for the amorous enjoyment of her lover, writer and critic Jean Paulhan, who called her creation "the most ardent love letter any man has ever received." Nordmann had each of his acquisitions festooned with his signature bookplate: a delicate wing imprinted with the words GERARD NORDMANN EX-LIBRIS, the letters E, R, O, and S highlighted in red to spell out EROS.

Nordmann's pursuit consumed much of his time and energy. He financed reprints of out-of-print pornographic novels and under-wrote scholarly treatises on the history of illicit publishing. He invited a select group of like-minded individuals into his inner sanctum, allowing them to peruse his selection of graphic Japanese handscrolls and first-edition volumes of the mysterious Victorian opus *My Secret Life*. And once, after purchasing valuable texts he'd located in England, rather than waiting for his prizes to arrive in the mail, he sent a private truck to the seller's doorstep.

He had never been particularly interested in Sade's hyperviolent writings, but he nonetheless yearned to own an item as mythical as *120 Days of Sodom*. For years he had inquired among his French sources whether the Noailleses would be willing to part with it. One of those contacts, a Parisian bookseller named Louis Botherel, had put Nordmann in touch with Grouet after the publisher had taken the scroll. On December 17, 1982, Grouet flew to Switzerland and offered up the manuscript, devoid of its container. Nordmann acquired it for 300,000 francs, or slightly more than $100,000 today.

Now installed as the centerpiece of his collection, the scroll needed a new receptacle. Working with a prominent Swiss bookbinder named Jean-Luc Honegger, Nordmann designed an elegant clam-shell box with geometric designs pressed into its bluish-gray calfskin leather; *120 Days of Sodom* was placed inside, wound tightly around a custom-made glass dowel.

Nordmann rarely discussed why he collected erotic texts. He and his Jewish family had survived the horrors of the Holocaust because of their affluence and Switzerland's diplomatic neutrality. But still, as a young man, he had witnessed the near eradication of an entire culture, not just through the Nazi gas chambers but also through mass book burnings and other systematic attempts to annihilate Jewish arts and literature. Nordmann's accumulation of pornographic materials, however, wasn't only due to altruistic preservation. He enjoyed the pursuit, and not simply in a sexual sense. As his Victorian predecessor Henry Spencer Ashbee had learned while amassing his own erotica collection, illicit books, thanks to their clandestine nature and their tendency to be destroyed, were among the most difficult texts to track down. It was the ultimate treasure hunt, one that required considerable diligence, perseverance—and wealth.

In that vein, *120 Days of Sodom* was a particularly attractive treasure, since by that point, it had come to be known for its starring role in one of the most famous censorship cases of the twentieth century. In the late 1940s, a pioneering twenty-year-old French publisher named Jean-Jacques Pauvert began publishing Sade's complete works, including *120 Days of Sodom*. Unlike earlier printings of Sade's writing, such as Iwan Bloch's 1904 version of *120 Days of Sodom* and Maurice Heine's "critical edition" put out thirty years later, these books were published openly, not via limited subscriptions, and included both the publisher's real name and the place of publication—Pauvert's parents' garage. It was a direct provocation, and authorities responded by taking the matter to court.

At the legal hearing in December 1956, Pauvert wasn't the only one on trial. As the government prosecutor told the court, "It is actually the illustrious and 'divine' Marquis de Sade who is now under examination, more than 140 years after his death." Many of the era's most esteemed intellectuals took the stand to defend the marquis, including avant-garde elder statesmen Jean Cocteau and André Breton. The literati argued that Sade's oeuvre didn't just possess scientific value, as Iwan Bloch had suggested a half century before, but also boasted ethical merit. Sade, they said, was a moralizer, exposing the dark truths of the human condition so that people could guard against them. As the philosopher Georges Bataille told the judge, "The Marquis de Sade was innovative because before him no one had said that human beings found satisfaction in contemplating pain and death." Banning Sade's texts, suggested literary critic Jean Paulhan, would be censoring works no more dangerous than passages of the Bible.

The arguments didn't sway the judge. He found Pauvert guilty of offending public morals, fined him two hundred thousand francs, and ordered the destruction of the incriminating texts, including *120 Days of Sodom*. But on appeal the following year, a higher court stripped away the punishment. Pauvert was free to print Sade's works, and the repercussions extended beyond France. Inspired by the Pauvert case and a landmark 1957 U.S. Supreme Court decision that narrowly defined obscenity as material "utterly without redeeming social importance," the maverick New York publishing house Grove Press began issuing uncensored editions of Sade's writing, marketing the volumes as works of cultural significance. None of them were banned or confiscated, not even *120 Days of Sodom*. In the years that followed, on both sides of the Atlantic, the floodgates opened. Books featuring all kinds of racy subject matter hit the market without official backlash. If the works of Sade could be published without restriction, everything else would have to be allowed, too.

Nordmann may have seen *120 Days of Sodom* as a symbol of triumph over censorship, but even that interpretation couldn't fully explain his attachment to the scroll. Among bibliophiles, he had a reputation for generosity. Even if Nordmann hadn't known that *120 Days of Sodom* had been taken unfairly from the Noailles family when he'd first purchased it, why hadn't he been willing to relinquish the manuscript once Perrone told him so in person? Why would he risk sullying his sterling reputation and disturbing his inconspicuous lifestyle by holding on to the scroll?

Perhaps he couldn't help it. For some collectors, the need to accumulate became debilitating, and these individuals had a name: bibliomaniacs. Stories abounded of bibliomaniacs who lied, cheated, stole, even murdered to augment their book collections. In 1836, fourteen-year-old Gustave Flaubert wrote one of his first short stories, "Bibliomania," about a man whose love of books "burned within him, used up his days, devoured his existence." He based the work on the tale of Don Vincente, a Spanish monk turned bookseller who allegedly killed eight people to seize their coveted tomes. When asked in court if he regretted his crimes, Don Vincente reportedly replied, "Every man must die sooner or later, but good books must be conserved."

While the story of Don Vincente was likely apocryphal, many

people had allowed bibliomania to consume their lives. That included Sir Thomas Phillipps, a Victorian aristocrat who became obsessed with amassing "one copy of every book in the world," to the dismay of his family and the ruin of his estate. As one visitor to his mansion reported, "Every room is filled with heaps of papers, [manuscripts], books, charters, packages & other things. . . . The windows of the house are never opened, and the close confined air and smell of the paper and [manuscripts] is almost unbearable." When Phillipps passed away in 1872, he left behind a sprawling clutter of one hundred thousand books and manuscripts; it would take his family more than one hundred years to disperse them.

Then there was the Marquis de Villeneuve-Trans, previous owner of the scroll. His fanatical need to cultivate his erotica collection likely helped bring about his financial ruin, forcing him to sell off much of his beloved library.

Nordmann's passion for erotic books never became so all-consuming. But there seemed to be something irrational about his obsession with *120 Days of Sodom*. Maybe he couldn't relinquish the scroll, despite his better judgment, because deep down, he harbored a streak of bibliomania.

THE NOAILLES FAMILY refused to give up the scroll without a fight. In France, Nathalie de Noailles filed a criminal complaint against Grouet, who claimed to authorities that she had allowed him to do what he wished with the scroll to support his business. After years of court battles and appeals, France's highest court ruled on the matter in 1990, finding Grouet guilty and upholding an earlier court decision that earned him a two-year suspended prison sentence and three hundred thousand francs in fines. More important, the court declared that Grouet had illegally transported *120 Days of Sodom* into Switzerland and sold it without its owner's permission. Now the Noailles family had a legal determination that Nordmann had purchased stolen and smuggled property.

The legal maneuvers were playing out against a backdrop of mounting public concern over the trafficking of cultural goods. Dur-

ing World War II, the world stood powerless as the Nazi regime engaged in the greatest destruction and displacement of artwork and
treasures in modern history. In 1954, a conference of concerned
nation-states drew up the Hague Convention for the Protection of
Cultural Property in the Event of Armed Conflict, a treaty that
aimed to safeguard antiquities during times of war. But in the years
that followed, it became clear that the plundering of precious artifacts wasn't limited to wartime. More and more relics from historical
sites and archaeological digs all over the world were finding their way
into auction halls, museum galleries, and the private homes of
wealthy collectors, mostly in Europe and the United States. Attempts
to return these items to their places of origin were often stymied by
diplomatic and legal difficulties, thanks to differences in how coun-
tries handled plundered materials. To streamline the process, the
United Nations Educational, Scientific and Cultural Organization,
or UNESCO, passed the 1970 Convention on the Means of Prohibit-
ing and Preventing the Illicit Import, Export and Transfer of Ownership of Cultural Property, which required all states that signed on
to assist in the restitution of stolen artifacts. Thanks to the French
court decision, *120 Days of Sodom* fit the definition.

There was only one problem: Switzerland, with its reputation for
neutrality and its deep commitment to its citizens' privacy, hadn't yet
signed the 1970 UNESCO convention. So while the Noailles family
filed an ownership claim in Geneva for the scroll, the only way they
could compel Switzerland to help them retrieve it was if they proved
in the Swiss courts that Nordmann hadn't been acting in good faith
when he'd purchased the manuscript. The idea of good faith, developed during the Age of Enlightenment and common in many legal
systems, presupposed that people tended to act with decency in arrangements with others. According to the concept, even if someone
purchased a stolen item, as Nordmann had appeared to do with *120
Days of Sodom,* that person was presumed to be not at fault, unless
they had ignored clear and compelling evidence that something
about the transaction was amiss.

The matter moved through the Swiss court system, and in 1998,
Switzerland's Federal Supreme Court took up the case. The justices

considered the evidence in Nordmann's favor, including that the transaction had been initiated by a reputable Parisian bookseller and that Grouet wasn't some dubious interloper but, instead, a personal friend of the scroll's previous owner. What's more, a French manuscript expert summoned by the court—Alain Nicolas, still several years away from doing business with Aristophil and having a falling-out with Castaing—had determined the three hundred thousand francs Grouet requested for the scroll wasn't unreasonably low compared to its actual value, so its price tag should not have raised suspicions.

The justices also took into account several facts that cast doubt on Nordmann's behavior. Grouet, for example, hadn't provided Nordmann with an export permit for the manuscript, and the scroll had been delivered strangely devoid of its signature container. Most damningly, Nordmann had long known that the Noailles family wasn't interested in selling the manuscript, and with all his contacts, it would have been easy for him to learn that by the time he'd acquired the scroll, Nathalie de Noailles had already reported to French authorities that the manuscript had been stolen.

On May 28, 1998, the Swiss Supreme Court ruled on the matter. One by one the five justices voiced their opinion, until there were two supportive of the Noailleses' claim, and two against. Then the final judge broke the deadlock, concluding that Nordmann had acted in good faith. As a result, *120 Days of Sodom* would not be returned to France.

The ruling was a blow to Nathalie de Noailles, who would pass away six years later. After nearly two decades of court battles, the highest court in the land had spoken; there was nothing else she or her son could do.

Nordmann, however, was not around to savor his victory. Six years earlier, on February 5, 1992, he had died quietly in his bed. Like two previous owners of the scroll, he had died fairly young, in his early sixties. Earlier that day, a book had slipped from a shelf and landed beside him, like a tribute from his collection. It was titled, in French, *The Loves of a Gentleman*. Nordmann had kept his word to Perrone: He had held on to the manuscript until the very end.

◄ ◄ ◄

ON A HILL overlooking Geneva, two elegant pavilions stand on an outcropping, framing a sweeping view of the lake below. At first glance, nothing about the site appears particularly remarkable. But behind a wall in a corner of the terrace, a staircase spirals downward into a hidden sanctum. Here, galleries have been carved into the earth, the dark spaces pierced by shafts of light filtering down from skylights above. Throughout the space, glass cases, fitted with temperature and humidity controls and fiber-optic lighting systems, display some of the most remarkable texts in human history: several of the earliest-known Gospels of the New Testament, written on ancient papyri; first editions of the Gutenberg Bible and Martin Luther's Ninety-five Theses; a complete copy of Shakespeare's First Folio, clad in its original binding. Each rests on translucent arms calibrated to reduce pressure on the materials, making the texts appear like birds taking flight.

This is the Bibliotheca Bodmeriana, designed to house one of the most remarkable personal libraries ever accumulated. Martin Bodmer, heir to a Swiss industrial fortune, spent most of the twentieth century amassing 150,000 precious texts, earning him the nickname "the king of bibliophiles." Not long before he died, in 1971, Bodmer launched the Martin Bodmer Foundation to preserve his library in perpetuity. In the late 1990s, the private foundation decided to erect a building that reflected the collection's scope and grandeur. It sold a single item from the collection, a drawing by Michelangelo, for $7.4 million at Sotheby's New York, then used the proceeds to construct an underground museum beneath Bodmer's original library.

When the new museum opened in 2003, the operation was looking to attract attention. The foundation turned to the heir of another noteworthy literary collection located not far away: Monique Nordmann, Gérard's widow, who was interested in her husband's erotica library receiving its proper due. The result was *Eros Invaincu,* a much-hyped special exhibit at the Bibliotheca Bodmeriana that showcased outstanding pieces from Nordmann's library. Visitors from all over the world came to scrutinize the obscene texts and peer at the lewd illustrations. The main attraction rested in a special display positioned in the deepest part of the museum: the first-ever public exhibition of *120 Days of Sodom*. Behind its security glass, the faintly illuminated scroll lay partially unrolled, its ends rising up from below.

At the conclusion of the exhibit, Monique Nordmann agreed to let the Bodmer Foundation undertake repairs on the scroll. To do so, the foundation turned to its longtime paper and papyrus conservation expert, Florence Darbre. Among her colleagues, Darbre was seen as a magician, someone who could work wonders with documents, no matter their age or condition. She had always been fascinated by how thin sheets of fiber could both be exceedingly fragile and endure for hundreds or thousands of years, how they could contain anything, from throwaway notes to compositions of world-changing significance. After studying the history of art and Egyptology, she delved into the field of restoration, a domain that required patience, deep knowledge, and, most of all, steady hands.

Preservation is as ancient as writing, and several Old Testament prophets left detailed instructions on how to best safeguard vital records. But it wasn't until the mid-twentieth century that the process of conserving books and documents emerged as a true profession, courtesy of a natural disaster. In 1966, the Arno River, in central Italy, overflowed its banks and flooded much of Florence. When the waters receded, the devastation included widespread damage to many of the city's archives and libraries, leaving hundreds of thousands of books, manuscripts, and records waterlogged and covered with mud. Conservation experts from around the world converged on the city to repair the destruction, and along the way they standardized procedures for document analyses, chemical paper treatments, and mending techniques, among other processes. A modern science was born.

By the time Darbre was tasked with conserving the scroll, she had become one of the biggest names in the discipline. Along with her efforts at the Bodmer Foundation, she worked as a private document restorer, and at the time she was helping the National Geographic Society preserve the long-lost Gospel of Judas Iscariot, whose papyrus pages, discovered in the 1970s, were so deteriorated that the text was barely readable.

Darbre understood that document preservation wasn't about making materials look new again. The marks and bruises the scroll had collected over the years were part of its history. For all she knew, a stain that spread across one end of the manuscript could have come from the scroll's internment in the Bastille, and removing it would be like erasing part of its story. Instead, her job was chiefly to preserve the manuscript's current state, to ensure that damage and deterioration wouldn't overwhelm it in the years to come.

She found that the work required to do so would end up being fairly minimal. The thirty-three pages from which the scroll had been assembled were made from high-quality paper, and whoever had pasted the sheets end to end—possibly Sade himself—had done a careful job, ensuring that all were well aligned. So she began by cleaning the manuscript, passing a soft brush across its surface. Then she focused on the edges of the scroll that had become crumpled and frayed, employing a fine-tipped brush to moisten and unfold each pleat. Finally, using special adhesive and thin strips of transparent Japanese paper, she repaired small tears in the pages and the joints between them, some of which were likely caused by the corrosive iron-gall ink Sade had used for the work.

As always, she worked with her bare hands. Gloves were unwieldy and could lead to snags, and the subtle work she engaged in required the sense of touch. Amid her efforts, she avoided pondering the history of the scroll beneath her fingers. She had long ago realized that if she thought too hard about the origins of the relics she worked on—the hallowed hands of Michelangelo, the twisted mind of the Marquis de Sade—she would never dare to touch them.

After three weeks of work, Darbre returned *120 Days of Sodom* to the Bibliotheca Bodmeriana, where it continued to be displayed—but since it was simply on an extended loan from Monique Nordmann, it would not remain there forever. Years earlier, however, the scroll had almost become a permanent part of the Bodmer library.

Nearly all collectors live with the knowledge that their beloved accumulations will likely be broken apart upon their demise, and erotica collections are especially susceptible to dispersion. Ashbee, in nineteenth-century England, had been well aware of this fact; it's why he had forced the hand of the British Museum, stipulating in his will that the institution could acquire his conventional literary treasures only if they preserved his illicit texts, too. Nordmann, as well, had tried to find a way to conserve his collection. Shortly before his death, he had quietly offered his entire library to the Bodmer Foundation.

At the time, not everyone at the organization welcomed the proposal. The materials, many believed, were too indecent to be placed alongside their noble assemblage of humanity's great works. It surely didn't help that the centerpiece of Nordmann's collection, *120 Days of Sodom,* was at the time entangled in an international legal battle. In the end, the foundation refused the gift.

Judging from the *Eros Invaincu* exhibit, the current leadership of the Bodmer Foundation had fewer misgivings about Nordmann's pursuits. But since ownership of Nordmann's collection now rested with his family, the donation offer was no longer on the table. It seemed only a matter of time until Nordmann's treasures would be scattered to the wind.

ON A WARM spring day in April 2006, the auction house of Christie's Paris, a limestone edifice just off the Champs-Élysées, opened its doors for what one newspaper called the "erotic sale of the century." Catalogs for the event had been sent out to a select group, their covers emblazoned with warnings about the explicit images within. Signs placed at the auction hall's door declared that no minors would be allowed inside. Such provisions stoked excitement for the event, and by the time the auction began, the wood-paneled hall was buzzing with bidders and onlookers, all eager for the sale of the erotic library of Gérard Nordmann.

As white-gloved porters paraded the volumes and manuscripts in front of the crowd, sales proceeded briskly. Nordmann's eleven-volume edition of *My Secret Life* sold for €38,400. A set of 102 lewd illustrations by Jules-Adolphe Chauvet, the French erotica illustrator who tried to help the Marquis de Villeneuve-Trans sell *120 Days of Sodom,* earned €2,040, four times its estimated price. The original manuscripts of *The Story of O* went to a Colombian businessman for €102,000. Pietro Aretino's groundbreaking "Lust Sonnets" commanded €325,600, the highest price of the auction. The one-of-a-kind Renaissance text fell into the hands of a private bidder and was never heard of again. By the end of a second round of auctions the following December, nearly everything from Nordmann's collection was gone, just as his widow had hoped. While she had always supported his pursuit, she had never shared his passion.

One item from Nordmann's library didn't make it to Christie's auction hall: *120 Days of Sodom*. Because of the simmering feud over its rightful owner, there was no way it could be put up for sale, especially in France, without triggering international scandal. So for the time being it remained in its subterranean crypt in the Bibliotheca Bodmeriana, too controversial for the erotic sale of the century.

CHAPTER ELEVEN

Erased from the Minds of Men

JULY 5, 1805

THE WELL-TO-DO OF EARLY-NINETEENTH-CENTURY PARIS ARRIVED IN their carriages at the Charenton mental asylum outside the city, eager to attend what had become a cultural sensation. They filed into a small theater above the women's ward, where, sitting alongside inmates from the hospital, they scanned the crowd for famous faces. The monthly sold-out events were known to attract pillars of high society, scions of royal blood, and advisers to Emperor Napoleon. At the sound of a gavel, the performance began: a one-act comedy whose actors sometimes wandered off the stage unexpectedly or forgot they were putting on a play. In the center of it all—playing the lead role, directing the pageant, and drawing attention "like one of those monstrous creatures they display in cages," as one attendee put it—stood the sixty-five-year-old Sade.

Since being arrested at his publisher's office four years earlier, Sade had been a prisoner of the police state established by Napoleon after he assumed power. As part of the cultural crackdown that shuttered many of Paris's newspapers and theaters, authorities had identified Sade as the author of the obscene novels *Justine* and *Juliette*. Even more damning, officials believed that Sade had penned *Zoloé,* an anonymous novel that satirized Joséphine, Napoleon's wife, noting that a character based on her enjoyed "an ardor for pleasure a hundred times greater than [her colleagues'], a [loan shark]'s avidity for money, which she squanders with the alacrity of a gambler, and a dizzying love of luxury grand enough to swallow up the revenue of ten provinces."

Zoloé was full of the sort of obscenity and political critiques that abounded in Sade's work. But the novel lacked his biting precision and penchant for nihilism. And concrete evidence would never emerge that the work had sprung from his pen. But even if Sade, rightly or wrongly, had never been suspected of writing *Zoloé*, he probably would have incurred the ire of the French emperor anyway. A firsthand account of Napoleon's later exile and death on the remote island of Saint Helena likely referred to *Justine* when it noted, "As emperor [Napoleon] had heard a summary and thumbed through the most abominable book ever engendered by the most depraved imagination: this was a novel which, even at the time of the [revolution], he said had revolted public morality so that its author had been locked up and had remained so ever since."

After Sade was detained, Paris's police commissioner rejected a public trial, concluding that legal proceedings "would provoke a scandalous furor not likely to be redeemed by a sufficiently exemplary punishment." Instead, the commissioner decided "to punish him administratively," quietly locking him up indefinitely. Once again, Sade found himself incarcerated without charges or opportunity for appeal.

The authorities first jailed Sade in Sainte-Pélagie, a Paris convent turned prison. He spent two years there before the guards caught him acting indecently toward a group of young male inmates and possessing "an enormous instrument that he fabricated with wax and used on himself." Outraged, officials transferred him to Bicêtre, a grim facility that had once been called "the rabble's Bastille." Sade passed only a month there before his long-estranged ex-wife and his children petitioned the police to transfer him to a more reputable facility—less out of concern for his well-being and more to protect what was left of their family honor. The authorities decided to once again commit him to Charenton, the mental hospital to which he'd been transferred right after he was removed from the Bastille. Sade's sexual manias, the police concluded with a hint of pseudoscientific creativity, had driven him into "a perpetual state of libertine dementia."

◄ ◄ ◄

THIS TIME AT Charenton, Sade found an ally: François Simonet de Coulmier, the hospital's director. Coulmier had served as a Catholic priest until he'd left the clergy during the French Revolution to devote himself to hospital and charity work. At Charenton, he redesigned the facility to employ therapeutic treatments tailored to patients' diagnoses, a revolutionary idea at the time. Coulmier, a dwarf with foppish manners and a refined intellect, also had a passion for the theater and beautiful women—leading him to strike up a friendship with his most notorious inmate. When state officials demanded that Sade be denied writing utensils and contact with the outside world, Coulmier refused, noting, "I should consider myself most unfortunate to use my time persecuting a man who, though no doubt guilty of many things, has long since demonstrated, through his consistent behavior, his desire to put his mistakes behind him."

Thanks to Coulmier's goodwill and a hefty annual hospital fee begrudgingly paid by his family, Sade enjoyed a privileged existence among Charenton's tree-lined facilities and picturesque meadows. He occupied a two-room suite furnished with hundreds of books and portraits of his favorite relatives, including his beloved former sister-in-law and paramour, who had passed away decades earlier. His companion Marie-Constance lived next door in the facility, under the guise of being an illegitimate daughter who needed to remain under his care. He could stroll about the grounds at will, had inmates read the newspapers to him, and hosted lunch and dinner parties several times a week. In a letter to Gaufridy, his long-standing lawyer, he noted, "*I am not happy,* but I am well."

As always, he wrote. He filled journals with tabulations of his time in captivity and calculations based on the mysterious numerical symbols only he could see. He penned two relatively tame novels, *Histoire Secrète d'Isabelle de Bavière, Reine de France* and *La Marquise de Gange.* He composed a far more scandalous work, *Les Entretiens du Château de Florbelle,* but police found and confiscated the manuscript, destroying it before it could ever be published.

Most notably, Sade threw himself into Charenton's theatrical program, which, according to the hospital's chief physician, "kept [the patients] active and warded off melancholy ideas, an all too common source of madness." Sade helped design the theater, wrote plays, directed rehearsals, planned the scenery, served as a stagehand, publicized the events, dispensed tickets, and sometimes starred in the show. He found a measure of dramatic and social success that had eluded him while he had been free. Before performances, he positioned himself at the asylum gates to welcome attendees, his posture as noble and erect as his girth and age would allow and his hair done up and powdered in the style of days gone by. Afterward, he would invite the prettiest ladies to supper in his quarters, charming them with his social graces and sometimes slipping love letters into the folds of their napkins.

While Sade's dramatic spectacles weren't exemplary works of theater, the mixture of high art and psychosis was unlike anything these audiences had ever experienced. As one visitor to Charenton noted after one of the performances, "After the miracles I had seen, I needed to leave this place before I could be sure that I had preserved my own reason."

SADE SUBMITTED NUMEROUS requests to be released, all of which the administrators ignored. Meanwhile, the police constantly searched his quarters, tried to prevent him from interacting with the outside world, and attempted to transfer him to a more restrictive prison. Even as his detention at Charenton stretched into its second decade, the authorities never stopped regarding him as a threat. While Coulmier managed to rebuff most of the state's attempts to subdue Sade, officials eventually grew weary of his revelries. In May 1813, the French minister of the interior ordered an end to Charenton's performances and parties.

A year later, France found itself beset by new political upheaval. With his army decimated and his European empire shattered by a coalition of foreign powers, Napoleon stepped down as emperor in April 1814. The following month the French populace, caught up in renewed royalist fervor, welcomed the return of Louis XVIII, the long-exiled brother of the last monarch of France, and crowned him king of a new constitutional monarchy. But while Sade's Napoleonic tormentors were swept from office, his own situation took a turn for the worse. The new government removed Coulmier from his post as director of Charenton, likely because of his past revolutionary activities. The well-connected lawyer who replaced him did not share his predecessor's fondness for the hospital's famed libertine. In the fall of 1814, the new director's reports on Sade led administrators to ask police officials to "examine ways of removing M. de Sade as promptly as possible from Charenton and sending him to a place where he can no longer do harm to society." Again, Sade was branded an enemy of the state. Despite their vast differences, each of the political regimes that had cycled through France over the previous quarter century had all agreed on one thing: Sade should be forever locked away.

Sade could expect little help or sympathy from what remained of his family. His ex-wife, Renée-Pélagie, had died in 1810 at age sixty-nine, having never reunited or made peace with her former husband. His youngest child, Madeleine-Laure, never married and, according to Sade, spent her life "pickled in stupidity and piety," with little interaction with her father. For a while, Sade enjoyed a closer bond with his oldest child, Louis-Marie. Like his father, Louis-Marie harbored literary aspirations, embarking on an ambitious written history of France, and developed a reputation as a libertine. While father and son both had volatile tempers that at times soured their relationship, Louis-Marie often visited Sade at Charenton and attended many of his plays. But in 1809, Louis-Marie was ambushed in Italy while serving in Napoleon's army, the forty-one-year-old's third stint in the military after living the capricious life of a bachelor. He didn't survive the attack.

That left Sade's middle child, Donatien-Claude-Armand, who went by Armand. Taking after his grandparents the Montreuils, Armand was more interested in wealth and standing than his fanciful older brother had been. He proved to be a reluctant caretaker of his namesake, since he had little patience for Sade's demands for ever more spending money, and much less for the notoriety his father had bestowed upon his family name. "Your unforgivable cruelty causes you to close your eyes to all I am suffering," Sade wrote to his remaining son in his typical melodramatic manner. "Will you love the child your wife is carrying if one day he treats you in this fashion?"

In November 1814, Armand offered a bit of warmth toward his father. "I greatly enjoyed reading *La Marquise de Gange*," he wrote in a letter, referring to Sade's recently published historical novel. But this small gesture of kindness couldn't outweigh years of embarrassment. Armand would eventually allow the police to destroy many of his father's papers and manuscripts.

Despite his increasingly dire state of affairs, Sade still refused to disavow the behaviors that had placed him in such circumstances. In fact, the septuagenarian was enjoying the favors of a new paramour: Madeleine Leclerc, the teenaged daughter of one of the hospital's nurses, who worked at the asylum as a laundress. Their relationship was condoned by Madeleine's mother as long as her daughter received payment and was tolerated by Sade's other companion, Marie-Constance. Sade tutored the girl in reading and writing, jealously forbade her to attend social functions, and enjoyed sexual dalliances with her, the specifics of which he recorded in his journal.

Even in the twilight of his life, Sade would never change. His attitudes and conduct, no matter how vile, made him who he was. As he put it in a letter to Armand's mother-in-law after she encouraged him to alter his ways, "Though you say it in words far kinder and more spiritual, what you are telling me literally means: *you will get out when you are good.* But I dare put it to you: Can one really speak this way to a wretched old man laid low by illness and imprisonment? Either I am what I ought to be, or I shall never be."

Still, Sade foresaw an end to his torment. As he noted in the same missive, "May my persecutors be patient. Woe and despair are opening my coffin, I am preparing to enter it."

THE NEW KING's officers never had time to move Sade to a new prison. Sade's health had been deteriorating—he complained of headaches, stomach pains, rheumatism, dizziness, body spasms, swollen legs, and partial blindness—and in late November 1814, horrible pains ran through his lower abdomen and groin. Soon he could no longer walk. His condition didn't stop him from enjoying another visit from the young laundress Madeleine, during which "she lent herself as usual to our little games," as Sade managed to note in his journal after she left.

But on December 1, he took to his bed with what the hospital's medical staff diagnosed as "prostrating gangrenous fever." Sade's son Armand came to see him the following afternoon, followed by a visit from the hospital's chaplain. On Saturday, December 2, a young intern at the asylum named L. J. Ramon took up vigil at Sade's bedside as the patient's breathing became increasingly labored. At ten that evening, the room grew quiet. The Marquis de Sade was dead.

The hospital's staff laid Sade to rest at the far end of the asylum's cemetery, giving him a religious burial and topping his grave with an untitled tombstone decorated with a simple cross. A few years later, when the hospital excavated that section of the cemetery, medical experts took the opportunity to examine Sade's skull, since phrenology, the practice of studying people's craniums to determine their mental traits, was very much in vogue. A phrenologist visiting from Germany borrowed the skull and never returned it, likely losing it while teaching either in his home country or the United States. But the specialist managed to produce an analysis of Sade's skull. He noted that "the harmony that governs the sublime combinations of the intellectual faculties and human feelings had ceased to exist in him," resulting in "such a depravity in the morals and philosophy of the Marquis de Sade that they consisted of the most amorphous composite of vices and virtues, acts of charity and crime, hatred and love."

But Ramon, the intern who had witnessed Sade's death and would later become Charenton's chief physician, also scrutinized Sade's cranium and came to a very different conclusion: "His skull was in all respects similar to that of a father of the church."

The wildly divergent evaluations weren't surprising, considering that phrenology would never prove to be an objective science. But the assessments were also among the first hints of the strange and often contradictory myths starting to take root about Sade, as the truth of his deeds and his writing mingled with legend.

Sade would not have wished for these developments. As a slightly younger man, he had welcomed eternal fame, but nearing the end of his life, he changed his mind about his legacy. More than anything else, he yearned to break free of the judgment of others, to put an end to the scandals once and for all. He suggested as much in the burial arrangements he requested in his last will and testament, nearly all of which his son Armand ignored. According to his last wishes, he wanted his body to be taken to a forest on one of his remaining estates and buried unceremoniously in an anonymous thicket. Acorns were to be strewn across his grave, so that the site would soon be overgrown. That way, he'd written, "all traces of my tomb will disappear from the face of the earth, just as I hope all trace of my memory will be erased from the memory of men."

CHAPTER TWELVE

The Grand Bargain

JULY 9, 2013

BRUNO RACINE SAT BY THE SWIMMING POOL OF HIS COUNTRY HOUSE IN southern Provence, basking in the summer sunshine. He felt at ease, content in the knowledge that he was about to obtain one of his greatest acquisitions for one of the largest and most famous libraries in the world.

Six years earlier, in 2007, Racine had become president of the Bibliothèque Nationale de France, the state library, which had been founded in 1368. The bulk of the institution's forty million–plus items were now stored in a multibillion-dollar ultramodern library in southern Paris, a 3.9-million-square-foot behemoth crowned by four sleek glass towers that resembled open books rising hundreds of feet into the sky. Racine was in charge of it all. He had the diminutive, unassuming look of the civil servant he'd been all his life, but the sixty-one-year-old also happened to be a prizewinning novelist with the ambition to propel himself to the top of France's political and cultural hierarchy. In his previous job, he had been president of the Centre Pompidou, the iconic multicultural complex and modern art museum in central Paris, where he'd spearheaded efforts to build satellite institutions in Shanghai and the French city of Metz. Since assuming the helm of the national library, Racine had set several far-reaching revitalization projects in motion. He had launched a multimillion-euro renovation of the library's old headquarters in central Paris, including restoring the building's expansive multi-domed reading room. He had scaled up the digitization of its manuscript archives, increasing the number of historic documents the public could access online by tenfold. And he had set about augmenting the library's permanent collection with as many literary treasures as possible.

That decision placed Racine in direct competition with major dealers and collectors in France and beyond. In theory, Racine boasted several advantages. The Ministry of Culture, which oversaw the national library, could declare particularly important works that were going to be offered for sale national treasures, which meant they couldn't leave the country or be put on the market for thirty months while the state worked to negotiate a suitable purchase price. Racine could also circumvent the vicissitudes of the auction halls by asserting the state's right to preemption on any of the texts up for sale, declaring as soon as the auctioneer's hammer fell for a given lot that France would be acquiring the item for the same price as the winning bid.

To pull off these efforts, however, the national library needed procurement funds. Racine shifted government budgets and used fiscal incentives to boost private donations. Soon he had amassed a sizable war chest, which he used to obtain major acquisitions, including the papers of Marxist theorist Guy Debord, the archives of French philosopher Michel Foucault, and the original memoirs of Giacomo Casanova. Now he was set to obtain a new prize: the Marquis de Sade's *120 Days of Sodom*.

The effort had begun several years earlier. Following the death of Gérard Nordmann's widow, Monique, in 2010, her children had made it known that the family was interested in finding a way to sell the scroll. Racine sprang into action. He convinced the French Ministry of Culture to announce that the scroll would be proclaimed a national treasure if it was returned to France and preserved in the national library. That potential designation helped Racine raise money to obtain it, since private donors who assisted in bankrolling the operation would then receive considerable tax benefits. At the same time, French law enforcement and Interpol placed the scroll on their registries of stolen goods. While the designations were largely symbolic, they had the potential to deter private parties interested in the manuscript. Now it would be very hard for anyone to argue in a

court of law, as Nordmann had done, that there was no way of knowing the scroll was considered contraband.

Racine, meanwhile, began working closely with Carlo Perrone,
Nathalie de Noailles's son, and they traveled to the Bodmer Foundation to assess the manuscript's condition. The viewing, deep in the
subterranean museum, left the grandson of the Red Vicomtesse vis-
ibly emotional. Afterward, Perrone agreed to not assert his family's
ownership of the scroll if it was returned to France and deposited in
the national library, and he even offered to help pay for its acquisition.
Working through legal liaisons, Racine then settled on a €3.5 million
payment to Serge Nordmann and his siblings. The Nordmanns, still
stung by the French legal decision that suggested that the scroll did
not belong to their family, refused to provide the scroll directly to
state authorities. Instead, they agreed to hand it off to an intermediary, who would then pass it on to the national library.

In the middle of the delicate negotiations, Racine told *The New
York Times*, "[The scroll] is a unique, exceptional work, and a miracle
that it survived. . . . Whether we like it or not, it belongs in the Bibliothèque Nationale." The arrangements had been finalized, the millions of euros at stake were ready to be transferred to various bank
accounts across Europe, and the final handoff in Geneva was scheduled to occur in two days' time, on July 11, 2013. Racine, sitting by
his pool and enjoying a summer break at his Provençal hideaway, appeared poised to get his wish.

That's when Racine's phone rang. There would be no handover,
he was told when he answered the call. The Nordmanns had changed
their minds. The deal was off.

BEHIND THE SCENES, someone else had been angling to obtain the
manuscript, the only other person around willing to offer enormous
sums for a document with such controversial provenance: Lhéritier.

Aristophil had reached out to the Nordmanns not long after the
family announced their intention to sell the scroll. While Perrone's
lawyer had tried to put a stop to the matter by threatening to have the
manuscript seized if Aristophil acquired the scroll and returned it to

THE CURSE OF THE MARQUIS DE SADE 163

France, Lhéritier wasn't deterred. He had never been particularly interested in the Marquis de Sade, but he understood the value of securing a document of such literary and historical significance. He
vowed to find a way to acquire it.

Not long before the scheduled handoff to the national library,
Lhéritier offered the Nordmanns €4 million, €500,000 more than
they would have received from the library. The last-minute proposal
led the family to back out of the deal Racine had spent months ham-
mering out. Since the state was either unwilling or unable to best
Aristophil's offer, the library had no way left to obtain the scroll.

Perrone found himself with little choice but to begin negotiations
with Lhéritier. Working with Aristophil appeared to be the only remaining way to deliver the manuscript back to France. But the idea
of allowing the scroll to go to a private entity rather than a state institution didn't sit well with him, so he increased his demands. In the
end, Lhéritier agreed to pay Perrone €2.33 million. In total, Lhéritier
wound up arranging to pay €7 million for the manuscript, including
taxes and a hefty commission to the individual who helped him or-
chestrate the arrangement: Jean-Claude Vrain, the prominent Parisian bookseller and archnemesis of Aristophil critic Frédéric Castaing.

Along with financial compensation, Aristophil agreed to recognize both families' role in the backstory of the scroll. In all related
exhibits, the company would include notices stating that Charles and
Marie-Laure de Noailles had acquired the scroll in 1929 but that the
manuscript had most recently been in possession of the Gérard Nordmann Collection in Geneva. There was no admission of wrongdoing
from either family, no attempt to repair decades of acrimony and
legal disputes.

Lhéritier also tried to appease the national library. He offered to
donate the manuscript to the institution in five years, after first selling joint-ownership shares of it to investors, then buying it back once
the company had promoted and exhibited it. That way, shareholders
could reap the rewards of buying stakes in the scroll—and Aristophil
would be able to boast that it had launched another successful investment vehicle. Thanks to the donation, the company would be able to
deduct up to 60 percent of the cost of the manuscript from its taxes,

according to a French law designed to encourage business contributions to French institutions.

Racine, who had worked with Lhéritier on past donations Aristophil had provided to the national library, signed off on the agreement. But the arrangement also had to be approved by the Ministry of Culture. Considering Lhéritier's past business tactics, that step threatened to be a problem.

The complication could be traced back to 2010, when Aristophil acquired a series of World War II letters written by Charles de Gaulle while he led the French Resistance from England. The correspondence had been quietly preserved for decades by the family of de Gaulle's private secretary in London, before Lhéritier's company had located and purchased them. But the following year, the opening of an Aristophil exhibit of the letters was thrown into turmoil when the state declared that the missives belonged in the national archives. According to French law, all documents produced by public servants could be claimed as state property, with no restitution required.

Aristophil took the matter to court, arguing that at the time de Gaulle wrote the letters, he wasn't technically a French public servant, since he had been stripped of his nationality and condemned to death in absentia by the Nazi-approved Vichy regime then in control of much of the country. In 2012, at the request of the court, government staffers went to Aristophil's museum and confiscated the letters. But at the national archives, experts discovered they'd been given photocopies of the missives—a deliberate insult from Aristophil. Once confronted, the company relinquished the originals, but ministry officials would not forget the slight. The incident was likely among the main reasons why, a year later, the Ministry of Culture ultimately decided it would not do business with Aristophil over *120 Days of Sodom,* declining to accept the company's offer to eventually donate the manuscript to the national library.

This development didn't derail Lhéritier's efforts. The decision meant that the company wouldn't receive a tax break on the purchase, but in exchange, Aristophil would be able to retain ownership of the manuscript in perpetuity, allowing it to sell it to investors again and again.

On the morning of March 25, 2014, a Cessna private jet slipped out of the clouds above Geneva and touched down at the city's airport. From the cabin stepped Lhéritier, wearing a tan overcoat, brown scarf, black suit, and a matching cobalt-blue tie and pocket square. Behind him trailed a French TV news crew. As the cameras rolled, Lhéritier waited at the airport terminal until the arrival of two red-clad representatives of a Swiss transportation and storage company specializing in fine art. One of the workers carried a nondescript cardboard carton not much larger than a shoebox. As various discharge documents were signed, Lhéritier gazed at the container with anticipation.

"I've been waiting for this for years," he told the news crew. "Happiness isn't far away. It's there, in that jewel box."

When the paperwork was complete, the workers handed the box to Lhéritier, who carried it back to the private jet. Once airborne, he removed the packaging, revealing the clamshell box designed for Nordmann many years earlier. Slipping on white cotton gloves, Lhéritier carefully opened the box. Inside rested the scroll, wound tightly around its glass dowel, just over four inches wide and roughly half that in diameter. Light from the airplane's window fell on the brittle yellow paper, illuminating the tiny, precise handwriting of the Marquis de Sade.

WHEN LHÉRITIER RETURNED to France with the scroll in hand, he was met with acclaim. The national press hailed the repatriation of the manuscript, noting that its purchase price made it the third most expensive manuscript in all of France. Recounting its convoluted provenance, the newspaper *Libération* proclaimed that Lhéritier had written "a new chapter in a saga with so many twists that Alexandre Dumas could have used the material for a novel." Lloyd's of London insured the scroll for €12 million, that figure based in part on an appraisal by Vrain, a devoted admirer of Sade's, who'd noted in his assessment that the manuscript was nothing less than "a mythical document."

At the weekly French newsmagazine *L'Express,* reporter Jérôme

Dupuis tracked the affair with unease. Dupuis had spent enough time sorting through the dealings of the scroll's new owner to be skeptical of anything to do with Aristophil. Dupuis, like many successful reporters, came across as down-to-earth and approachable, with his flattop haircut and casual attire. In the early 2000s, after years of tackling political investigations and fending off libel lawsuits, Dupuis had turned his attention to a new beat: the book industry.

The subject lay close to his heart. As a boy, Dupuis had developed a voracious literary appetite, often reading a book a day. He'd also figured that the field would prove to be fertile ground for stories. In France, a high achiever who wanted to be recognized as a person of substance would typically try to write a literary volume, aiming to have it put out by the best publisher possible. By covering the book industry, Dupuis would have an inside track on the nation's power brokers and those angling to join their ranks. He soon discovered that the passions and elitism inspired by the country's love of books—not to mention the massive sums passing between dealers and collectors of rare texts—had a tendency to breed bad behavior.

Dupuis began in 2001 by detailing in *L'Express* the backstory of the manuscript for Louis-Ferdinand Céline's celebrated novel *Journey to the End of the Night,* which had recently reappeared after being lost for decades. Soon he was uncovering other literary scoops—including how celebrities were trying to leverage the publishing industry to burnish their reputations. In 2011, he reported that Patrick Poivre d'Arvor, the famous French newscaster and a close friend of Lhéritier's, had plagiarized a good portion of his forthcoming biography of Ernest Hemingway, lifting nearly one hundred pages of material from an American book. The scandal led Arvor's publisher to publish a shortened version of the biography, scrubbed of all problematic passages.

By that point, Dupuis had been hearing stories from sources about Aristophil. He learned the company was buying up wide swaths of materials from auction houses, and that it was employing aggressive business practices that left some dealers ill at ease. In 2012, he began looking into the operation in earnest. He cornered rare-book sellers in the hallways of Drouot and grilled them at out-of-the-way bistros in Saint-Germain-des-Prés, since he knew that French sources were most forthcoming over a meal and wine. He spoke with Aristophil investors, struck by how little they seemed to know about the operation to which they'd consigned much of their savings. He found himself amazed by the sheer magnitude of Lhéritier's empire—the vast quantity of letters and manuscripts involved, the amounts of money being thrown about, the staggering number of investors who had signed on to the operation.

Unlike Dupuis's typical assignments, this wasn't a story of industry insiders and cultural power brokers. This was a chronicle of ordinary people, far removed from Paris's auction halls, who in many cases were risking all they had ever earned on the financial promise of the written word. It felt troubling to him, but he didn't know what to make of Aristophil. That's when he recalled what his mentor had always told him: The most difficult part of an investigation is figuring out what exactly you're searching for.

The main question, Dupuis realized, was this: How, exactly, was Aristophil managing to run its business so successfully? Its books and manuscripts were real, as was the money it was paying out to its investors. But how was it able to produce such stable and sizable returns on materials whose value had long risen and fallen by subjective appraisals and the whims of a cloistered market? To answer this question, Dupuis decided that he needed to think like a storyteller. To get to the heart of an operation involving tens of thousands of documents and millions upon millions of euros, he needed to tell the story of the historical texts in the middle of it: how these books and manuscripts moved through the Aristophil system from initial acquisition, to division into joint-ownership shares, to distribution to company investors, to the firm's repurchasing of the materials five years later. Most important, he had to figure out whether there was anything about this process that should give those who bought into the operation reason to worry.

In the middle of his investigation, Dupuis received a strange email from Lhéritier. The head of Aristophil told him that a source had alerted him to Dupuis's efforts. Lhéritier let on that he knew that Dupuis spent several months a year in Scotland, fly-fishing for salmon. Perhaps, suggested Lhéritier, the two of them could bond over their shared love of fishing. Dupuis read the tone as friendly but slightly menacing. It seemed that Lhéritier was investigating the investigator—and wanted Dupuis to know it.

Undeterred, Dupuis continued his research, working away in his flat in Montparnasse. In May 2013, he published his first story on Aristophil in *L'Express*. He described Lhéritier's "empire of paper": the €100 million the company spent every year on books and manu-scripts, the grand galas that drew the city's elite, Lhéritier's exorbi-tant acquisitions of Parisian mansions and Mediterranean real estate. Thanks to records and accounts Dupuis had spent months working to obtain, he also detailed how the company's historical documents seemed to rise in value in ways that defied all expectations. In 2007, for example, he noted that Aristophil had acquired a Van Gogh letter from Sotheby's for €250,000, only to offer it to investors five years later for nearly €900,000. Another time it obtained a manuscript by the French poet Paul Verlaine for €300,000, then sold it to clients for €1.4 million. And according to company estimates, the Einstein doc-ument that had launched the Aristophil model was now worth €26.5 million, more than fifty times what Lhéritier had paid for it in 2002.

Such hefty markups had never been scrutinized or challenged, since Aristophil functioned as a closed system. Once acquired, its books and manuscripts were never offered for sale again at public auction, where the company's sky-high valuations would be put to the test. Instead, the materials' newly established prices were split among hundreds of investors, most of whom had no idea that Aris-tophil had significantly hiked their price. And while the manuscript trade was booming, bolstering the company's claims, the boom was largely due to Aristophil itself, since it dominated the market and shelled out steep prices for materials. Instead of the typical buyer, who was always looking for the best deal, Aristophil's business model seemed to incentivize spending as much money as possible for its ac-quisitions, then selling them for even more to its investors.

France's strict libel laws and Lhéritier's litigious nature meant Du-puis had to be careful about what he wrote. But the reporter had come to suspect that the company was in fact a giant con. In particular, he believed that Lhéritier had constructed an elaborate Ponzi scheme, a kind of scam in which profits weren't generated by any sort of real, functional business enterprise. In such operations, new investments were used to pay off old investments, in order to make the operation appear sound as it grew ever bigger. Despite their various permutations and vast differences of scale, most Ponzi schemes shared fundamental similarities. The most obvious red flags were promoters promising high yields with little apparent risk, business mechanisms that fell beyond the purview of financial regulators, and stakeholder payouts that remained strangely consistent despite market shifts. Aristophil met all the criteria.

The company also played on the same sort of romantic impulses that financial swindlers often used to fuel their scams. As Boston University law professor Tamar Frankel notes in her 2012 book *The Ponzi Scheme Puzzle: A History and Analysis of Con Artists and Victims,* "The investment stories of con artists have the aura of a thrilling treasure hunt. A treasure hunt promises a high reward, an adventure, a risk-bound mystery." The mysteries, adventures, and rewards of collecting historical letters and manuscripts had long captivated book and autograph collectors—but they could also be used to entice potential targets of fraud.

If Aristophil was in fact a Ponzi scheme, it meant that sooner or later, the firm would fail to find enough new investors to offset its expenditures and payouts. When that happened, Dupuis realized that those who had money in the operation—not to mention the letters market itself—would be poised for disaster. As one bookseller told Dupuis, "If one day the system collapses, it will be a cataclysm."

DUPUIS'S EXPOSÉ, A sweeping, thoroughly vetted piece in one of the country's largest newsmagazines, couldn't be easily wiped away by lawsuit threats or other Aristophil tactics. As his reporting and other eye-opening media accounts emerged, the public image of Lhéritier's venture began to shift from a success story to a potentially unstable enterprise. Between the troubling coverage, the ongoing warnings from critics like Castaing, the recent government alert about investing in letters and manuscripts, and the fact that Aristophil had recently struggled to reimburse some of its investors, pressure was mounting on French authorities to take action.

Five months after Dupuis's exposé came out, the government's consumer affairs and fraud prevention division launched an investigation into Aristophil. Investigators searched the company's offices and interviewed many of its employees. They met with Castaing and other dealers in the area, asking about how the book and manuscript market typically operated, and why it was that Aristophil seemed to be able to break all the rules.

This moment would have been the perfect time for Lhéritier to temper his exploits. Instead, he had become more ostentatious than ever. A few months earlier, Dupuis had noticed Lhéritier's smiling face on news kiosks all over Paris, courtesy of a cover story in a glossy magazine titled, in English, *Winner: The Magazine of Success.* Inside the publication, filled with flashy photos of Aristophil's holdings, a lengthy feature written in both French and English lauded Lhéritier and his firm in a manner that read like a thirty-six-page advertisement for the company. "Lhéritier is the acknowledged king, the lord of letters and manuscripts, disconcerting and spellbinding," declared the piece. "He lives at high speed. Hence his irresistible acceleration and his chronic desire to conquer, create, and imagine."

Then, in January 2014, the company launched "Cercle Aristophil," a VIP program that provided high-paying clients with rewards like a five-star Parisian hotel stay, tickets to the Cannes Film Festival, and trips on a private jet. The firm also threw its biggest gala yet: a massive celebration for the tenth anniversary of the Museum of Letters and Manuscripts and the twentieth anniversary of *Plume* at the Monte-Carlo Bay Hotel and Resort in Monaco that reportedly cost nearly €1 million. Lhéritier, meanwhile, was quietly laying the groundwork for a bold new enterprise. He planned to launch his own auction company, to cut out established houses like Drouot and their pricey commissions.

It didn't seem to matter that Aristophil's staff had begun to worry that the company's maneuvers and expenditures were unsustainable. Or that Lhéritier's confidant, the bookseller Vrain, had warned him to keep a low profile, writing in an email, "You're getting into trouble, Gérard. Please note, we're surrounded by a bunch of assholes." Or that in February 2014, government investigators completed a twenty-six-page report that accused the company of deceptive commercial practices, which it sent to the Paris prosecutor's office. While the report wasn't made public at the time, it was the first step in a potential criminal case.

The head of Aristophil insisted on moving forward with his most ambitious plans, even as his empire teetered on the verge of collapse. So a month after the investigators completed their report, he hadn't thought twice about traveling to Geneva to take possession of one of the world's most valuable and notorious manuscripts.

LHÉRITIER COULD NOT have chosen a better moment to return *120 Days of Sodom* to France. The country was in the middle of a year-long celebration of Sade, a culmination of its long reevaluation of the writer that would climax on December 2, 2014, the bicentennial of Sade's death. As part of the fête, several leading French writers wrote provocative new Sade biographies, and the famed Bibliothèque de la Pléiade publishing house issued a luxurious new eleven-hundred-page edition of Sade's works. *Le Figaro* and *The Paris Review* published think pieces on the marquis, while the newsmagazine *Le Point* issued an entire special edition dedicated to "The Sade Mystery," asking on its cover, "Is he a modern-day hero?"

The French writer Michel Onfray tried to counter the adulation with a new book, *La Passion de la Méchanceté,* which pointed out that Sade had been a sex offender and possibly a murderer. The rebuke did little to temper the festivities. In Geneva, the Bodmer Foundation mounted an exhibit titled *Sade, an Atheist in Love.* While the institution's recently relinquished scroll was noticeably absent, the show included a twenty-five-volume version of *120 Days of Sodom* that a German artist had spent three years transcribing into Braille, allowing people to read Sade's opus through the press of their own skin.

Most notably, just around the corner from Lhéritier's Institute of Letters and Manuscripts in Paris, the Musée d'Orsay announced that it would be hosting an exhibit titled *Sade: Attacking the Sun*. To publicize the show, the popular art museum released a promotional video featuring a soft-core orgy with writhing bodies arranged to spell out "SADE." As part of the exhibit, the Musée d'Orsay asked Lhéritier if it could borrow *120 Days of Sodom*. The show's title, after all, came from the novel: At one point, one of the novel's debauched protagonists grows so dispirited by the lack of crimes left to commit on earth that he declares, "How many times, good God, have I not wished it were possible to attack the sun, to deprive the universe of it, or to use it to set the world ablaze."

Lhéritier refused. The Musée d'Orsay operated under the authority of the Ministry of Culture. If he lent the manuscript to the museum, he feared, his enemies in the ministry might find a way to never give it back.

Instead, on September 25, 2014, a month before the Musée d'Orsay planned to launch its Sade exhibit, Aristophil opened the first exhibition in its new headquarters: *Sade: The Marquis of Shadows, the Prince of Lights*.

For the show, the institute's ground-floor gallery had been decorated like a belle époque bordello. Blood-red display walls curved through the space, framing salacious writings from Blaise Pascal, Giacomo Casanova, and Molière. Sheer veils displayed erotic images, tracing the evolution of libertinage through the centuries. In the center of the room, stretching from one end of the exhibit to the other, stood an elongated glass display case. Aristophil had built the fixture two years earlier when it hosted a traveling exhibition of the first draft of Jack Kerouac's *On the Road,* which the author had typed out on a 120-foot scroll during a three-week writing frenzy in 1951. Now the case held the centerpiece of the Sade exhibit: the unrolled manuscript of *120 Days of Sodom*.

Lhéritier, dressed in a striking blue suit and matching paisley tie, welcomed the crowd to the first-ever French exhibit of the scroll, boasting that it had taken him three years of tense negotiations to pull off the feat. Experts weighed in on the importance of the manuscript, with one specialist warning parents to keep children away from the relic, lest it corrupt them beyond repair. As the festivities stretched into the evening, red floodlights around the mansion lit the trees the celebratory color of blood.

Technically, the centerpiece of the exhibit no longer belonged to Aristophil. Immediately after obtaining the scroll from the Nordmanns, the company had divided the manuscript into joint-ownership shares valued at €5,000 each and offered them to investors all over France. Hundreds agreed to the offer, including Sylvie Le Gall, an insurance company employee in the northeastern French city of Strasbourg. Le Gall had just sold her car, and she was looking to use the proceeds to diversify her assets. An independent broker suggested Aristophil's latest investment proposal. As a student she had read Sade's *Philosophy in the Boudoir,* which she'd found daring if a bit boring. She was fascinated by the backstory of the scroll, but she wasn't really interested in rare books and manuscripts; for her the old text was an investment vehicle. So on April 14, 2014, three weeks after Lhéritier had acquired the manuscript, Le Gall signed a four-page legal document noting that she was purchasing six shares of "The Scroll of the Bastille of the Marquis de Sade" for a total price of €30,000. According to the contract, at the end of five years she would offer to sell her shares back to Aristophil for a price of €43,425, a potential profit of 44.75 percent. And with that, Le Gall became one of 420 investors who, for a total price of €12 million, became the latest in the long line of people to gain ownership of the scroll.

The Aristophil exhibit proved to be a hit; across the Channel, the British tabloid *The Daily Mail* declared, "The Original *Fifty Shades of Grey* Goes on Display." But not everyone with an interest in the scroll appreciated the fanfare. After years of fighting to repatriate the manuscript, Carlo Perrone didn't attend the company's unveiling of the scroll. He was frustrated that the document hadn't ended up in the national library, and he had a bad feeling about Aristophil. The Nordmanns, too, avoided the festivities. The negotiations had been too acrimonious for them to take part in the homecoming. Racine attended the show, although the collapse of the national library's bid for the manuscript had proven to be one of his greatest professional regrets. The fiasco had further stoked the hostilities between Aristophil and the Ministry of Culture. Soon, feared Racine, the tension could spill out in public.

In Strasbourg, Sylvie Le Gall made tentative plans to visit Paris and see the scroll, which she now partly owned. But for her, the effort wasn't a major priority. She figured there was no rush: For the first time in generations, the manuscript didn't appear to be going anywhere.

CHAPTER THIRTEEN

The Divine Marquis

JANUARY 22, 1948

THE BARE BRANCHES OF CENTURIES-OLD OAK TREES STRETCHED INTO the winter sky as Gilbert Lely approached the old château, in search of the secrets of the Marquis de Sade. Lely, a Surrealist poet, had become good friends with Sade expert Maurice Heine a decade earlier, around the time Heine had published his version of *120 Days of Sodom*. When Heine had died in 1940, Lely had taken up the mantle of rescuing Sade from the shadows. Despite the cult of Sade embraced by the Surrealists and others in the avant-garde, very little was known about the author himself. Up to that point, there had been few attempts to detail the marquis's life since Iwan Bloch had written about him at the turn of the century, and his story remained mired in rumors and myth.

Lely had arranged a visit to this secluded château amid the forested hills of the Champagne region, east of Paris, since he had come to believe he could find information about the marquis here that no one had discovered before. The Renaissance castle, with two stately wings framing a cobblestoned courtyard, had seen better days. Its pinnacled towers were crumbling, its white-limestone façade pockmarked with bullet holes from the German soldiers who had ransacked the property a few years before. The gentleman who opened the creaking front door gazed at the caller with watery eyes, a remnant from medical experiments he'd been subjected to while imprisoned in a Nazi labor camp during the war. For Lely, there was no mistaking the man's prominent forehead, his pouty lips, his hooded eyes, the aquiline nose. He was staring at the Marquis de Sade.

◂ ◂ ◂

STARTING WITH ARMAND, Donatien Alphonse François de Sade's younger son, the house of Sade had worked to wipe away all vestiges of their infamous relative. No one bestowed the name Donatien on any of their sons, unlike how the clan still named daughters after their celebrated Renaissance ancestor Laura de Sade. When, in the 1930s, Charles de Noailles reached out to family members, asking them to discuss the ancestor they shared with his wife, they refused. And for generations, the title "marquis" hadn't been used to refer to the oldest son in the family. It was why when Xavier de Sade was born, in 1922, he was told nothing of his great-great-great-grandfather. And it was why, when his father and older siblings died in a train accident when he was a young boy, making Xavier the family's most senior surviving male family member, he never took up the official title of the Marquis de Sade.

But now, thanks to his meeting with Lely at his family's château, the twenty-five-year-old Xavier learned that part of his history had been kept from him. A genteel aristocrat with conservative views and a deep Catholic faith, Xavier had little in common with his ancestor— but his curiosity was piqued. He made his way through the château, passing shattered stone fireplaces and moldering ceiling frescoes, lingering mementos of years of abandonment and the Nazi occupation. On the top floor, in the dusty library, he found what he was looking for: an immense old trunk. When Xavier had returned from the war, he'd found that, adjacent to the library, the Nazis had uncovered a secret, walled-up room filled with old family records and had scattered its contents around the property. He'd gathered up the clutter and placed it in this trunk; the materials had included two ancient storage boxes, fastened with red seals dated 1815. Now, breaking open the boxes, he beheld thousands upon thousands of documents, all covered with the handwriting of the Marquis de Sade.

While his family had hidden their ancestor away, they had stopped short of completely obliterating his sprawling output. It was a chaotic mess of musings, speeches, travel memoirs, unpublished plays, original manuscripts, and numerous letters written to and from Sade.

Together they detailed Sade's upbringing and relationship with his parents, his scandals and struggles with the law, his prolonged internments and the resulting literary creations. Some of the documents appeared to be written in Sade's blood.

Xavier gave Lely access to the papers, and over the following decade, Lely published several volumes of Sade's correspondence and a two-volume biography that revealed the details of a life that had been lost to time. As Sade emerged from the artistic and literary fringes, scholars and intellectuals found him ripe for analysis. His writings were so unique, so extreme, they figured there had to be an underlying reason for his efforts. No one, however, could agree on exactly what that was.

The French intellectual Simone de Beauvoir, in an influential essay titled "Must We Burn Sade?," argued that the marquis had posed vital questions about personal freedom: "Can we, without renouncing our individuality, satisfy our aspirations to universality? Or is it only by the sacrifice of our individual differences that we can integrate ourselves into the community?" The writer Pierre Klossowski theorized that Sade had been examining the clash between nature and God, while the philosopher Michel Foucault wrote that the marquis was obsessed with the many facets of human desire. Still others deemed Sade a proto-feminist. Thanks to the unrestrained lust of his female characters, novelist Angela Carter asserted that he was "claiming rights of free sexuality for women" and "installing women as beings of power."

Some glimpsed a darker truth in Sade's oeuvre. While the Surrealists held up Sade as a chronicler of humanity's potential shorn of all rules, in the wake of World War II, many readers saw the opposite. In Sade's depictions of absolute evil, they perceived a premonition of the concentration camps and mushroom clouds of the twentieth century. As the French author Albert Camus noted not long after the war, "Two centuries ahead of his time and on a reduced scale, Sade extolled totalitarian societies in the name of unbridled freedom." Max Horkheimer and Theodor W. Adorno, two social philosophers who were forced to flee Nazi Germany, elaborated on this idea in their 1947 book *Dialectic of Enlightenment,* equating the regimented tortures of Sade's fictional Silling Castle with the rise of fascism. "The strict regime of the libertine society of the *120 Days of Sodom*," they wrote, "prefigures the organization, devoid of any substantial goals, which was to encompass the whole of life." Mankind, Sade seemed to be saying, wasn't destined for greatness. It was barreling into annihilation.

The one thing scholars could agree on was that Sade offered relevant ideas to modern-day readers. In France and the United States, as publishers began issuing general editions of Sade's works, they often padded the volumes with one or more critical essays, since the analyses suggested that Sade's writings boasted enough significance that they shouldn't be suppressed. As French literary theorist Roland Barthes put it in his linguistic studies of Sade, "When written, shit does not have an odor; Sade can inundate his partners in it, we receive not the slightest whiff." The horrible crimes Sade described, in other words, were safely imprisoned on the page.

In 1966, some of those literary atrocities appeared to break free. In April of that year, the world watched as twenty-eight-year-old Ian Brady and twenty-three-year-old Myra Hindley were led into court in the quaint English town of Chester to be tried for murder. The two had been charged with killing three youths, including a boy and girl whose bodies had been found buried in a desolate stretch of North West England called Saddleworth Moor. Authorities believed the couple had also killed several other missing children, but so far no other bodies had been found. The so-called Moor Murders became international news. As the legal proceedings began, Brady and Hindley sat behind bulletproof glass for their own protection, and all women were removed from the jury. During the trial, a photography expert who examined photos the couple had taken of their crimes testified that "no adjective in the English language is appropriate" for what he had seen. When lawyers played a sixteen-minute audio clip the two had recorded while torturing one of their victims, many in the courtroom broke down in tears.

Prosecutors made special note of Brady's reading material, which included an English-language version of *Justine* and a book on the life and ideas of the Marquis de Sade. They described how Brady had used Sade's philosophy to try to indoctrinate others, reading from a notebook in which one of Brady's colleagues had paraphrased the marquis by writing, "Rape is not a crime, it is a state of mind. Murder is a hobby, and a supreme pleasure." When an attorney cross-examined Brady about the pornographic nature of the books, the defendant replied, "They cannot be called pornographic. They can be bought at any bookstall."

It didn't seem to matter that Brady had committed several of the murders before he obtained his copy of *Justine*. The literary critic George Steiner spoke for many when he noted in a letter to *The Times Literary Supplement* that there was a "high probability that the reading of Sade and related material was a significant factor" in the accused killers' behavior.

The jury took just two hours to convict Brady and Hindley of murder, for which they received life imprisonment. After the trial, the United Kingdom banned the publishing or importation of all of Sade's writing, a prohibition that would remain in place for more than three decades. Many considered the decision warranted. As English novelist Pamela Hansford Johnson concluded, "There are some books that are not fit for all people, and some people who are not fit for all books."

IN THE DIMMING light of a dwindling Provençal summer day, a band of farmers made their way up a steep hillside, perched atop rumbling tractors and in some cases armed with pitchforks. It was July 14, 2010—Bastille Day—and like their revolutionary forebears, they focused their ire on the looming fortress up ahead: the ruins of La Coste, Sade's onetime estate, now referred to as Lacoste. They were there for the current lord of the castle, a man who reveled in provocation and controversy. His name was Pierre Cardin, and he was one of the most powerful fashion designers in the world.

Cardin had become famous—and very rich—for selling his space-age designs to the masses and had been among the first designers to turn his name into a global brand, churning out "Pierre Cardin"–emblazoned perfume, cosmetics, household goods, cigarettes, private jets, even boxer shorts. In 2000, he visited the remnants of Lacoste, which had been deteriorating and stripped for building materials ever since it had been ransacked during the revolution, and decided that the site deserved the Cardin treatment. He purchased the property from an English teacher who had been slowly renovating it and set about shoring up the remains and embellishing its hollowed-out rooms and courtyards with modern sculptures like life-size technicolor giraffes and cows. On a dusty pitch beyond the castle bridge, he erected a bronze statue of Sade, his head enclosed in a metal cage. And in the sleepy village that clung to the hillside below, he began buying up houses and retrofitting them—into art galleries, a high-end bakery, and a gourmet food shop with bold color schemes and modern décor. Soon the main cobblestoned street winding through town was decorated with signs for businesses like Boulangerie du Marquis and Moulin de Sade. Cardin declared that his goal was to create a "cultural Saint-Tropez" and told a journalist that while some people liked to collect paintings or stamps, he collected houses and land.

Some in the village of four hundred welcomed the improvements and attention. Others balked at how Cardin seemed to be turning their home into a haute-couture Disneyland. The situation reached a breaking point when Cardin announced plans to build a golf course decorated with immense sculptures on a hundred acres of fallow farmland outside Lacoste. Outraged at what they saw as a squandering of water reserves and the desecration of pristine Provençal land, farmers in the area demanded to meet with Cardin, but received no response. So now they were bringing the fight to his doorstep. As Sade had done before him, Cardin had launched a theater festival at the château that drew cultural elites from far and wide, and Bastille Day was the opening of the annual event. As the sun slipped below the rolling hills to the west, the farmers parked themselves in front of the castle and refused to let anyone enter until Cardin agreed to hear their concerns.

An immaculately dressed figure stepped from within the illuminated stone walls of the château: Cardin, his white hair tousled and his signature black glasses framing an irritated glare. To allow the festivities to proceed, he acceded to the farmers' demand. The following day, after meeting with them, he called off the golf course. The decision might not have been completely altruistic. At eighty-eight years old, the designer likely figured the effort wouldn't be worth the trouble.

While Sade's onetime environs were saved from being overrun with golf carts and statuary, the stoppage did little to slow the commercialization of the once-scorned writer. As Guillaume Apollinaire had predicted in 1909, the man he'd titled "the Divine Marquis" had in many ways come to dominate the latter half of the twentieth century, but not necessarily in the ways the avant-garde poet might have imagined. The rise of a new, more stylish version of Sade began in the United States. A 1965 *New York Times* review of an English-language edition of *Justine* hinted at what was to come when it noted that a modern-day incarnation of Sade, instead of being imprisoned, "might very well have ended up in Hollywood as a consultant for Vincent Price horror films, the secret collaborator of James Bond novels."

Sure enough, the details of Sade's life and writing proved to be ready-made for the world of pop culture. The 1965 Broadway debut of the play *Marat/Sade,* a fictional account of Sade putting on a play in the Charenton mental asylum, became a sensation, leading to a movie adaptation, an LP of the show's star reading selections of Sade's work, and a cover of *Life* magazine declaring the arrival of the "Mad New World of Batman, Superman, and the Marquis de Sade." Four years later, the English-language film *De Sade* turned the marquis's life into a psychedelic sex romp, filled with soft-core orgies and accompanied by a promotional spread in *Playboy.* Then, in 1975, the Italian art-house director Pier Paolo Pasolini transferred the debaucheries of Silling Castle to a World War II Fascist republic in his film *Salò, or the 120 Days of Sodom.* The film, a critique of consumerism, political corruption, and the voyeurism of cinema itself, drew controversy for its graphic depictions of sex and torture, as well as the fact that Pasolini, an outspoken critic of Italy's power brokers, was brutally murdered under mysterious circumstances not long after its completion. Finally, in 2000, Hollywood returned to the subject of Sade's internment in Charenton with the film *Quills,* featuring Geoffrey Rush as an aging Sade battling for artistic freedom and penning some of his works in his own blood.

In France, too, Sade was evolving into a pop star. In 1990, on the 250th anniversary of his birth, the Bibliothèque de la Pléiade, an iconic French publishing imprint, announced that it would be issuing authoritative editions of Sade's novels with advertisements declaring "Hell on Bible paper," a reference to the thin, wispy paper the publisher used for its books. The dungeon of Vincennes, now surrounded by the largest public park in Paris, opened a reconstruction of Sade's onetime cell as a tourist attraction. Across town, the trendy Parisian restaurant Morot-Gaudry developed a dish of blood-red slices of raw meat and "well-whipped" mousseline sauce and called it "Boeuf à la Marquis de Sade."

Xavier de Sade, who helped inspire his ancestor's popularity by uncovering the details of his life, tracked the shift with mixed emotions. On occasion, he spoke out or filed lawsuits to try to quell endeavors he believed were giving Sade a bad name, such as the launch of a "Prix Sade" literary prize he felt was rewarding pornographic drivel, as well as the widespread use of the term "sadism." At the same time, he wasn't strictly opposed to commercializing his namesake. He trademarked the family name and launched a Sade-branded line of champagne.

But more than any other venture, Xavier dedicated himself to making sense of the papers of the Marquis de Sade. He collaborated with Lely until the biographer died in 1985, then provided materials to other Sade biographers. He ignored relatives who said he was tarnishing the legacy of the noble house of Sade, and he kept working even as his wealth dwindled away and he was forced to sell the longtime family château. Finally, as he lay dying in 2010, he called members of his family to his bedside.

"The one thing I am proud of," he whispered to them in his last handful of intelligible words, "is rehabilitating the Marquis de Sade."

WITH PRIM COMPOSURE, Thibault de Sade did little to attract attention as he sipped an espresso on a sidewalk terrace of a small Parisian bistro, taking in the springtime view of the city's Luxembourg Gardens. Around the corner lay the Théâtre de l'Odéon and the famed literary stretch of Rue de l'Odéon, meaning he was just a few steps away from the birthplace of his great-great-great-great-grandfather. He, like his father, Xavier, displayed the high forehead, full lips, and hooked nose of his ancestor, but that was where the similarities ended. In behavior and philosophy, Thibault espoused restraint. A government adviser, the sixty-two-year-old kept his graying hair short and tidy, his jackets and ties subdued. He chose his words carefully, avoiding anything extreme. He had learned the value of keeping a low profile after the newspapers had a field day with the news that he, a Sade, had been put in charge of family values and women's rights as part of his job at a state agency.

But he, more than his four siblings, had come closest to carrying on his father's work. His two sisters, Marie Laure and Marie Aigline, were interested in their heritage, but they never made it a major facet of their lives. His oldest brother, Elzéar, sometimes trotted out the title of Marquis de Sade when reporters interviewed him about his ancestor, but that was largely the extent of his efforts. The middle brother, Hugues, the most flamboyant of the bunch, with a long silver mane and a fondness for colorful attire, shattered the family omertà by naming one of his sons Donatien and embracing the business potential of their namesake, selling wine, spirits, and candles under the name Maison de Sade. Hugues had even been in contact with Victoria's Secret about developing a line of Sade-branded lingerie.

But Thibault was the one who had spent the most time with his father in the château library. He was the most enthralled when the family passed afternoons sitting in Empire armchairs and trading anecdotes they had gleaned from the papers. When he studied at the Sorbonne, Thibault wrote his dissertation on Sade's political worldview, and he had since worked with scholars to further research his ancestor. He hoped to one day launch a foundation to support academic work on Sade, and he encouraged his two grown sons to continue the family legacy.

In 2014, Thibault was excited when he learned that *120 Days of Sodom* had been brought back to France. He and his brother Hugues even attended the grand opening of Aristophil's exhibit on the scroll, at the personal invitation of Lhéritier. But he also believed that the scroll had returned home tainted. Thanks to his studies, Thibault was convinced that Sade, during his years in the dungeons of Vincennes and the Bastille, had become utterly obsessed with vengeance—not just against the individuals he blamed for his imprisonment but also against emancipated people everywhere, all those who enjoyed freedom while he languished behind bars.

Thibault believed that Sade had therefore written *120 Days of Sodom* with a singular purpose in mind. To him, it wasn't an accident that in the novel, Sade addressed his readers far more often than he ever did in his other works, writing things like "The time has come, friendly reader, for you to prepare your heart and mind for the most impure tale ever written since the world began." Thibault thought it was all part of Sade's plan that as the novel progressed, the story became ever more blunt and appalling, until all that remained was a mind-numbing onslaught of horror. The marquis, he and other prominent Sade experts had concluded, had designed the tale to lead his readers by the hand, to lure them ever deeper into his world of madness, until they were all but complicit in the crimes he described. Sade, he believed, had constructed *120 Days of Sodom* to be a prison.

In Thibault's mind, the scroll was foredoomed, poisoned by the logic of its twisted conception. His idea was bolstered by the mayhem and misery the manuscript had left in its wake as it had journeyed across Europe: depleted fortunes, ruined relationships, social turmoil, theft and legal disputes, loneliness and pain, disease and death. As he laid out his theory on the bistro patio, Thibault's impassive countenance fell away, leaving behind an impassioned, even manic grin. The clear spring sky over his head would soon be filled by billows of ominous smoke. Later that day, an accidental fire at Notre-Dame would light central Paris in towering flames, consuming the cathedral's roof.

"The manuscript," Thibault declared between sips of his espresso, "has always been cursed."

CHAPTER FOURTEEN

The Prisoner by the Sea

NOVEMBER 18, 2014

THE POLICE ARRIVED NOT LONG AFTER DAYBREAK, EXACTLY TWO WEEKS shy of the bicentennial of Sade's death. Emerging from the early-morning fog, they approached the imposing red doors of the Institute of Letters and Manuscripts. Lhéritier was in his office, meeting with staff members, when his personal assistant rushed in with the news. Downstairs there were twenty plainclothes officers from the Parisian judicial police's economic delinquency repression brigade.

Trying to maintain his calm, Lhéritier ushered the squad's commander into his office and asked what was going on. Perhaps, he offered, they were looking into allegations of stolen cultural goods? Or maybe there had been a mistake? The commander refused to tell him anything, other than that he was there as part of an investigation launched by the Paris prosecutor's office. As the squad fanned out through the mansion, collecting documents and requisitioning hard drives, dozens of other officers descended on the outposts of Lhéritier's domain all over Paris and beyond. A few blocks away, gendarmes marched into Aristophil's Museum of Letters and Manuscripts, as well as Vrain's bookshop. In a Lyon office building, 290 miles to the southeast, law enforcement began to pore over the company files of Aristophil's main distributor. And in the hills of the French Riviera, agents converged on Lhéritier's multimillion-euro villa.

Aristophil was being shut down. Everything, every last manuscript, had to be seized—and that included *120 Days of Sodom*.

◂ ◂ ◂

ARISTOPHIL COLLAPSED WITH startling speed. What had started in 2013 as a discreet government inquiry into the company was now a very public criminal investigation. On the day of the police raids, the Paris prosecutor's office froze the operation's bank accounts, sequestered its properties, and shut down its website. The French media jumped on the story, announcing, "Justice Dehorns Aristophil" and "Will the Emperor of Manuscripts End Up Like Madoff?" Employees continued to operate the museum and the *120 Days of Sodom* exhibit, even though the collections had been placed under government seal and no one knew if they would continue to get paid.

In early March 2015, the Parisian judicial police's financial brigade summoned Lhéritier to its headquarters for questioning. After a lengthy interrogation that stretched over several days, officers escorted him to the High Court of Paris. There, he learned the details of the case being built against him. According to prosecutors, every aspect of Aristophil—its unique investment program, its takeover of the letter and manuscript market, its overzealous valuation of its assets, its glitzy festivities—was part of an elaborate Ponzi scheme, just as Dupuis and others had come to suspect. The investigating judge assigned to the case listened to the arguments, then handed down her indictments. As the founder and president of the operation, Lhéritier was charged with organized fraud, money laundering, misappropriation of corporate assets, misleading marketing practices, breach of trust, and publication of inaccurate financial statements. For the organized-fraud charge alone, he faced up to ten years in prison and a fine of €1 million.

As part of the investigation, authorities seized everything Lhéritier owned—his EuroMillions winnings, his Mediterranean villa, his racehorses, his hot-air balloons. After posting bail of €500,000, Lhéritier was allowed to continue living in his villa in Nice and to travel freely around France, pending the resolution of his case. But he couldn't leave the country without judicial permission. The only reason he had any money at all was thanks to his son, Fabrice, to whom he'd bestowed €25 million of his lottery windfall.

Lhéritier wasn't the only one authorities targeted for Aristophil's alleged misdeeds. For her role in the business, the judge charged

Lhéritier's daughter, Valérie, with organized fraud and placed her under investigation for complicity in the company's other activities. Authorities also indicted several of Lhéritier's associates, including his notary, the company's accountant, the directors of the operation's manuscript-distribution companies Finestim and Art Courtage, and the Sorbonne law professor who had helped craft the company's sales contracts. Vrain, too, found himself ensnared in the dragnet. For his part in the operation, the judge charged the book dealer with fraud.

Through his contacts, Dupuis scored access to the investigation's case files, giving him a direct view into the inner workings of Aristophil. He reported on how Lhéritier had paid a tech firm to scrub critical Aristophil coverage from the internet and had hired investigators to track his foes, including Castaing. He detailed how the head of Aristophil had spent €250,000 to commission two journalists to write a play featuring him, a production that was never performed. And he revealed how Lhéritier had taken the original Einstein manuscript that had inspired his investment program and, after repurchasing it from Aristophil investors, tried to sell it to a variety of celebrities, including Bill Gates, Steven Spielberg, and Harvey Weinstein. None of them had agreed to the sale, likely because the manuscript, originally purchased by Lhéritier for $559,500, had been priced at $32 million.

Most important, Dupuis discovered the missing piece in how the company was able to drastically inflate its holdings' values before selling them to investors. The price hikes appeared to be driven by generous estimates provided by the company's well-compensated specialists. As one of the company's brokers put it in a telephone conversation intercepted by investigators, "Lhéritier has a network of experts around him who evaluate his works. The guy buys works of art and, two or three years later, he makes them quadruple the price, based on a network of experts with whom he was friends."

Dupuis discovered an example of this arrangement when he obtained emails between Lhéritier and Vrain. According to a December 2012 exchange, Lhéritier had written to Vrain asking him to evaluate a manuscript signed by Helen Churchill Candee, an American writer who'd survived the sinking of the *Titanic*. While Aristophil had purchased the text for a few hundred thousand euros, Lhéritier wrote to Vrain that he thought €1.1 million would be a more accurate value for the document. Two hours later, Vrain replied with his valuation. While he hadn't seen the original text, Vrain noted that the €1.1 million figure Lhéritier had proposed was, in fact, exactly right. "I declare that I have appraised the manuscript for an insurance value of 1,100,000 euros," he wrote. "Certified sincere and genuine."

While dealers like Vrain provided the company with sky-high document appraisals, according to case files they also sold their own materials to the firm for two, six, or even fifty times the price they had paid for them, netting huge profits. Vrain alone was responsible for providing Aristophil with nearly €80 million worth of items between 2009 and 2014. As the revelations emerged, shock waves rippled through the book and manuscript market. "Members of the French trade are complicit," said a prominent American historical document dealer of the affair. "To me, the story is that these people were at some level enablers of this thing. And they were not minor players in the industry."

Former French prime minister Dominique de Villepin was caught up in the scandal after the news media discovered that pricey selections from his historical document collection had ended up being sold to Aristophil, often courtesy of an intermediary: Vrain. And news that the police had detained and questioned the newscaster Patrick Poivre d'Arvor over his relationship with the king of manuscripts drew salacious headlines, especially since Dupuis had already been reporting on how Lhéritier had showered his high-profile friend with texts written by Eugène Delacroix and Louis-Ferdinand Céline, not to mention a €400,000 loan.

By that point, Aristophil had ceased to exist. Three months after the raids, left with no way to continue their business activities, the company and its subsidiaries crumpled into bankruptcy. The Commercial Court of Paris assigned a legal administrator to try to resuscitate the operation, but prosecutors nixed the resulting reorganization plan, arguing that no amount of effort would ever leave the business solvent. So the facilities were shuttered and sold. Sixty-one employees lost their jobs, and the manuscripts were carted away. Soon, where people had once entered the Museum of Letters and Manu-scripts on Paris's Boulevard Saint-Germain, a branch of Bang & Oluf-sen sold high-end Danish electronics. Not far away, part of the grand mansion that had housed Lhéritier's Institute of Letters and Manu-scripts and exhibited *120 Days of Sodom* was reconfigured into a carpet showroom.

"THE PRESS NOW call me the Bernie Madoff of France," said Lhéritier, his French tinged with bitterness. "I will tell you how they killed Aristophil. It will feel good to talk about this, to explain how they destroyed it."

Lhéritier sat in the timber-ceilinged living room of his villa in the hills overlooking Nice, a sprawling stone edifice built from the rem-nants of an old church that once occupied the site. On this early De-cember day two years after the police raids, the city below was quiet—the summer crowds long since departed, the Christmastime revelers yet to arrive. Here in his villa, a plant-filled sunroom fea-tured a hot tub and a small indoor pool, and photos of Lhéritier's children and grandchildren stood haphazardly among antiques and gold-framed paintings. In a downstairs bathroom, an electronic toilet featured a heated seat and self-opening lid, the ultimate extravagance for the offspring of plumbers. As usual, Lhéritier was impeccably dressed: a cobalt-blue suit over a plaid open-collared shirt, with a matching pocket handkerchief. But in the bright white light coming off the Mediterranean, the sixty-eight-year-old looked older, more tired, than he appeared in the many photos of him presiding over regal galas.

The house was Lhéritier's final redoubt, all that was left of his em-pire. Gone was the bustle of the Aristophil headquarters and the buzz of the Paris auction houses. He had spent years scaling France's social hierarchy: forging bonds with book and manuscript dealers, cultivat-ing alliances with celebrities and power brokers. Now nearly every-one save his family had abandoned him.

But Lhéritier wasn't giving up. He had emerged victorious from one scandal and disaster after another. He aimed to do so again. "If I really deceived people, I would go hide somewhere," he said, anger flashing in his greenish-blue eyes. "Since I know I am right and I didn't deceive anyone, we are not going to let them win."

He spent his days poring over legal briefs and penning accounts of his business activities that he was certain would clear his name. Now, with a cup of espresso in his hand and Frank Sinatra on the stereo, he was ready to share the results of his efforts. As the afternoon stretched on, he pulled from his shelves various Aristophil marketing materials and reference books on historical documents, the stacks of tomes and papers accumulating on the table around him. He was building his case that Aristophil was an upstanding company that exposed people all over France and beyond to the world of letters and manuscripts. At the same time, thanks to its acquisition strategies, the firm had been able to safeguard numerous French treasures that otherwise could have been snatched up by foreign collectors and institutions.

It had all come tumbling down—but not, he insisted, because of internal mismanagement or deceit. He blamed what had happened on a secret government conspiracy. Bit by bit, he laid out his account: He had earned the animosity of senior officials in the ministries of culture, finance, and justice by threatening the status quo. He had done so by upending the book and manuscript markets monopolized by France's elite, by distributing to the people literary riches that had been hoarded by those in power. The new state of affairs would not be tolerated; those in charge had decided to take him down. "I did everything to develop this market," he said. "And they cut our wings because it was going too well."

It didn't help that Lhéritier had the gall to move far beyond his station, that he had the audacity to flaunt his success. "In order to live happily in France, you have to live hidden," he said. That is not how he had wanted to live.

He insisted that his adversaries were helped by journalists like Dupuis, who were all too eager to publicize a make-believe scandal. Castaing, too, deserved part of the blame, for working to demonize Aristophil simply out of jealousy. "Castaing is a hoodlum," said Lhéritier. "He was a god in the world of books and manuscripts, and then all of a sudden we were stepping on his toes. So he attacked us."

Finally, after his purchase of *120 Days of Sodom,* his enemies had decided it was time to act. "The minister of culture and some malicious prosecutors thought that the manuscript would be seized for free after Aristophil's destruction," he said. "They preferred to place a bomb in the heart of Aristophil and its museums—and it exploded."

The investigation into Aristophil seemed to be stretching on indefinitely. No one knew when the criminal inquiry would be complete or when the case would come to trial. Considering the complexity of the alleged fraud, the myriad financial transactions involved, and the thousands of potential victims, many more years would likely pass before the matter ever reached a courtroom.

Lhéritier felt emboldened by the delay. Sitting in his villa in Nice, he waved away the case against him. "It might take two or three years, but they are not going to get me," he said. He insisted that he couldn't be convicted of fraud, breach of trust, or misleading business practices, since his company had never done anything to deceive its customers. Aristophil, he explained, had never technically guaranteed that it would buy back people's joint-ownership shares. Its carefully worded contracts had stated that investors would offer to sell their shares back to the company after five years, but Aristophil had been under no obligation to repurchase them every time. As for the 40 percent returns company shareholders expected from their investments? Those were the overzealous promises of independent brokers, he said, not company policy.

Plus, as Lhéritier pointed out, after he had won the lottery, he had poured millions into the company. If Aristophil had been a hoax, that investment would make him its number one victim. "You need to have a motive in order to defraud people," he said. "I didn't need money, absolutely not. Any day I could have taken my retirement."

But questions remained about his EuroMillions prize. The odds of him winning that jackpot were one in 139 million. Had he really done so just when his company needed a major cash infusion? Or had he used clandestine millions he'd siphoned from Aristophil to buy the winning ticket from somebody else, therefore making his windfall look legitimate? Such a scheme had been pulled off before. In 1991, the American mobster James "Whitey" Bulger had reportedly purchased part of the winnings from a $14.3 million Boston lottery ticket to make it look like he'd obtained his riches through lawful means.

To rig what was then the largest jackpot in French history, Lhéritier would have had to track down and pay off the actual winner before the news went public. Otherwise, he would have had to manipulate the inner workings of a transnational lottery system to produce a winning ticket whose numbers perfectly matched his birthdays and those of his children. Pulling off such a maneuver would have made him one of Europe's greatest criminal masterminds, eclipsing everything he'd been accused of doing with Aristophil. "It sounds like an American police series," said Lhéritier. Yet after years of digging into his various ventures, authorities had yet to suggest that anything was amiss with his lottery payout.

Lhéritier insisted that he wasn't France's Bernie Madoff. Madoff's Wall Street firm hadn't been selling anything tangible; Aristophil, meanwhile, had traded in real manuscripts with real value. The truth, declared Lhéritier, would emerge when he finally had his day in court. When asked how many years in prison he thought he'd receive, he flashed his roguish smile and made a circle with his fingers: zero.

AS THE SUN set over Nice, painting the sky a dramatic shade of lavender, Lhéritier stepped into his backyard. He ambled across his stone patio and around his outdoor pool, to a decorative pond near the far end of his property, just before the land dropped away toward the city and the sea far below. He tossed fish food to the colorful koi carp that swam up to meet him, then closed up his henhouse, which sheltered forty birds. His two Belgian shepherds, Skipper and Gypsy, scampered about, darting through the whistling ducks and emperor geese that wandered freely among the fruit and olive trees. "It is like my simple origins," he said, referring to his childhood home amid the pastures of northeastern France.

"Unlike people, animals do not betray you," said Lhéritier, glancing at his wild companions. "They let you down only when they die."

Lhéritier wasn't alone in feeling betrayed by the collapse of Aristophil. The company's bankruptcy proceedings laid bare the scope of the damage. Roughly eighteen thousand people had €850 million invested in the program when it imploded. With the interest they expected to receive, the company's clientele were now owed €1.2 billion. The sum meant Lhéritier stood accused of running the largest Ponzi scheme in French history.

The numbers stunned even those, like Castaing, who had long believed that Aristophil was a scam. No one had realized the extent of the operation, how many people had been drawn into its grasp. Even with his lottery winnings, liquidating all of Lhéritier's assets wouldn't come close to allowing his clients to recover their investments, much less their expected earnout.

Seeking other alternatives, investors had formed consumer associations and filed lawsuits against the ancillary businesses that had helped facilitate Aristophil's rise. Some groups took aim at the financial advisers who had sold Aristophil contracts. Others were launched by Aristophil brokers themselves, since many had invested in the system alongside their customers. An organization called ADILEMA gathered roughly six hundred members and sued Aristophil's notary for signing off on its investment contracts. The largest group, organized by two prominent investment-law attorneys, had amassed more than fifteen hundred clients and was going after the banks that did business with Aristophil, arguing that the institutions had ignored warning signs about the company. One association made headlines when authorities discovered that its founder had received a €200,000 donation from Lhéritier's son, Fabrice.

None of these efforts promised quick resolutions. The success of most, if not all, was dependent on the outcome of the Aristophil criminal case, the conclusion of which was likely years away. The majority of Aristophil's clients, meanwhile, hadn't joined any of the associations. Some shared Lhéritier's view that the operation would have continued to flourish if not for government meddling. Others simply had no idea what to do. All of them had nothing to show for their investment save for an ownership contract produced by a company that no longer existed.

Night had fallen by the time Lhéritier finished looking after his animals and returned to his villa. After talking for hours about the collapse of Aristophil, not once had he brought up the plight of his clients.

"It is a sad affair," he finally said when prompted about his company's investors. But he insisted that he wasn't responsible for what had happened to them: "Maybe I made some management mistakes, but I never tried to defraud anyone."

There are others the investors should blame, not him. "I would tell the clients to address themselves to the authors of this destruction, not to me," he said. "There is only one thing I can say to the clients, and I have said this since the beginning: They have to be patient and confident. Their collections still exist. They haven't lost anything."

Not all of them could be patient. Robert Cipollina, the former motorcycle racer from Avignon who had planned to use the returns on his investment to buy a new car, had changed his mind in 2014, deciding that the profits should go to his children as he lay dying from leukemia. Now he was gone, and his daughter Aude Nehring, a bank manager in Luxembourg, had taken up his cause, fighting out of principle to retrieve his lost investment.

Then there was Jean-Claude Le Coustumer, the hair salon owner who had spent €1.7 million on various collections of letters and manuscripts. In March 2015, the sixty-nine-year-old's stepson had been quoted in a newspaper describing how his family had been caught up in the Aristophil affair. In response, the financial adviser who had sold Le Coustumer his Aristophil shares had repeatedly called his client, outraged by what he saw as a betrayal. Two days later, Le Coustumer's wife had found him dead in his bed, an empty pill bottle resting nearby.

IN THE SPRING of 2019, after years of waiting for any sort of development in the status of their lost investments, thousands of former Aristophil clients found a surprise in the mail: a copy of *Affaire Aristophil: Liquidation en Bande Organisée,* a 336-page paperback that promised to reveal the truth about "the story of the plumber's son who, in the field of letters and manuscripts, became the greatest collector, investor, patron, and creator of private museums in the world, before losing everything." According to the preface, the volume would prove once and for all whether Lhéritier was "one of the greatest crooks in the world or a victim of an unprecedented plot to confiscate his business and personal property."

The book, with detailed references to the criminal investigation and internal Aristophil financial matters, made its answer to this question clear: Blame for the collapse of Aristophil lay with corrupt government officials, backstabbing colleagues, and scandal-hungry reporters. The account also faulted unscrupulous liquidators, lawyers, and auctioneers who were quick to capitalize on the catastrophe.

The one person not responsible, claimed the book, was Gérard Lhéritier. According to the work, if the king of manuscripts was guilty of anything, it was trusting too much in those he thought were his friends, in misjudging the clout of his foes. "[His enemies] could never admit that a self-taught former soldier was able to best them," noted the book. "Gérard Lhéritier's big mistake was to underestimate their power." *Affaire Aristophil* concluded with exhaustive lists of Lhéritier's accomplishments: major works acquired by his company, exhibitions he helped mount, books and catalogs he wrote, gifts and donations he bequeathed to various causes.

The book's author was Isabelle Horlans, a longtime French journalist who had written other books on legal scandals. But Lhéritier's critics saw his fingerprints all over the effort in an elaborate attempt to clear his name, just as he had done in the wake of the Monaco stamp affair. The book's preface was written by Didier van Cauwelaert, a novelist and the onetime president of the Institute of Letters and Manuscripts. And it had been sent to Aristophil investors by "The Association of Friends of the Museum of Fine Letters and Manuscripts," or AMBLEM, a newly formed organization whose president, Karine Duchochois, had been the first-ever recipient of Lhéritier's Count of Monte-Cristo Prize, a literary award he gave to authors of books on French miscarriages of justice. Many of the logistics behind AMBLEM were being handled by Footprint Consultants, a Paris communications firm that had long worked with Aristophil and still represented Lhéritier.

Lhéritier didn't deny that he had worked closely with Horlans on the book. He said he'd provided her with access to his business records and court files and that she, in turn, had let him read through drafts of her manuscript. When Lhéritier's criminal defense attorney had expressed concerns about his client working with Horlans, Lhéritier had instructed the journalist not to let his lawyer read an advance copy. A few months after its publication, Lhéritier even indicated that he'd helped pay for the book itself. "There's a contract for the fees, for everything, for the platforms," he said. "If I ask you to write a book, you're going to tell me, 'Okay, sure, but I won't do it for free.' That is completely normal in France." Two days later, after speaking with Horlans, he recanted the statement, claiming it had been a joke.

Whatever Lhéritier's true involvement in *Affaire Aristophil,* he shared its central conceit: He was innocent of all charges and had never done anything wrong. He insisted that he wasn't a criminal mastermind who had singlehandedly pulled off the largest Ponzi scheme in French history.

Lhéritier spoke with a degree of truth. No matter if one believed that he had concocted a massive scam or that he had simply built a groundbreaking company, it was easy to imagine him as some sort of savant, a man of depth and nuance. But in person, he never came across as especially profound. In conversation, he was most comfortable holding forth on his business prowess. He had little to say about the significance of the manuscript collection he'd amassed, or what it said about French society that a onetime insurance salesman from the middle of nowhere had been able to upend the world of Paris's cultured elite. There were no ruminations on the deeper significance of Paris's celebrated rare-book and manuscript trade. For him, it was simply a long-overlooked market waiting to be exploited.

Whatever Lhéritier's true motives, he hadn't been able to pull it off alone. The operation never would have reached the heights it did without help. Well-compensated financial advisers and document experts had been happy to prop up the system with stories of fantastic returns and excessive valuations. Caught up in the excitement, government officials, journalists, and a majority of Paris's book and manuscript market looked the other way. And thousands of investors, seduced by the incredible opportunity, had been willing to sink their savings into the venture without asking hard questions about where their money would be going.

None of this made Lhéritier innocent. Like the Marquis de Sade, the author of his most famous acquisition, he was so focused on his foes, real or imagined, he refused to consider how he had become his own worst enemy. He seemed utterly incapable of acknowledging the role his own ego played in the Aristophil catastrophe, in the upended lives he'd left in his wake—including his own.

TO TAKE HIS mind off his troubles, Lhéritier liked to immerse himself in his adopted home: passing time among the wildlife he kept on his property, going deep-sea fishing on his son's yacht, and surrounding himself with the beauty of the city by the sea that he'd dreamed of since he was a boy. On a warm December afternoon, his diversion of choice was lunch at an open-air restaurant on the roof of one of the sleek hotels that stretched along the city's waterfront. As he washed down beef carpaccio with an expensive bottle of French Syrah, motorcycles raced down the Promenade des Anglais, nine stories below, and beyond that, sailboats glided through the endless blue of the Mediterranean. In the afternoon sunlight, Lhéritier appeared energized, ready to embark on his next venture. He had made a comeback before; he could do so again. "I am working on a new affair," he said with one of his conspiratorial smiles. "Linked to the siege of Paris."

But even his attorney, a hotshot criminal defense lawyer named Francis Triboulet who had defended suspects in headline-grabbing murders, sex-assault scandals, and Nigerian investment scams, was doubtful he would ever completely recover. "He is sixty-eight years old, not far from seventy. This is quite a heavy thing to live with," said Triboulet. "Will he get out of his legal problems? Yes, really there is a possibility. But one thing is for sure: He will never fully come back."

Like everyone else who'd sought or claimed ownership of *120 Days of Sodom,* Lhéritier had found that his prize had left him with nothing but heartbreak and loss. "It is incredible," he said. "I acquire the manuscript, and seven months later, Aristophil collapses." Maybe the scroll really was cursed. "Maybe if I hadn't touched the manuscript," he said, "maybe Aristophil would still be here."

But he said this with a laugh, drinking a post-meal espresso and looking out at the sea. In truth, he had never thought too hard about the implications of Sade's magnum opus, never really pondered the dark corruption it described. He had once tried to read the novel, but he'd been repulsed by its dreadfulness. After a few pages, he had put it down and never picked it up again.

CHAPTER FIFTEEN

The Black Sale

DECEMBER 19, 2017

AS PARISIANS BUNDLED UP AGAINST THE BITTER COLD AND HURRIED about the city for last-minute holiday gifts, *120 Days of Sodom* sat in a large second-floor gallery of the Hôtel Drouot auction house, its first public appearance in three years. Encased in security glass and wound tightly around its dowel, the manuscript lay in the same calfskin container in which Lhéritier had retrieved it from Geneva, the clamshell box yawning open like an oyster revealing its pearl.

Onlookers stooped and pressed their faces close to the glass, eager to catch a glimpse of the legendary object. Thick bands of ink ran along both edges of the scroll, delineating thin margins beyond which the paper had flaked away. In between, the meticulous script flowed unceasingly across the parchment. It was hard to imagine anyone having written something so small and precise, much less someone suffering from bad eyesight and working by candlelight. To complete such an endeavor in thirty-seven days would have required an extreme force of will. It did not appear to be the work of a madman.

All around the dimly lit auction gallery, its walls draped in somber black curtains, visitors and television news crews examined long display cases holding other treasures from Aristophil's collections: A richly illustrated fifteenth-century manuscript, its pages adorned with images of knights in battle. A guestbook French author Antoine de Saint-Exupéry had signed in 1942 with a doodle of his most celebrated creation, the Little Prince, a year before the character first appeared in print. An original manuscript of Honoré de Balzac's 1841 work *Ursule Mirouët,* displaying the fine, sloping script of the novel-ist. In the center of it all rested the diminutive scroll. It stood alone, the star of the show.

The wall directly behind the scroll displayed the logo for Aristophil—but not the regal emblem Lhéritier had designed for his company. Now the insignia featured a single bold "A" enclosed in an elegant border. The logo was about starting anew. It stood for Les Collections Aristophil, an extended series of public auctions an-nounced two months earlier to liquidate Aristophil's 130,000 letters and manuscripts. According to the announcement, the series would involve numerous sales over the next half dozen years. The effort would begin with a blockbuster auction of more than one hundred of the company's most celebrated acquisitions—including *120 Days of Sodom.* Everything—Lhéritier's claims that his empire was built on real value, the ability of his eighteen thousand clients to recoup their investments, the stability of the manuscript market—hinged on whether the auctions were a success. The first test would be the open-ing sale, taking place at Drouot the following day.

The plan had already gone awry. Two days before the auction, the French government had proclaimed that two of the items up for bid deserved to be national treasures: André Breton's Surrealist Manifestos and *120 Days of Sodom.* Everything about the scroll was remarkable, declared France's minister of culture in the official an-nouncement: its extraordinary creation, its journeys across Europe, its influence on twentieth-century French literature, its standing as "the most radical and the most monumental" of all of Sade's works. The same government that had once suppressed all of Sade's output had now concluded that his most obscene creation should be ele-vated to an emblem of French heritage.

The items in question couldn't leave the country and had to be removed from the auction while the state worked with the courts and auction experts to negotiate a fair-market price. The scroll that had been prominently featured in all of the event's promotional materials and press coverage, the manuscript that experts had figured would alone fetch at least a third of the €11 to €16 million the auction was intended to bring in, would not be for sale.

Still, the auctioneers decided to showcase the scroll at the pre-sale exhibition at Drouot, hoping the manuscript would draw attention to the auction the following day. But everyone who peered at the relic knew that as soon as the exhibit ended, the manuscript would be carted off to its vault, locked away for untold years as government officials and auction-house experts haggled over its worth. Just as it was poised to be delivered to a new home, the scroll had once more slipped out of reach.

THE PREVIOUS YEAR, the Commercial Court of Paris had put out a call for an auction company willing to be in charge of liquidating Aristophil's assets in exchange for a 25 percent buyer's premium on all items sold. The undertaking would be daunting: No one in the business had ever before tried to organize, catalog, and sell 130,000 unrelated documents, most of which came saddled with complicated ownership claims. To pull it off, an auction company would have to be wildly ambitious, if not a bit foolhardy.

The job was awarded to the French company Aguttes, the only firm to apply. The operation had been founded in 1974 by Claude Aguttes, a self-taught auctioneer whose demure bearing and attire concealed a history of bold business moves. In 2009, Aguttes and his team had mounted an auction of the contents of the storied Art Deco hotel La Mamounia, in Marrakech, Morocco, after spending six months carefully inventorying armchairs and dressing tables used by the likes of Édith Piaf, Josephine Baker, and Omar Sharif. More recently, his firm jockeyed into the fossil business by auctioning off a thirty-foot dinosaur skeleton at a special sale on the first floor of the Eiffel Tower. Aguttes now helmed the most successful independent auction company in the country, allowing him to purchase a thousand-year-old castle on the side of a dormant French volcano and retrofit it into his country house.

At times, Aguttes's chutzpah landed him in trouble. In 2012, his company had been banned from holding sales for two months after it sold a nineteenth-century Russian painting of questionable authenticity. But many in the art world waved away the matter as an unavoidable slipup of a risk-taker, just the sort of person needed to take on a challenge like Aristophil.

As a first step, Aguttes's firm took possession of Aristophil's letters and manuscripts. The company removed hundreds of boxes of documents from a fine-arts storage facility outside Paris where the authorities were storing them, carefully transported them across the city in a convey of armored trucks, and deposited them in a climate-controlled, fireproof bunker in an undisclosed location kept under permanent armed guard. A dozen workers then began systematically inspecting each document, confirming its identity and authenticity, then entering its details into a tracking system, all under the watchful eye of a court bailiff. The process consumed six months. After that, the team set about restituting letters and manuscripts to investors who had purchased undivided ownership of Aristophil documents under one of the company's pricey "Amadeus" contracts and who now wanted to take possession of their materials.

That still left the vast majority of the collection, the bulk of which were letters and manuscripts whose ownership was split among various investors under Aristophil's "Coraly's" contracts. Since there was no way to physically divide the materials among their owners, the court had given Aguttes the authority to auction all of these assets for the best possible price, then use each item's proceeds to reimburse its co-owners. It didn't matter if some of the investors didn't agree with the plan. With thousands of documents, most split among numerous owners, the court had concluded that it would be impossible to get a unanimous sign-off on any particular approach.

Hôtel Drouot had been the obvious choice for the auctions. Run by a collective of French auction companies, it ranked as one of the oldest and most venerated auction houses in the world. For generations, Drouot thrived as the public clearinghouse of the nation's riches, thanks to a monopoly on French auctions established by royal decree. The house had sold the personal property of the nineteenth-century French king Louis Philippe, pieces of the Eiffel Tower, paintings by Monet and Renoir, and even Napoleon's underpants. For a long while, Drouot had been a hub for postage stamp sales, leading many dealers to open on Rue Drouot near the auction house. That included Roumet, the stamp shop that had inspired Lhéritier's obsession with letters three decades earlier.

Legal reforms had done away with Drouot's sales monopoly in 2000, forcing the house to cede some of its high-end market to Christie's and Sotheby's. The operation lost additional luster in 2010 when it came to light that the "Cols Rouge," the squad of red-collared art porters who had handled Drouot's inventory since the time of Napoleon III, had been pilfering millions of euros' worth of art and jewels. But in terms of sheer variety of items up for sale, Drouot remained unmatched. Every day thousands of visitors to its sixteen auction halls gawked and bid on lots that ranged from Banksy graffiti artwork to one-of-a-kind Astérix drawings. And more than anywhere else, Drouot handled French auctions of books and written materials.

Now Aguttes and Drouot were poised to hold the first Aristophil sale. Every aspect of the event had been designed to draw out the highest prices possible. In the end, nothing else mattered. In the world of letters and manuscripts, expert appraisals went only so far. In this field, where every item was one of a kind and every judgment inherently subjective, to truly determine a collection's worth you had to put it up for sale. Aristophil's sky-high valuations, based on market surveys and the overzealous appraisals of well-compensated associates, had existed in a vacuum. Now, for the first time ever, the value of this empire of letters would be put to the test.

AS THE DATE of the auction had approached, Lhéritier had sat in his villa in Nice and seethed. Since the Aristophil sales had first been announced, he had repeatedly written to the Commercial Court of Paris condemning the plan. Everything about the idea, he'd argued, was a mistake: The choice of Aguttes to run the auctions, since, he claimed, the company had a questionable reputation and little experience in letters and manuscripts. The inclusion of photos, paintings, and antiques in the first sale, since, while they came from Aristophil's assets, they had little to do with the company's speciality. The decision to schedule the event right before Christmas, since it was an inopportune time to hold a major auction, especially one slated to feature letters by Hitler and Mussolini.

Lhéritier predicted that Aristophil's investors would end up paying dearly. "The liquidation of Aristophil is becoming more and more like a self-fulfilling prophecy," he concluded in one letter. The poorly organized sales would be the final nail in the coffin of his once-magnificent empire.

Lhéritier wasn't simply thinking about his former clients. Also at stake was what was left of his reputation. By bungling its liquidation, he believed, Aguttes risked undermining the materials' true significance. These documents, he insisted, were worth the prices he had promised because of a monumental development he had been predicting for years: The age of handwriting had nearly come to an end.

Lhéritier wasn't lying. Over the past few decades, written communication had undergone one of its greatest transformations since ancient Sumerians first began imprinting cuneiform script on clay tablets. The U.S. Common Core State Standards, which detailed what students should be learning throughout the country, now advised instructors to teach handwriting in depth only in kindergarten and first grade, and didn't recommend teaching cursive at all. In the early 2010s, the Pew Research Center found that Americans aged eighteen to twenty-nine sent and received an average of nearly eighty-eight text messages a day; a British survey of two thousand people found that one in three respondents hadn't written anything particularly important by hand in six months. And while every day 215 billion new emails streamed back and forth across the internet, their physical counterparts had nearly become extinct. The U.S. Postal Service had found that the average American household mailed or received just five personal letters a year.

In archives and libraries all over the globe, those charged with maintaining the world's written heritage were grappling with a fundamental shift in the nature of written culture. As important texts evolved from journals and manuscripts to bytes of electronic data, experts had to find a way to value the resulting hard drives, disks, and other "born-digital" materials. They had to figure out how to store and protect these items from "bit rot," the magnetic degradation and natural decomposition that leaves most electronic storage media unusable within a few decades. Now that public figures had moved from writing letters to producing emails, texts, and social media posts, they had to determine how to parse such gargantuan output and uncover important missives. And now that modifying written works involved a few keystrokes rather than penning multiple drafts, many wondered whether the world had lost the ability to track the birth and evolution of literary masterpieces.

Collectors of letters and manuscripts, meanwhile, found themselves staring down a threat to their continued existence. As a rare-book dealer put it in an article for the International League of Antiquarian Booksellers, "We have progressed from a unique handwritten document, which gives us a clear insight into the author's creative process, to a sterile, clean printout that can be produced in potentially limitless numbers and that tells us nothing about the author's creative process. . . . The future of manuscript collecting and literary scholarship is truly in danger."

Lhéritier had always been less interested in what the end of handwriting meant for archivists and collectors than what it meant for his bottom line. Far from a cataclysm, he saw the demise of written documents as a bonanza for those who had taken proper precautions. He was sure that as people realized that future generations wouldn't have access to personal letters from the hand of Barack Obama, songs scribbled out by Lady Gaga, or manuscripts drafted and redrafted by Stephen King, remnants from the days of pens, quills, and pencils would grow as precious as a Stradivarius violin.

"In people's basements in the United States and Europe, people have boxes and boxes of letters," Lhéritier had said a year earlier, sitting at the hotel restaurant overlooking the sea in Nice. "They are completely hidden treasures." Lhéritier had been among the first to realize this fact, and he had prepared by amassing as many handwritten treasures as possible. If the people behind the new Aristophil auctions had understood what his collections truly signified, if they had been a little more savvy with how they planned the sales, Lhéritier was convinced that all those who had believed in him would be amply rewarded. Instead, he predicted, the auctions would turn out to be a fiasco.

"L'ADJUGÉ!"

Claude Aguttes's authoritative voice rang through the auction hall, announcing with a knock of his wooden gavel that the first lot up from the Aristophil collection had been sold. Video screens positioned around the room displayed the item—a painting of the Madonna and Child attributed to the Renaissance painter Giovanni Pietro Rizzoli—and the winning bid: €30,000, followed by its equivalents in dollars, pounds, yuan, and other currencies. A respectable figure, at the high end of its pre-sale estimate, but far from spectacular.

As onlookers crammed into the room and spilled into the hallway, news cameras zoomed in on Aguttes, resembling a stern professor as he leaned over the podium at the front of the room. In the audience sat Jérôme Dupuis, reporter's notebook in hand. Nearby sat an attorney for one of the largest consumer associations formed by Aristophil investors, there to track the differences between the auction's going rates and the values promised by Lhéritier. In the crowd at the back stood Hugues de Sade, Thibault's extravagant brother, drawn to the event by the news that his ancestor's manuscript had nearly been auctioned off. All around them sat bidders—mostly older men—whispering, mouths covered, into their cellphones, gesturing subtly when the price was right.

The second lot came up for bid: a sixteenth-century sketch of clasping lovers by Italian artist Girolamo Francesco Maria Mazzola. Pointing back and forth across the room, Aguttes took up bids with rapid motions drawn from years of practice, then gaveled the final price. "Seventy-five thousand euros," he announced, a relative steal at €5,000 less than the low estimate for the work. A porter handed an orange claim ticket to the winning bidder, sitting near the front: Jean-Claude Vrain, conspicuous as ever in his wide-brimmed hat.

The auction continued, but with increasing lethargy. For long stretches the room remained sedate, with hardly any of the spectacu-

lar bids or lively tête-à-têtes that usually triggered gasps of excitement or restrained rounds of applause at sales such as this. A
handwritten music score by Richard Wagner sold for below estimate,
as did a series of correspondences between the French poet Paul
Valéry and his daughter. Many items didn't sell at all: a first edition of
Marcel Proust's *Les Plaisirs et les Jours,* a lock of Napoleon's hair. Little
by little the crowd began to thin. The auction organizers had included the *Titanic* survivor's manuscript that Aristophil had sold to
its investors for €1.1 million to attract attention from U.S. collectors.
But when the work came up for bid, the bank of telephones off to
the side remained silent, with no offers coming in from across the
Atlantic. Aguttes moved on to the next sale.

Many of the biggest lots went to Vrain: A one-of-a-kind text by
Alexandre Dumas for €82,000. An original Balzac manuscript for
€1.17 million. But even Vrain, perhaps chastened by his own involvement in the scandal that had led to the sale, appeared unusually demure. For most of the auction, the book dealer remained in his seat,
avoiding the sort of ostentatious displays that so incensed his rival
Castaing.

During the bidding for a letter by Horatio Nelson, a man stood up
and interrupted the sale. "I am a former investor of Aristophil," he
told the crowd. "For anyone else like me who doesn't know what is
happening, let's meet in the hall." As stern-faced security guards
wearing translucent earpieces tried to defuse the commotion, camera
crews and reporters swarmed the small crowd of Aristophil investors
who gathered outside. "It is absolutely unprofessional," declared one
of the men in the crowd. "Some of us weren't even notified of the
sale."

"I am scared, I can't do anything," complained another investor,
gesturing into the auction hall, where the sale had resumed. "These
people can do whatever they want with our property."

The auction concluded with an aura of quiet disappointment.
Nearly a third of the items up for bid had gone unsold. Many that did
sell didn't reach the low end of the pre-sale values experts had assigned to them. In total, the sale brought in just under €3 million, a
far cry from the €11 million to €16 million experts had predicted be-

fore the top two lots had been declared national treasures. Most wor-
ryingly, none of the materials, no matter the price they fetched, came
close to reaching the prices Aristophil's clients had paid for them. As
the headline to Dupuis's article on the sale would declare the following day, "The market tells the cruel truth about the Aristophil scandal."

As auction-goers trickled out of Drouot, several longtime Parisian
book and art dealers gathered downstairs at L'Adjugé!, the auction
house's bistro, to ponder what had transpired. Usually when Drouot
auctioned off a major collection, the sales felt like a celebration, a
memorial to the efforts put into its creation. But this event was different. "The atmosphere was like a funeral," said Serge Plantureux, a
specialist in photographic prints who had attended the sale garbed in
bright red suspenders. He took a sip of his espresso, then summed up
the afternoon with a somber shake of his head: "It was a black sale."

CASTAING DID NOT attend the first Aristophil auction. The manuscript
dealer preferred the genteel approach of one-on-one sales, and he
refused to take advantage of the collapse of Lhéritier's empire of letters. He ignored the whispers that it was easy for him to take a moral
stand when he'd been born into privilege. Call it principle or snob-
bery, he still insisted on having nothing to do with Aristophil.

The Aristophil sales continued in the following months. A sequence of seven auctions at Drouot in June 2018 yielded more promising results, generating €17.6 million. The strong sales persisted a
few months later when a five-auction run totaled €8.8 million. Then,
in 2019, fourteen sales throughout the year brought in €18 million
more. The narrative around Aristophil began to shift from lingering
scandal to auction-hall triumphs. Treasures like a Frida Kahlo letter
signed with red-lipstick kisses and World War II missives penned by
Joseph Stalin lured tens of thousands of visitors to Drouot and drew
coverage from the likes of BBC News and *The New York Times*. Disappointing results, like an original partial draft of Mozart's *The Marriage
of Figaro* failing to find a buyer, were overshadowed by achievements
like the Einstein manuscript that had launched Aristophil's innova-

tive investment program selling for €11.6 million, roughly four times the pre-auction estimate.

Works that had been locked away in Aguttes's top secret vault were now flowing to institutions all over the world. France's national library obtained an original manuscript of Gustave Flaubert's and dozens of other materials, while the Van Gogh Museum in Amsterdam snatched up an important letter by its namesake. In November 2019, the Brontë Parsonage Museum succeeded in acquiring the miniature Charlotte Brontë manuscript it had lost to Aristophil in a previous bidding war, using €780,000 it had collected with fundraising help from Judi Dench, president of the Brontë Society.

Still, insiders like Castaing knew the truth: Those with the most at stake in the auctions were losing enormous sums of money. The miniature manuscript sold to the Brontë Parsonage Museum for roughly half the amount Aristophil's clients had invested in it years earlier. The Einstein manuscript's €11.6 million haul was still less than the €12 million investors had paid for it nearly two decades earlier. And the vast majority of lots produced far poorer returns. After three years of auctions, the average going rate for Aristophil documents hovered between 10 and 15 percent of what Aristophil's clients had paid for them. This meant, on average, that investors were losing nearly 90 percent of their investments. Despite their complaints, there was nothing investors could do to stop the process. The Commercial Court of Paris had made its decision: This was how the materials would be dispersed.

In March 2019, Dupuis dropped a bombshell in *L'Express:* Some investors were going to lose their assets without any reimbursement at all. The French government was preparing to seize hundreds of Aristophil documents without compensation, including King Louis XVI's farewell letter to his subjects and the Charles de Gaulle missives over which Lhéritier had clashed with the Ministry of Culture. According to French law, the texts belonged to the state—not those who'd bought them from Aristophil.

Castaing followed the developments with frustration. He watched as Vrain continued to spend liberally at the sales, at times buying back materials at a fraction of the price for which he had first sold them to

Aristophil. He noticed that for one of its document specialists, Aguttes turned to prominent manuscript expert Thierry Bodin, who had reportedly made millions selling documents to Aristophil and had criticized Castaing for speaking out about the company. The current situation was like a cruel twist in one of the detective novels Castaing had written: People like Vrain and Bodin profited from Aristophil's rise and disparaged Castaing for sounding the alarm. Now they were the ones benefiting from its collapse.

Like everyone in his field, Castaing was concerned about the decline of handwritten documents, anxious about what the change would mean for his profession and the future of written heritage. But he scoffed at Lhéritier's assertions that the digitization of the written word would turn existing letters and manuscripts into ultra-valuable relics. He saw that as simply one more false promise in Lhéritier's empire of lies.

As president of the private organization Compagnie Nationale des Experts, Castaing had petitioned the authorities to take their time with the Aristophil auctions, to spread them out over twenty or thirty years. No one had listened. Now signs were emerging that the letter and manuscript market was suffering from oversupply. When a series of Marcel Proust letters put up for sale at Christie's Paris failed to find a buyer, some blamed the Aristophil sales for flooding the market. When an auction of Sade materials, including the marquis's favorite writing chair, resulted in disappointing sales, the event's organizers—the three Sade brothers—attributed the lack of interest to Aristophil-related upheaval. And so far, only a few thousand items from the Aristophil collection had been put up for sale. That still left more than one hundred thousand letters and manuscripts, of ever-diminishing value.

The book and manuscript shops of central Paris had long operated on deals sealed with a handshake, on mutual love of the written word. Now that world simmered with suspicions and discontent. "Aristophil has left a stain on the world of autographs," said Castaing, sitting in his shop on Rue Jacob on a tranquil summer morning in 2019. In the quiet of his manuscript gallery, surrounded by vestiges of his grandmother's designs and remnants of one of the first manuscript shops on the planet, he seemed to exist in a domain out of time. Every day, in fact, he walked in the very footsteps of the Marquis de Sade. A few doors down stood the building where Sade, lured to Paris by news of his dying mother, had once been arrested by Inspector Marais.

But Castaing knew that letters and manuscripts didn't exist in a vacuum. He knew that these artifacts' owners had power over their fate—adding to their legacy, shaping how the world came to see them, using them to shed light on the human condition. But he also knew that people could end up being defined by these treasures—forever associated with the texts they sought and possessed, for good or for ill. Literary relics, he understood, could be escapes, or they could be prisons. The riches of Aristophil had ensnared them all—and he believed no one would escape anytime soon. "This affair will last for years and years," he said. "I am not going to live to see the end of it."

Entombed

THE ANNOUNCEMENT ARRIVED WITH LITTLE FANFARE: THREE AND A half years after declaring that *120 Days of Sodom* deserved to be a national treasure and a few days shy of the 232nd Bastille Day, the French government announced that it had acquired the scroll.

The €4.55 million the state used to buy the manuscript from the 420 Aristophil investors who had purchased joint-ownership shares of it came from a single donor: Emmanuel Boussard, a wealthy French investment banker. For Boussard, who had worked on Wall Street before launching a multibillion-euro French hedge fund, the donation, which came with considerable tax benefits, was an example of American-style philanthropy—pragmatic, professional, dispassionate. While Boussard had grown up in central Paris surrounded by its famous booksellers and had amassed a formidable book collection, he wasn't particularly intrigued by Sade or his work. He was far more interested, in fact, in the scroll's most famous recent owner, Lhéritier, and for years he had warned associates and regulators that Aristophil would turn out to be a scam. But when he heard from a philanthropist colleague that state officials were concerned that they wouldn't find enough private donations to acquire the controversial scroll, the investment banker offered up the full amount. He would have preferred to finance the purchase of the other Aristophil documents the government had declared to be national treasures, André Breton's Surrealist Manifestos—but those acquisitions had been bankrolled by a handful of other wealthy donors, including Carlo Perrone, the grandson of the Red Vicomtesse.

The €4.55 million sum was several million less than Lhéritier had spent to retrieve *120 Days of Sodom* from Switzerland, and less than half of the total amount Sylvie Le Gall and other Aristophil investors had spent to purchase shares of it. If the ministry had accepted Lhéritier's 2014 offer to donate *120 Days of Sodom* after five years in exchange for tax incentives, the scroll would likely have already been placed in the state's possession, for no additional expense. Lhéritier, still awaiting a trial that may or may not ever come, saw treachery in the government's actions. "It is a pure scam by the French state," he declared in an email from his villa in Nice.

The state's acquisition of the scroll went largely unnoticed, since France and the rest of the world were at the time occupied by the global COVID-19 pandemic. For much of the previous year, the Eiffel Tower had been closed to visitors, the Louvre had been empty, and nearly all of the *bouquinistes* that lined the Seine had been shuttered. In the Saint-Germain-des-Prés and Odéon neighborhoods in the heart of the city, most of the book and manuscript dealers had closed their doors, and many feared that a good number would never reopen, a major blow to a market that had already been shrinking. In the previous two decades, more than 40 percent of the bookshops in the area had closed, due to gentrification and the rise of online shopping.

The scroll was consigned to the national library's Arsenal building on the Right Bank, locked away amid thousands of other documents related to the French Revolution. The manuscript's new home was especially appropriate: Boussard's grandfather had worked as chief curator of the Arsenal Library, and his father had spent his childhood exploring its collections.

The manuscript of *120 Days of Sodom* had been written in one of history's most formidable prisons and had witnessed the first salvos of the French Revolution. It had moved through clandestine circles of eighteenth-century erotica collectors and had nearly become property of the British Empire. It had helped inspire a sexual revolution and barely escaped the fires of the Holocaust. It had produced one of the twentieth century's most notorious works of art, triggered riots, and turned a pillar of French society into a revolutionary.

It had been stolen, been smuggled across Europe, and fallen into the possession of one of the richest people on the planet. And it had become the centerpiece of an endeavor that aimed to transform global ownership of the written word, but instead left the world's greatest book and manuscript market in shambles. Now the scroll's journey had come to an end in a state library facility—less than a thousand yards from where it had been written, at the onetime site of the Bastille.

It would be easy to envision the manuscript's arrival in its final resting place resembling the end of the film *Indiana Jones and the Raiders of the Lost Ark:* the central treasure entombed in an anonymous storage vault, destined to be forgotten. But in reality, the vast majority of historic materials in archives and research libraries are readily accessible to the public. Items that are too fragile or valuable for such exposure are often digitally scanned and made available electronically, part of the mass digitization of written works that has made access to historic documents far more widespread than ever before. Texts, both typed and handwritten, are being uploaded to the internet by the millions. Many of the central documents that tell the story of *120 Days of Sodom*—the prison-cell letters of the Marquis de Sade, the bibliographic writings of Henry Spencer Ashbee, the quasi-scientific dispatches of Iwan Bloch, the newspaper accounts of Marie-Laure de Noailles's final revolutionary stand, the court records of the international battle over the scroll, the news reports and blog posts detailing the rise and fall of Aristophil—are accessible from anywhere in the world, and in many cases can be instantaneously translated into nearly any language.

As communication has become digitized, thanks to the Internet and e-readers, news reports have heralded "the end of books" and the arrival of "the post-text future." But doomsayers have been predicting the death of writing for centuries, and they have always been wrong. When Gutenberg invented the printing press, scholars proclaimed, "Printed books will never be the equivalent of handwritten codices, especially since printed books are often deficient in spelling and appearance." In the nineteenth century, a French poet asserted, "The newspaper is killing the book," and others bemoaned the rise of "mechanical writing" ushered in by the typewriter. In 1913, Thomas Edison announced that with the advent of motion pictures, "Books . . . will soon be obsolete in the public schools." Instead, writing has become ever more versatile, and access to the results ever more ubiquitous. In the twenty-first century, courtesy of social media, internet slang, hyperlinks, novel punctuations, emojis, GIFs, and memes, communication is more collaborative and dynamic than at any other point in history.

Now that France has obtained *120 Days of Sodom,* it will belong to no one—and to everyone. Likely no one ever again will be able to suppress it, hoard it, exploit it, or smuggle it away. Instead, people everywhere will likely be able to go online and access high-resolution images of every inch of the scroll. They will be able to read for themselves the diabolical script that for centuries has inflamed passions, triggered upheaval, and inspired insurrections large and small. They will be able to scrutinize the impossibly tiny, perfectly crafted pen strokes produced in a prison cell by someone who may or may not have been a lunatic. For the first time in its existence, the manuscript will finally be free—and its curse can carry on.

ACKNOWLEDGMENTS

AS WITH THE LONG HISTORY OF *120 DAYS OF SODOM*, A GREAT MANY people had a hand in the journey of this book. The first people who deserve credit are Grace Hood and Vince Darcangelo, who in 2015 told me an incredible story: They had recently tried to visit a Paris museum to view a notorious manuscript written by the Marquis de Sade, only to be stopped at the door by police officers clearing out the facility and speaking of a man who had become known as the Bernie Madoff of France. When I expressed interest in the matter, the two had the grace and generosity to let me run with it.

A great many people lent a hand in the subsequent research and writing of this book. They include Jean-Christophe Abramovici, Sascha Alper, Naomi Baron, Barbara Basbanes, Nicholas Basbanes, Dan Baum, John Baxter, Robert Beachy, Terry Belanger, Kate Bredeson, Libby Burton, Ash Carter, Frédéric Castaing, Robert Darnton, Ron Doyle, Andrea Dupree, Jacques Duprilot, Jérôme Dupuis, Abigail Edge, Stephen Enniss, Rachel Foss, Rick Gekoski, Jean-Paul Goujon, Erwin J. Haeberle, Neil Hannum, Michael Henry, Jean-Pascal Hesse, Glenn Horowitz, Meghan Houser, Benoit Huet, Philippe Julien, Patrick J. Kearney, Ben Kinmont, Matthew Kirschenbaum, Anne Lamort, Ralph Leck, Thomas Ledoux, David Lowenherz, Jeff Martin, Peter McGraw, Will McMorran, Charles Méla, Caron Mineo, Leslie Morris, Bradford Mudge, Naomi Nelson, Serge Nordmann, David Patterson, Maximillian Potter, Nicole Prause, Leah Price, Bruno Racine, Ken Rendell, Marc-André Renold, Julian Rubinstein, David Sirota, Nicole Sullivan, Anne Trubek, Hélion de

Villeneuve Esclapon, John von Sothen, Francis Wahlgren, and Larry Weissman. There are surely many others.

Special thanks go to the first book people in my life: Barbara, Jim, and Kelly Warner, who instilled in me a love of words and supported me when I decided to turn that passion into a career. And this book would not have been possible without the assistance of Cole Stangler, who started out as a translator extraordinaire and ended up a good friend.

But most of all, thank you to my family: Emily, Gabriel, Charlotte, and our dog, Lafayette. You sustained me through years of effort, you cheered me on during moments of struggle and uncertainty, you gave me the gift of space and patience. I am so grateful to have you.

NOTES

Unless otherwise indicated, all translations are the author's.

EPIGRAPH

vii **"In the end"**: Maurice Lever, *"Je Jure au Marquis de Sade, Mon Amant, de Nêtre Jamais Qu'à Lui . . ."* (Paris: Librairie Arthème Fayard, 2005), 120.

vii **"Friend Reader"**: Alfred Bonnardot, *The Mirror of the Parisian Bibliophile: A Satirical Tale*, trans. Theodore Wesley Koch (Chicago: Lakeside, 1931), 1.

PROLOGUE: The Prisoner in the Tower

3 **"The extensive wars"**: Donatien Alphonse François de Sade, *120 Days of Sodom*, trans. Will McMorran and Thomas Wynn (London: Penguin Classics, 2016), 3.

3 **The man's fine-tipped quill**: Iwan Bloch, *Neue Forschungen über den Marquis de Sade und Seine Zeit: Mit Besonderer Berücksichtigung der Sexualphilosophie de Sade's auf Grund des Neuentdeckten Original-Manuskriptes Seines Hauptwerkes "Die 120 Tage von Sodom"* (Berlin: Max Harrwitz, 1904), 389–91.

3 **As he wrote**: Simon Nicolas Henri Linguet, *Memoirs of the Bastille*, vol. 2 (Edinburgh: privately printed, 1885), 33.

3 **In the cold evening**: Francine du Plessix Gray, *At Home with the Marquis de Sade* (New York: Penguin Books, 1999), 263.

4 **Expensive bottles**: Donatien Alphonse François de Sade, *Letters from Prison*, trans. Richard Seaver (New York: Arcade, 1999), 346–47.

4 **And a prized collection**: Gray, *At Home*, 238.

4 **Inactivity and a penchant for delicacies**: Maurice Lever, *Sade: A Biography* (New York: Farrar, Straus and Giroux, 1993), 310–11, 208; Gray, *At Home*, 283.

4 **He was plagued:** Neil Schaeffer, *The Marquis de Sade: A Life* (New York: Alfred A. Knopf, 1999), 312.

5 **With his eyesight nearly ruined:** Lever, *Sade,* 312–13.

5 **In his mounting delusion:** Sade, *Letters from Prison,* 166; Lever, *Sade,* 326; Sade, *Letters from Prison,* 148.

5 **At other times, he concluded:** Lever, *Sade,* 321.

5 **"It is impossible":** Sade, *Letters from Prison,* 359–60.

5 **He composed endless letters:** Gray, *At Home,* 11, 412–13.

5 **Experts would come to call:** Schaeffer, *The Marquis de Sade,* 336; Jean Paulhan, *Le Marquis de Sade et Sa Complice* (Brussels: Éditions Complexe, 1987), 28.

5 **As the duke:** Sade, *120 Days of Sodom,* 56.

6 **In 1957, the French philosopher:** Georges Bataille, *Literature and Evil* (London: Marion Boyars, 1985), 121.

6 **The Sade publisher Jean-Jacques Pauvert:** Jean-Jacques Pauvert, *Sade's Publisher: A Memoir* (New York: Paris Writers Press, 2016), 145.

6 **Austryn Wainhouse:** Loren Glass, *Rebel Publisher: Grove Press and the Revolution of the Word* (New York: Seven Stories, 2018), 136–37.

6 **In the 1980s:** Annie Le Brun, *Sade: A Sudden Abyss* (San Francisco: City Lights Books, 1990), 12.

6 **And most recently:** Will McMorran, "Translating Violence," *The Bad Books Blog,* September 26, 2016, www.thebadbooksblog.com/2016/09/26 /translating-violence/ (accessed October 21, 2020).

6 **McMorran would come away:** Will McMorran, interview with the author, September 24, 2020.

7 **Sade worked on the text:** Bloch, *Neue Forschungen über den Marquis de Sade und Seine Zeit,* 383.

7 **Finally, in 2014:** "L'Épilogue Français des 'Cent Vingt Journées de Sodome,' " *Le Point,* April 3, 2014, www.lepoint.fr/livres/l-epilogue-francais -des-cent-vingt-journees-de-sodome-03-04-2014-1808871_37.php (accessed December 16, 2019).

7 **The price made it:** John J. Goldman, "Gutenberg Bible Is Sold for Record $4.9 Million," *Los Angeles Times,* October 23, 1987, www.latimes.com /archives/la-xpm-1987-10-23-mn-10733-story.html (accessed March 5, 2020); "Sale 6012: Wentworth: Lot 2: Chaucer, Geoffrey (c. 1345–1400). The Canterbury Tales," Christie's, www.christies.com/lotfinder/lot/chaucer -geoffrey-the-canterbury-tales-wes-998506-details.aspx (accessed March 5, 2020); "Sale 9878: The Library of Abel E. Berland: Lot 100: Shakespeare, William (1564–1616). Comedies, Histories, & Tragedies," Christie's, www .christies.com/lotfinder/lot/shakespeare-william-comedies-histories-tra -3098350-details.aspx (accessed March 5, 2020).

7 **The scroll settled into:** John Lichfield, "Marquis de Sade: Rebel, Pervert,

Rapist . . . Hero?," *Independent,* November 14, 2014, www.independent.co
.uk/news/world/europe/marquis-de-sade-rebel-pervert-rapist-hero-9862270
.html (accessed January 30, 2021).

8 **Some would conclude:** Pascal Fulacher, interview with the author, April 14,
2019; Jean-Pierre Guéno, interview with the author, May 29, 2019.

8 **When Sade began:** Sade, *120 Days of Sodom,* 59.

CHAPTER ONE: Relic of Freedom

9 **The summer sky:** David M. Ludlum, "Bad Weather and the Bastille,"
Weatherwise 43, no. 3 (June 1989): 141.

9 **Beyond the walls:** David Garrioch, *The Making of Revolutionary Paris*
(Berkeley: University of California Press, 2002), 1, 18–20, 48.

10 **As the drought-ravaged fields:** Peter McPhee, *Liberty or Death: The French
Revolution* (New Haven, Conn.: Yale University Press, 2016), 7.

10 **The final provocation:** McPhee, *Liberty or Death,* 70–71.

10 **With rumors spreading:** Christopher Hibbert, *The Days of the French Revolution* (New York: Harper Perennial, 1980), 69–70.

11 **This was where numerous state convicts:** Hans-Jürgen Lüsebrink and
Rolf Reichardt, *The Bastille: A History of a Symbol of Despotism and Freedom,*
trans. Norbert Schürer (Durham, N.C.: Duke University Press, 1997), 15.

11 **Tales of prisoners:** Lüsebrink and Reichardt, *The Bastille,* 11–18.

11 **So early that afternoon:** Lüsebrink and Reichardt, *The Bastille,* 42–43.

11 **In the Bastille:** Hibbert, *The Days of the French Revolution,* 72.

11 **As the morning rain let up:** Hibbert, *The Days of the French Revolution,*
70–80; Georges Pernoud and Sabine Flaissier, *The French Revolution* (New
York: G. P. Putnam's Sons, 1960), 40–41.

12 **The revolutionaries refused:** Pernoud and Flaissier, *The French Revolution,*
41–42.

13 **Later that night at Versailles:** Simon Schama, *Citizens: A Chronicle of the
French Revolution* (New York: Vintage Books, 1989), 420.

13 **Back at the prison:** Hibbert, *The Days of the French Revolution,* 72.

13 **It had escaped notice:** Michel Delon, *La 121ème Journée: L'Incroyable Histoire
du Manuscrit de Sade* (Paris: Albin Michel, 2020), 75.

14 **Instead, the manuscript came into:** Jacques Duprilot and Jean Paul Goujon, "Le Rouleau de la Mer Morte, *120 Journées de Sodome,* de 1789 à l'Aube
du XXIe Siècle," *Histoires Littéraires* 18, no. 70 (2017), 37.

14 **Perhaps he was one:** Schama, *Citizens,* 409–3, 416–18.

15 **Arnoux hailed from:** Monique Cubells, "Les Mouvements Populaires du
Printemps 1789 en Provence," *Provence Historique* 36, no. 145 (1986), 309–23.

15 **He wasn't among the 954 citizens:** "Tableau des Vainqueurs de la Bastille,
par Ordre Alphabétique, Noms, Surnoms, Qualités & Professions: Publiée

pour la Première Fois d'Après le Manuscrit Authentique, Conservé au Musée des Archives Nationales," *Journal Officiel de la Bastille,* supp. (Paris: 1889).

15 **His name would never appear:** "Archives Nationales," www.archives -nationales.culture.gouv.fr/en/web/guest (accessed November 12, 2020); Jean-Paul Goujon, "Une dernière question," email, October 23, 2020.

15 **There, in the neighboring town:** Duprilot and Goujon, "Le Rouleau de la Mer Morte," 26, 34.

16 **As the years stretched into decades:** Jonathan Fenby, *France: A Modern History from the Revolution to the War on Terror* (New York: St. Martin's, 2015), 124.

16 **The scroll traveled east:** Duprilot and Goujon, "Le Rouleau de la Mer Morte," 34; Romée de Villeneuve-Trans-Flayosc, *Notice sur les Villeneuve Arcs, Trans, Flayosc, Suivie d'un Appendice Où Se Trouvent Relatés les Titres Ayant Existé ou Existant Encore dans la Maison de Villeneuve en Provence* (Lyon: Société Anonyme de l'Imprimerie A. Rey, 1926), 88.

16 **Thus *120 Days of Sodom* might have remained:** L. Romée de Villeneuve Esclapon, *Histoire de la Maison de Villeneuve en Provence: Généalogie et Preuves des Nouvelles Générations de 1850 à Nos Jours* (Fontenay-le-Comte, France: Imprimerie Loriou, 1989), 31, 251

16 **The lineage was related through marriage:** Guillaume Barles, "Le Dernier Seigneur de Trans: Louis Henri de Villeneuve, 1739–1794," *Bulletin de la Société d'Études Scientifiques et Archéologiques Draguignan et du Var* 25 (1980), 14.

16 **From a young age, Hélion harbored:** Villeneuve Esclapon, *Histoire de la Maison de Villeneuve,* 251.

17 **Leather bindings of calf- and goatskin:** John Carter, *ABC for Book Collectors* (New Castle, Del.: Oak Knoll, 1995).

17 **For most collectors:** John Baxter, interview with the author, April 14, 2019.

18 **The number of bookshops:** Willa Z. Silverman, *The New Bibliopolis: French Book Collectors and the Culture of Print, 1880–1914* (Toronto, Ont.: University of Toronto Press, 2008), 5, 64, 79–80.

18 **At the time, as thousands:** Gershon Legman, *The Horn Book* (New Hyde Park, N.Y.: University Books, 1964), 61–62.

18 **Publishers furtively churned out:** Marie-Françoise Quignard and Raymond-Josué Seckel, *L'Enfer de la Bibliothèque: Eros au Secret* (Paris: Bibliothèque Nationale de France, 2019), 194–219.

18 **They reissued classic works:** Legman, *The Horn Book,* 82, 91, 102.

18 **While some collectors relegated:** Silverman, *The New Bibliopolis,* 178.

18 **When French authorities attempted:** Patrick J. Kearney, *A Catalogue of the Publications of Jules Gay, Jean-Jules Gay and Gay et Doucé,* rev. ed. (Santa Rosa, Calif.: Scissors & Paste Bibliographies, 2019), 5–6.

19 **As one observer noted:** Gray, *At Home,* 414.

19 **Some claimed Sade's notorious novel:** Laurence L. Bongie, *Sade: A Biographical Essay* (Chicago: University of Chicago Press, 1998), 282.

19 **One critic went further:** Sade, *120 Days of Sodom,* xxii.

19 **A young Gustave Flaubert:** Gray, *At Home,* 414.

19 **Villeneuve-Trans likewise became enamored:** Frederick Hankey, Jacques Duprilot, and Jean-Paul Goujon, *Ce N'Est Pas Mon Genre de Livres Lestes . . . : Lettres Inédites à Richard Monckton Milnes, Lord Houghton (1857–1865)* (n.p.: Miss Jenkins, 2012), 78.

19 **He financially supported:** Jacques Duprilot, *Gay et Doucé: Éditeurs sous le Manteau, 1877–1882* (Paris: Éditions Astarté, 1998), 49.

19 **And employing the services:** Duprilot and Goujon, "Le Rouleau de la Mer Morte," 40.

19 **At the death of his father:** Villeneuve-Trans-Flayosc, *Notice sur les Villeneuve Arcs, Trans, Flayosc,* 90.

20 **He offered the manuscript:** Duprilot and Goujon, "Le Rouleau de la Mer Morte," 30.

20 **Unlike their more freewheeling:** Ronald Pearsall, *The Worm in the Bud: The World of Victorian Sexuality* (Toronto, Ont.: Macmillan, 1969), xi, endpapers, 371–72.

20 **In the middle of it all:** William Roberts, *A Portrait of Holywell Street and Its Environs* (Santa Rosa, Calif.: Scissors & Paste Bibliographics, 2019), 3.

21 **Their first choice was the individual:** Patrick J. Kearney, *Frederick Hankey (1821–1882): A Biographical Sketch* (Santa Rosa, Calif.: Scissors & Paste Bibliographies, 2019), 2, 6.

21 **He cultivated a small but select:** Edmond de Goncourt and Jules de Goncourt, *Journal des Goncourt: Mémoires de la Vie Littéraire,* vol. 2, *1862–1865* (Paris: G. Charpentier, 1888), 134–35.

21 **Knowing his reputation:** Duprilot and Goujon, "Le Rouleau de la Mer Morte," 30; Robert Allen, "Prices and Wages in Paris, 1400–1914," Nuffield College at the University of Oxford, www.nuff.ox.ac.uk/users/Allen/studer/paris.xls (accessed December 5, 2020).

22 **After examining the manuscript:** Duprilot and Goujon, "Le Rouleau de la Mer Morte," 30.

22 **He often seemed more concerned:** Kearney, *Frederick Hankey,* 9.

22 **Around that time, he sold:** Kearney, *Frederick Hankey,* 14–15.

22 **He turned to another English bibliophile:** Ian Gibson, *The Erotomaniac: The Secret Life of Henry Spencer Ashbee* (Cambridge, Mass.: Da Capo, 2001), 22–23.

23 **Aware of his interests:** Hankey, Duprilot, and Goujon, *Ce N'Est Pas Mon Genre de Livres Lestes,* 76–77.

23 **The effort demanded daunting:** Steven Marcus, *The Other Victorians: A Study of Sexuality and Pornography in Mid-Nineteenth-Century England* (New Brunswick, N.J.: Transaction, 2009), 72.

23 **In 1877, he privately published:** Gibson, *The Erotomaniac*, 26, 39.

24 **"My object":** Pisanus Fraxi, *Index Librorum Prohibitorum: Being Notes Bio- Biblio- Icono-graphical and Critical, on Curious and Uncommon Books* (London: privately printed, 1877), li.

24 **While he hadn't viewed:** Fraxi, *Index Librorum Prohibitorum*, 422–24.

24 **Ashbee insisted:** Fraxi, *Index Librorum Prohibitorum*, lxx.

24 **Yet Ashbee again declined:** Hankey, Duprilot, and Goujon, *Ce N'Est Pas Mon Genre de Livres Lestes*, 77.

24 **In the late 1880s:** Gibson, *The Erotomaniac*, 166, 194–229.

25 **In 1891, Ashbee's wife:** Gibson, *The Erotomaniac*, 128.

25 **He died in 1900:** Gibson, *The Erotomaniac*, 153; Legman, *The Horn Book*, 115.

25 **When Villeneuve-Trans passed away:** Villeneuve Esclapon, *Histoire de la Maison de Villeneuve en Provence*, 250.

CHAPTER TWO: *Par Ballon Monté*

26 **This particular letter stood out:** Gérard Lhéritier, *Intime Corruption: L'Affaire des Timbres Rares de Monaco* (Paris: L'Archipel, 2006), 31–33.

27 **Lhéritier had been born:** Lhéritier, *Intime Corruption*, 23–24.

27 **Among his few escapes:** Lhéritier, *Intime Corruption*, 26–27.

28 **Eager to prove himself:** Lhéritier, *Intime Corruption*, 28–31; Gérard Lhéritier, interview with the author, July 18, 2019.

29 **In September 1870:** Richard Holmes, *Falling Upwards: How We Took to the Air* (New York: Pantheon, 2013), 251–52.

29 **As refugees from the countryside:** Holmes, *Falling Upwards*, 256–57.

30 **That is, until Félix Nadar:** Holmes, *Falling Upwards*, 262.

30 **With the regional railways:** Holmes, *Falling Upwards*, 279; John Fisher, *Airlift 1870: The Balloons and Pigeons in the Siege of Paris* (London: Max Parrish, 1965), 39, 268, 280.

30 **Soon carrier pigeons:** Gérard Lhéritier, *Collection 1870: Ballons Montés, Boules de Moulins* (Paris: Éditions Aristophil, 2000), 361–65.

31 **In early 1871:** Holmes, *Falling Upwards*, 291–93.

31 **He authored four reference books:** Lhéritier, *Collection 1870*, 44.

31 **And in 1995:** Lhéritier, *Intime Corruption*, 137–38.

32 **Ancient Sumerians:** Joseph E. Fields, "The History of Autograph Collecting," in *Autographs and Manuscripts: A Collector's Manual*, ed. Edmund Berkeley, Jr. (New York: Charles Scribner's Sons, 1978), 40–41; Christine Nelson, *The Magic of Handwriting: The Pedro Corrêa do Lago Collection* (Cologne, Germany: Taschen, 2018), 18.

32 **In ancient Rome:** Mary A. Benjamin, *Autographs: A Key to Collecting* (New York: Dover, 1986), 7.

32 **The Great Library of Alexandria:** Fields, "The History of Autograph Collecting," 42.

32 **Similarly, along with founding Baghdad:** Nicholas A. Basbanes, *On Paper: The Everything of Its Two-Thousand-Year History* (New York: Alfred A. Knopf, 2013), 49.

32 **After the fall:** Nicholas A. Basbanes, *A Gentle Madness: Bibliophiles, Bibliomanes, and the Eternal Passion for Books* (New York: Henry Holt, 1995), 72.

33 **By the sixteenth century:** Benjamin, *Autographs: A Key to Collecting,* 9.

33 **In nineteenth-century Europe:** Gates P. Thruston, *Autograph Collections and Historic Manuscripts* (Sewanee, Tenn.: University Press, 1902), 16; A. N. L. Munby, *The Cult of the Autograph Letter in England* (London: Athlone, 1962), 11.

33 **Celebrities of the day:** Munby, *The Cult of the Autograph Letter in England,* 10.

33 **France became an epicenter:** Étienne Charavay, *La Science des Autographes: Essai Critique* (Paris: Charavay Frères, 1887), viii, xi.

33 **Over the next four decades:** Joseph Rosenblum, *Prince of Forgers* (New Castle, Del.: Oak Knoll, 1998), 8–9.

33 **As Étienne Charavay:** Charavay, *La Science des Autographes,* xiv.

34 **"They think that I carry":** Adrian Hoffman Joline, *Meditations of an Autograph Collector* (New York: Harper & Brothers, 1902), 2–3.

34 **A document authored by John Hancock:** Mary A. Benjamin, "Values," in *Autographs and Manuscripts: A Collector's Manual,* 182.

34 **A missive by Charlotte Brontë:** Kenneth W. Rendell, *History Comes to Life: Collecting Historical Letters and Documents* (Norman: University of Oklahoma Press, 1995), 65, 203, 207.

34 **The type of document:** Clifton Waller Barrett, "Introduction," in *Autographs and Manuscripts: A Collector's Manual,* xvii.

34 **In 1988, *Les Autographes:*** Alain Nicolas, *Les Autographes* (Paris: Maisonneuve & Larose, 1988), 10.

35 **As Mary Benjamin:** Benjamin, "Values," 187.

35 **He felt the first inkling:** Lhéritier, *Intime Corruption,* 33.

35 **Lhéritier started small:** Lhéritier, *Intime Corruption,* 34–35.

36 **Investing in postage stamps:** Stephen Datz, *Stamp Investing* (Loveland, Colo.: General Philatelic Corporation, 1997), 5–7.

37 **But law enforcement:** Roger-Louis Bianchini, "Enquête sur la Fortune des Grimaldi," *L'Express,* June 15, 2000, www.lexpress.fr/actualite/monde /europe/enquete-sur-la-fortune-des-grimaldi_491985.html (accessed February 3, 2020).

37 **The newest scandal:** Jon Henley, "Stamps Scandal Leaves Mark on Roy-

als," *Guardian,* March 7, 1999, www.theguardian.com/world/1999/mar/08/jonhenley (accessed February 3, 2020).

37 **As one website:** "Monaco Stamp Scandal," Stamp-Scandal.com, viewed on Internet Archive's Wayback Machine, web.archive.org/web/20040219035058/http://www.stamp-scandal.com/Stamp_Scandal1.htm (accessed March 23, 2022).

37 **In December 1995, Murciano:** Jean-Pierre Murciano, *Juge sur la Côte d'Azur: Missions Impossibles* (Neuilly-sur-Seine, France: Michel Lafon, 2001), 36, 40, 48.

37 **"The Monaco stamps":** Lhéritier, *Intime Corruption,* 18–20; Jean-Pierre Murciano declined multiple interview requests.

37 **Three months later:** Lhéritier, *Intime Corruption,* 127.

38 **Sitting in the solitude:** Lhéritier, *Intime Corruption,* 137–38.

38 **Lhéritier's crusade for redemption:** Lhéritier, *Intime Corruption,* 149, 165, 203, 230, 255.

39 **"It is a demonic assembly":** Lhéritier, *Intime Corruption,* 12.

39 **Lhéritier went so far:** Lhéritier, *Intime Corruption,* 256.

39 **It didn't matter:** Judgment of the Cour d'Appel d'Aix-en-Provence, February 28, 2007.

CHAPTER THREE: In the Bosom of Luxury and Plenty

41 **Jeanne Testard hammered:** Lever, *Sade,* 120.

41 **Erotic novels evaded:** Robert Darnton, *The Forbidden Best-Sellers of Pre-revolutionary France* (New York: W. W. Norton, 1996), 3.

41 **The procurement of a *petite maison*:** James A. Steintrager, *The Autonomy of Pleasure: Libertines, License, and Sexual Revolution* (New York: Columbia University Press, 2016), 81–82.

41 **members of all-male:** Chad Denton, *Decadence, Radicalism, and the Early Modern French Nobility: The Enlightened and Depraved* (Lanham, Md.: Lexington Books, 2017), xiv.

41 **Marais had been assigned:** Nina Kushner, *Erotic Exchanges: The World of Elite Prostitution in Eighteenth-Century Paris* (Ithaca, N.Y.: Cornell University Press, 2013), 10, 29–42.

42 **According to her:** Lever, *Sade,* 119–20.

43 **As one of the oldest:** Lever, *Sade,* 3–10.

43 **Jean-Baptiste:** Lever, *Sade,* 36–39.

43 **He was also an unabashed libertine:** Lever, *Sade,* 25–26, 27, 82.

44 **Instead, his dissolute interests:** Lever, *Sade,* 31–32.

44 **Several days after the incident:** Lever, *Sade,* 120.

44 **As he'd been led:** Honoré Gabriel Riqueti, Comte de Mirabeau, *Des*

Lettres de Cachet et des Prisons d'État, Seconde Partie (Hambourg: n.p., 1882), 47.

44 **The young courtier:** Olivier Bernier, *Pleasure and Privilege: Life in France, Naples, and America 1770–1790* (Garden City, N.Y.: Doubleday, 1981), 7.

45 **But here in his dismal chamber:** Riqueti, *Des Lettres de Cachet,* 47–48.

45 **He was accustomed to sumptuous foods:** Lever, *Sade,* 310–11.

45 **Now he had to make do:** Riqueti, *Des Lettres de Cachet,* 15–16.

45 **The prisoner stood:** Schaeffer, *The Marquis de Sade,* 519; Gray, *At Home,* 21; Lever, *Sade,* 530.

45 **Sade had come into the world:** Lever, *Sade,* 38, 49–50.

45 **The boy adopted a skewed view:** Donatien Alphonse François de Sade, *Aline et Valcour* (Paris: Gallimard, 1990), 403. Cited in Lever, *Sade,* 51.

46 **Once, when the young Prince:** Bongie, *Sade,* 29.

46 **Sade's mother, Marie Éléonore:** Bongie, *Sade,* 20–21, 71.

46 **As a pastime:** Lever, *Sade,* 50.

47 **Sade found his new home:** Schaeffer, *The Marquis de Sade,* 262; Lever, *Sade,* 14–15.

47 **The abbé also enjoyed:** Lever, *Sade,* 57–58.

47 **As a first step:** Lever, *Sade,* 61–62.

48 **A police report:** Bongie, *Sade,* 82.

48 **Sade joined the Chevaux-légers:** Gray, *At Home,* 46.

48 **As an adolescent:** Lever, *Sade,* 69.

49 **When he heard:** Lever, *Sade,* 84–85.

49 **On leave:** Lever, *Sade,* 86.

49 **Renée-Pélagie wasn't particularly beautiful:** Gray, *At Home,* 53.

49 **Sade had nurtured hopes:** Schaeffer, *The Marquis de Sade,* 38.

49 **On May 15:** Lever, *Sade,* 108–09.

50 **In the years to come:** Lever, *Sade,* 116.

50 **He insisted that he felt:** Schaeffer, *The Marquis de Sade,* 49.

50 **Like Sade:** Gray, *At Home,* 52, 60, 61.

50 **With his new bride:** Gray, *At Home,* 56; Lever, *Sade,* 109.

50 **"Oh, the rascal":** Lever, *Sade,* 111.

51 **As Marais noted:** Lever, *Sade,* 120.

51 **Three years later:** Bongie, *Sade,* 105.

51 **He pleaded:** Lever, *Sade,* 122.

52 **He consorted:** Kushner, *Erotic Exchanges,* 5.

52 **"When he has passed":** Lever, *Sade,* 144.

52 **He attacked a coachman:** Lever, *Sade,* 152.

52 **Finally, on Easter Sunday:** Lever, *Sade,* 153–56.

53 **Known by everyone:** Gray, *At Home,* 54, 141.

53 **The Présidente also likely spread:** Lever, *Sade,* 164.

54 **"A disreputable deed":** Lever, *Sade,* 171.

54 **Marais had little doubt:** Lever, *Sade,* 152.

CHAPTER FOUR: *Psychopathia Sexualis*

55 **Around him, bookshelves displayed:** Günter Grau, *Iwan Bloch: Hautarzt, Medizinhistoriker, Sexualforscher* (Teetz: Hentrich & Hentrich, 2007), 10, 16–17.

55 **A few decades earlier:** Rory MacLean, *Berlin: Portrait of a City Through the Centuries* (New York: Weidenfeld & Nicolson, 2014), 172.

55 **Everywhere Bloch looked:** David Clay Large, *Berlin* (New York: Basic Books, 2000), 82–87.

56 **"It is a new city":** Eva-Maria Schnurr, "Berlin's Turn of the Century Growing Pains," *Spiegel International,* November 22, 2012, www.spiegel.de /international/germany/the-late-19th-century-saw-the-birth-of-modern -berlin-a-866321.html (accessed November 21, 2020).

56 **In 1867, Karl Heinrich Ulrichs:** Robert Beachy, *Gay Berlin: Birthplace of a Modern Identity* (New York: Alfred A. Knopf, 2014), 5.

56 **Two years later, an Australian journalist:** Beachy, *Gay Berlin,* 31.

56 **While the law remained:** Beachy, *Gay Berlin,* 55–58.

57 **Born in 1872:** Erich Ebstein, "In Memoriam: Iwan Bloch with Biblio-graphia Blochiana," *Medical Life* 30, no. 2 (February 1923): 57–70.

57 **And he came face-to-face:** Deborah Hayden, *Pox: Genius, Madness, and the Mysteries of Syphilis* (New York: Basic Books, 2003), xviii.

57 **"The epitome of sexual hygiene":** Iwan Bloch, *Beiträge zur Aetiologie der Psychopathia Sexualis* (Dresden: Verlag von H. R. Dohrn, 1902), 377.

57 **The women's-rights movement:** Edward Ross Dickinson, *Sex, Freedom, and Power in Imperial Germany, 1880–1914* (New York: Cambridge University Press, 2014), 164.

57 **And he believed that the seeds:** Benjamin Kahan, *The Book of Minor Per-verts: Sexology, Etiology, and the Emergences of Sexuality* (Chicago: University of Chicago Press, 2019), 1.

58 **The abolition of Paragraph 175:** Bloch, *Beiträge zur Aetiologie der Psycho-pathia Sexualis,* 251–52.

58 **As the rise of diverse:** Vern Bullough, *Science in the Bedroom: A History of Sex Research* (New York: Basic Books, 1994), 6, 10.

58 **Like Bloch:** Bullough, *Science in the Bedroom,* 59.

58 **The nascent field of study:** Anna Katharina Schaffner, *Modernism and Per-version: Sexual Deviance in Sexology and Literature, 1850–1930* (New York: Pal-grave Macmillan, 2012), 60.

58 **In France, the psychologist Alfred Binet:** Schaffner, *Modernism and Perver-sion,* 176–77.

58 **In Britain, physician Havelock Ellis:** Schaffner, *Modernism and Perversion,* 182–84.

58 **In Austria, Sigmund Freud:** Anna Katharina Schaffner, "Fiction as Evidence: On the Uses of Literature in Nineteenth-Century Sexological Discourse," *Comparative Literature Studies* 48, no. 2 (2011), 165.

59 **According to Krafft-Ebing's analysis:** Richard von Krafft-Ebing, *Psychopathia Sexualis,* trans. Charles Gilbert Chaddock (Philadelphia: F. A. Davis, 1894), 57, 71.

59 **He began his publishing career:** Iwan Bloch, *Der Marquis de Sade und Seine Zeit: Ein Beitrag zur Kultur-und Sittengeschichte des 18* (Berlin: H. Barsdorf, 1906), 57.

59 **The two grew close:** Iwan Bloch to Henry Spencer Ashbee, July 21, 1900, the estate of Iwan Bloch/Robert Bloch, Magnus Hirschfeld Society archives, Berlin, Germany.

59 **In their correspondence:** Gibson, *The Erotomaniac,* 141–42.

59 **Bloch, touched by the gesture:** Bloch, *Sex Life in England* (New York: Panurge, 1934), 348, 352–53.

60 **In 1904, 119 years:** Donatien Alphonse François de Sade, *120 Journées de Sodome, ou l'École du Libertinage,* trans. Eugène Dühren (Paris: Club des Bibliophiles, 1904), ii, vii.

60 **All were luxury items:** Allen, "Prices and Wages in Paris, 1400–1914."

60 **Nearly everything about the book's publication:** Sade, *120 Journées de Sodome,* iii.

60 **According to Bloch's lengthy introduction:** Bloch, *Neue Forschungen über den Marquis de Sade und Seine Zeit,* 390.

61 **Bloch had always been:** Ebstein, "In Memoriam: Iwan Bloch," 59.

61 **He noted that his discovery:** Sade, *120 Journées de Sodome,* vii.

61 **Why else would he have written:** Sade, *120 Days of Sodom,* 28.

61 **Sade, he believed, had blazed:** Iwan Bloch, *Marquis de Sade's Anthropologia Sexualis of 600 Perversions: "120 Days of Sodom, or the School for Libertinage" and the Sex Life of the French Age of Debauchery from the Private Archives of the French Government* (New York: Falstaff, 1934), x.

61 **Looking ever more professorial:** Ebstein, "In Memoriam: Iwan Bloch," 70.

62 **Between 1901 and 1912:** Grau, *Iwan Bloch,* 59–60.

62 **Within its pages:** Arthur Bernstein, "Iwan Bloch: Ein Nachruf," *Zeitschrift für Sexualwissenschaft* 9, no. 10 (January 1923), 265.

62 **And Bloch's long-held belief:** Sade, *120 Journées de Sodome,* 11.

62 **To solve this new conundrum:** Iwan Bloch, *The Sexual Life of Our Time in Its Relations to Modern Civilization* (London: Rebman, 1909), 488–90.

63 **Hirschfeld had been forever transformed:** Beachy, *Gay Berlin,* 86–87, 97, 113, 172.

63 **Bloch began taking regular walks:** Erwin Haeberle, "Interview About Iwan Bloch and the Marquis de Sade," email, August 29, 2019.

63 **Bloch would take to heart:** Beachy, *Gay Berlin,* 88.

63 **The insight would lead Bloch:** Grau, *Iwan Bloch,* 14.

63 **Instead, he came to believe:** Bloch, *The Sexual Life of Our Time,* 236.

63 **Now, rather than dreading:** Bloch, *The Sexual Life of Our Time,* 250.

64 **After everything he had seen:** Bloch, *The Sexual Life of Our Time,* 490, 524.

64 **On a warm July evening:** Laurie Marhoefer, *Sex and the Weimar Republic: German Homosexual Emancipation and the Rise of the Nazis* (Toronto, Ont.: University of Toronto Press, 2015), 3–4.

64 **Visitors that night toured:** Beachy, *Gay Berlin,* 163–84.

65 **After their recent defeat:** MacLean, *Berlin: Portrait of a City,* 173–74.

65 **"Here was the seething brew":** Christopher Isherwood, *Christopher and His Kind, 1929–1939* (New York: Farrar, Straus and Giroux, 1976), 49.

65 **He used the institute:** Beachy, *Gay Berlin,* 184.

65 **Over the years, Bloch had worked:** Elena Mancini, *Magnus Hirschfeld and the Quest for Sexual Freedom: A History of the First International Sexual Freedom Movement* (New York: Palgrave MacMillan, 2010), 40; Ralph M. Leck, *Vita Sexualis: Karl Ulrichs and the Origins of Sexual Science* (Urbana: University of Illinois Press, 2016), 181.

65 **Because of his expertise:** John R. McDill, *Lessons from the Enemy: How Germany Cares for Her War Disabled* (Philadelphia: Lea & Febiger, 1918), 101.

66 **In 1918, Louis Morin:** Louis Morin, *Comment le Docteur Boche, pour Justifier à l'Avance les Infamies Allemandes, Accusait de Sadisme Sanglant les Français en Général et les Parisiens en Particulier* (Paris: C. Bosse, 1918).

66 **As someone who counted:** Johannes Werthauer, "Iwan Bloch: An Obituary," *Abendblatt,* January 26, 1923.

66 **Bloch emerged broken:** Grau, *Iwan Bloch,* 24.

66 **Early in the autumn of 1922:** Werthauer, "Iwan Bloch: An Obituary."

66 **Sigmund Freud wrote:** Sigmund Freud, letter to Julius Schuster, January 7, 1923, the estate of Iwan Bloch/Robert Bloch, Magnus Hirschfeld Society archives, Berlin, Germany.

67 **That year, a government committee:** Beachy, *Gay Berlin,* 220.

67 **Nazi thugs distributed flyers:** Beachy, *Gay Berlin,* 169.

67 **As shopkeepers unfurled:** Isherwood, *Christopher and His Kind,* 128; Beachy, *Gay Berlin,* 244.

67 **Just after nine A.M.:** Isherwood, *Christopher and His Kind,* 128.

67 **The students kicked in:** Isherwood, *Christopher and His Kind,* 128–29.

68 **Four days later:** MacLean, *Berlin: Portrait of a City,* 184.

68 **Hirschfeld, abroad on a world:** Beachy, *Gay Berlin,* 243.

68 **In the coming years:** Richard Plant, *The Pink Triangle: The Nazi War Against Homosexuals* (New York: Henry Holt, 1986), 110, 149, 180.

68 **In East and West Germany:** Beachy, *Gay Berlin,* 246.
69 **In 1972:** Murray J. White, "The Legacy of Iwan Bloch (1872–1922)," *New Zealand Psychologist* 1, no. 2 (1972).

CHAPTER FIVE: Rise of an Empire

70 **Jean-Claude Le Coustumer listened:** Xavier Deroche (stepson of Jean-Claude Le Coustumer), interview with the author, October 30, 2019; the financial advisor did not respond to multiple interview requests.
70 **It boasted the densest concentration:** Barbara Chabbal, "Les Librairies Parisiennes: Résistance et Mutations, Evolution 2003–2014," L'Apur: Atelier Parisien d'Urbanisme, May 2016; Vincent Monadé, interview with the author, April 11, 2019.
71 **In 1984:** Matthew G. Kirschenbaum, *Track Changes: A Literary History of Word Processing* (Cambridge, Mass.: Belknap Press of Harvard University Press, 2016), xiv–xv.
71 **"Writers of all descriptions":** Thomas Pynchon, "Is It O.K. to Be a Luddite?," *New York Times,* October 28, 1984, www.archive.nytimes.com/www .nytimes.com/books/97/05/18/reviews/pynchon-luddite.html (accessed September 16, 2020).
72 **A century earlier, Mark Twain:** Kirschenbaum, *Track Changes,* ix.
72 **"What is to become":** Gore Vidal, "In Love with the Adverb," *New York Review of Books,* March 29, 1984, www.nybooks.com/articles/1984/03/29/in -love-with-the-adverb/ (accessed September 16, 2020).
73 **In Avignon, Robert Cipollina:** Aude Nehring (daughter of Robert Cipollina), interview with the author, November 5, 2016.
73 **In a suburb of Paris, Geoffroy:** Geoffroy (last name withheld upon request), interview with the author, October 23, 2019.
73 **Jean-Marie Leconte:** Jean-Marie Leconte, interview with the author, November 10, 2016.
73 **They joined priests:** Isabelle Horlans, *Affaire Aristophil: Liquidation en Bande Organisée* (Paris: Le Passeur, 2019), 181.
73 **Not long after he learned:** Xavier Deroche, interview with the author, October 30, 2019.
73 **Gérard Lhéritier had founded Aristophil:** Gérard Lhéritier, interview with the author, December 8, 2016.
73 **Bidding over the phone:** "EINSTEIN, Albert and Michele BESSO. Autograph manuscript, comprising a series of calculations using the early version ('Entwurf') of the field equations of Einstein's general theory of relativity . . . ," Christie's, www.christies.com/lotfinder/lot/einstein-albert-and -michele-besso-autograph-manuscript-3983409-details.aspx (accessed November 14, 2019).

74 **Within two weeks:** Vincent Noce, "Aristophil Gavé en Lettres d'Or," *Libération,* February 1, 2013, www.liberation.fr/societe/2013/02/01 /aristophil-gave-en-lettres-d-or_878630 (accessed November 14, 2019).

74 **Thanks to Lhéritier's innovation:** Alain Poncet, interview with the author, June 13, 2019.

74 **They also appreciated:** Horlans, *Affaire Aristophil,* 272.

74 **In the 1980s and '90s:** "Welcome to HistoryForSale," www.historyforsale .com/profile (accessed July 6, 2020).

75 **To ensure that everything:** Horlans, *Affaire Aristophil,* 166; Jean-Jacques Daigre declined to be interviewed because legal proceedings were still ongoing.

75 **As *Le Figaro* declared:** Mohammed Aïssaoui, "Les Beaux Jours du Manuscript," *Le Figaro,* December 20, 2012, www.lefigaro.fr/livres/2012/12/20 /03005-20121220ARTFIG00642-les-beaux-jours-du-manuscrit.php (accessed June 4, 2020).

75 **At the Fontainebleau Auction House:** "Napoleon's Coded Kremlin Letter Sold for $243,500 at Fontainebleau Auction House," *ArtDaily,* December 3, 2012, www.artdaily.cc/news/59301/Napoleon-s-coded-Kremlin-letter-sold -for-243-500-at-Fontainebleau-Auction-House-#.Xc3j6FdKg2w (accessed November 14, 2019).

75 **At Sotheby's in London:** Bryony Jones, "Miniature Bronte Manuscript Sparks Bidding War," CNN, December 15, 2011, www.cnn.com/2011/12/15 /world/europe/bronte-manuscript-sold-at-auction/index.html (accessed November 14, 2019).

75 **And in 2008, when Sotheby's Paris:** Henry Samuel, "André Breton's Surrealist Manifesto Sold at Auction in France," *Telegraph,* May 22, 2008, www .telegraph.co.uk/news/worldnews/europe/france/2003659/Andre-Bretons -Surrealist-Manifesto-sold-at-auction-in-France.html (accessed November 14, 2019).

76 **The company's treasure trove:** Horlans, *Affaire Aristophil,* 313–16.

76 **Jurors for most of the country's:** Norimitsu Onishi and Constant Méheut, "Pedophile Scandal Can't Crack the Closed Circles of Literary France," *New York Times,* November 28, 2020, www.nytimes.com/2020/11/28/world /europe/france-literary-prizes-matzneff.html (accessed December 4, 2020).

76 **And for seventy years:** William Grimes, "Pierre Berès, Tenacious Book Collector, Dies at 95," *New York Times,* August 3, 2008, www.nytimes .com/2008/08/03/world/europe/03beres.html (accessed December 4, 2020).

76 **In June 2004:** Thomas Anquetin, "Les Autographes Ont Leur Musée: Des Lettres et Manuscrits d'Artistes et de Personnages Historiques Rassemblés à Saint-Germain-des-Prés," *Le Figaro,* August 20, 2004; Alexis Geng, "Les Manuscrits Ont Leur Musée à Paris," *Le Monde,* September 17, 2004.

77 **Six years later:** Horlans, *Affaire Aristophil,* 26.

77 **It lent documents:** Horlans, *Affaire Aristophil,* 324–26.

77 **It hosted symposiums:** Jérôme Dupuis, "Aristophil: La Chute d'un Empire de Papiers," *L'Express,* March 10, 2015, www.lexpress.fr/actualite/societe/justice/aristophil-la-chute-d-un-empire-de-papiers_1659704.html (accessed November 15, 2019); Patrick Poivre d'Arvor and Didier van Cauwelaert declined to be interviewed.

77 **When Lhéritier, through his company, acquired:** Horlans, *Affaire Aristophil,* 88.

77 **And when the Bibliothèque Nationale:** Horlans, *Affaire Aristophil,* 89–90.

77 **The media started calling:** Vincent Monnier, "Affaire Aristophil: Gérard Lhéritier, le Madoff des Lettres?," *L'Obs,* December 5, 2014, www.nouvelobs.com/societe/20141205.OBS7091/affaire-aristophil-gerard-lheritier-le-madoff-des-lettres.html (accessed March 5, 2020); Didier van Cauwelaert, "Gérard Lhéritier—Chasseur de Textes," *Le Point,* June 21, 2012, www.lepoint.fr/livres/gerard-lheritier-chasseur-de-textes-21-06-2012-1477643_37.php (accessed March 5, 2020); Vincent Noce, "Aristophil Gavé en Lettres d'Or," February 1, 2013, www.liberation.fr/societe/2013/02/01/aristophil-gave-en-lettres-d-or_878630 (accessed March 5, 2020).

77 **Lhéritier's ambitions extended beyond:** Horlans, *Affaire Aristophil,* 305, 254.

78 **One of the most respected:** Ken Rendell, interview with the author, August 8, 2019.

78 **So Rendell was happy:** Horlans, *Affaire Aristophil,* 192–93; Jacques de Saint Victor, "Le Testament Politique de Louis XVI Retrouvé," *Le Figaro,* May 20, 2009, www.lefigaro.fr/actualite-france/2009/05/20/01016-20090520ARTFIG00025-le-testament-politique-de-louis-xvi-retrouve-.php (accessed November 22, 2019).

79 **During one of Rendell's visits:** Ken Rendell, interview with the author, August 8, 2019.

CHAPTER SIX: The Tyranny of Lust

80 **As the church bells struck:** Lever, *Sade,* 195–96.

80 **For the previous four years:** Lever, *Sade,* 180.

81 **As part of his rehabilitation:** Lever, *Sade,* 187, 192–93.

81 **After Sade departed:** Lever, *Sade,* 198–199, 202, 206.

82 **Sade waved away:** Schaeffer, *The Marquis de Sade,* 174.

82 **As for the vomiting:** Lever, *Sade,* 203.

82 **After a lifetime of entitlement:** Lever, *Sade,* 160.

82 **Sade even developed:** Lever, *Sade,* 396.

82 **As the eighteenth century progressed:** McPhee, *Liberty or Death,* 25–28.

82 **As he noted:** Schaeffer, *The Marquis de Sade,* 122–23.

83 **Sade's obsession with debauchery:** Donatien Alphonse François de Sade, *Juliette,* trans. Austryn Wainhouse (New York: Grove, 1968), 269–70.

83 **He told his wife:** Schaeffer, *The Marquis de Sade,* 132.

83 **One of Sade's accusers testified:** Gray, *At Home,* 94.

83 **He had come to yearn:** Schaeffer, *The Marquis de Sade,* 142.

83 **On September 12:** Lever, *Sade,* 210.

84 **What had transpired in Marseille:** Paul Friedland, "Beyond Deterrence: Cadavers, Effigies, Animals and the Logic of Executions in Premodern France," *Historical Reflections / Réflexions Historiques* 29, no. 2 (2003), 314.

84 **As the crowd watched:** Lever, *Sade,* 211.

84 **Over the previous two centuries:** Friedland, "Beyond Deterrence," 309.

84 **Along with satisfying:** Bongie, *Sade,* 133.

84 **Sade wasn't especially troubled:** Sade, *120 Days of Sodom,* 256.

85 **During her stay at the château:** Lever, *"Je Jure au Marquis de Sade,"* 31.

85 **It wouldn't take long:** Lever, *"Je Jure au Marquis de Sade,"* 47.

85 **For the first and only time:** Lever, *"Je Jure au Marquis de Sade,"* 56.

86 **There were no indications:** Jeffrey Merrick, "Patterns and Prosecution of Suicide in Eighteenth-Century Paris," *Historical Reflections / Réflexions Historiques* 16, no. 1 (1989), 4, 10.

86 **A few days later:** Lever, *Sade,* 215–16.

86 **The officers took Sade:** Lever, *Sade,* 223, 227.

86 **Two weeks later:** Lever, *Sade,* 229.

87 **In the dim light:** Lever, *Sade,* 230.

87 **To recapture her son-in-law:** Schaeffer, *The Marquis de Sade,* 169.

87 **Now, on the night:** Lever, *Sade,* 230–32.

88 **The Marquise de Sade, having:** Schaeffer, *The Marquis de Sade,* 301.

88 **The twelve years she had spent:** Lever, *Sade,* 117, 144.

88 **"I know my world better":** Schaeffer, *The Marquis de Sade,* 180.

88 **While he was incarcerated:** Schaeffer, *The Marquis de Sade,* 223; Gray, *At Home,* 143.

89 **"Once out of her grip":** Lever, *Sade,* 286.

89 **"I shall never be able":** Lever, *Sade,* 324.

89 **No matter the calamities:** Gray, *At Home,* 59.

89 **The villagers knew to avert:** Lever, *Sade,* 254.

89 **Reaching the top:** Gray, *At Home,* 89, 163.

90 **"We have decided":** Lever, *Sade,* 249.

90 **By the following January:** Lever, *Sade,* 251, 256, 258.

90 **"I take them with me":** Schaeffer, *The Marquis de Sade,* 175, 187.

91 **But when the father:** Lever, *Sade,* 278.

91 **Those who knew Sade:** Lever, *Sade,* 282.

92 **Even Sade's uncle:** Lever, *Sade,* 283.

92 **"When will I get out":** Lever, *Sade,* 289.

92 **But his supplications:** Gray, *At Home,* 187.

92 **The inspector soon had agents:** Gray, *At Home,* 208.

93 **Marais had gone too far:** Schaeffer, *The Marquis de Sade,* 255–56.

93 **They hoped to catch a glimpse:** Lever, *Sade,* 173–74, 208.

CHAPTER SEVEN: Reign of the Red Vicomtesse

94 **With electric lights blazing:** Lancelot Hamelin and Luca Erbetta, *Dans les Eaux Glacées du Calcul Égoiste,* vol. 1, *Le Bal des Matières* (Grenoble: Éditions Glénat, 2018), 6.

94 **From the vehicles stepped:** Alexandre Mare and Stéphane Boudin-Lestlenne, *Charles et Marie-Laure de Noailles: Mécènes du XX Siècle* (Paris: Bernard Chauveau Édition, 2018), 93–94.

94 **Inside, through the glass double doors:** James Lord, *Six Exceptional Women: Further Memoirs* (New York: Farrar, Straus and Giroux, 1994), 103–06; Mare and Boudin-Lestlenne, *Charles et Marie-Laure de Noailles,* 92–93.

95 **Clothed in a gown:** "Le Bal des Matières: La Fête Comme Célébration Artistique," *Festival de L'Histoire de l'Art,* www.festivaldelhistoiredelart.com /programmes/le-bal-des-matieres-1929/ (accessed December 10, 2020).

95 **While she was not beautiful:** Mare and Boudin-Lestlenne, *Charles et Marie-Laure de Noailles,* 18.

95 **She relished parties:** Laurence Benaïm, *Marie Laure de Noailles: La Vicomtesse du Bizarre* (Paris: Bernard Grasset, 2001), 168, 230.

95 **Marie-Laure was born:** Benaïm, *Marie Laure de Noailles,* 12.

95 **At twenty-one, Marie-Laure married:** Benaïm, *Marie Laure de Noailles,* 107.

96 **Earlier that year:** Mare and Boudin-Lestlenne, *Charles et Marie-Laure de Noailles,* 296.

96 **In the years to come:** Benaïm, *Marie Laure de Noailles,* 165.

97 **The black-and-white images:** "*L'Age d'Or* (1930)," YouTube video, 1:02:37, Eric Trommater, June 2, 2014, www.youtube.com/watch?v= RDbav8hcl5U (accessed December 12, 2020).

97 **Emerging from the devastation:** Maurice Nadeau, *The History of Surrealism* (New York: Macmillan, 1965), 11–12.

97 **The movement was spearheaded:** Sue Roe, *In Montparnasse: The Emergence of Surrealism in Paris, from Duchamp to Dalí* (New York: Penguin Press, 2019), 29; Mary Ann Caws, *Creative Gatherings: Meeting Places of Modernism* (London: Reaktion, 2019), 242.

97 **Decrying the pretentiousness:** Roe, *In Montparnasse,* 135, 157, 162.

98 **The Noailleses had attended:** Marie Audran, "Les Noailles, Ces Personnages de Roman Qui Ont Vraiment Existé," *Le Point,* July 29, 2010, www .lepoint.fr/culture/les-noailles-ces-personnages-de-roman-qui-ont -vraiment-existe-29-07-2010-1220323_3.php (accessed December 13, 2020).

98 **The couple had already decorated:** Mare and Boudin-Lestlenne, *Charles et Marie-Laure de Noailles*, 17–18, 151–53.

98 **The Noailleses would end up:** Mare and Boudin-Lestlenne, *Charles et Marie-Laure de Noailles*, 181–84.

98 **After Dalí and Buñuel suffered:** Luis Buñuel, *My Last Sigh: The Autobiography of Luis Buñuel* (New York: Vintage Books, 2013), 115–16.

99 **In *L'Oeuvre du Marquis de Sade*:** Guillaume Apollinaire, *L'Oeuvre du Marquis de Sade* (Paris: Collection des Classiques Galants, 1909), 24–30.

99 **In Sade's frenzied:** Alyce Mahon, *The Marquis de Sade and the Avant-Garde* (Princeton, N.J.: Princeton University Press, 2020), 93.

99 **Surrealists generated explicit artworks:** Mark Polizzotti, *Revolution of the Mind: The Life of André Breton* (New York: Farrar, Straus and Giroux, 1995), 367, 529.

99 **And like the marquis:** Roe, *In Montparnasse*, 182.

99 **Breton, in his pivotal:** André Breton, *Manifeste du Surréalisme* (Paris: Éditions du Sagittaire, 1924), 26.

99 **Buñuel found the novel:** Buñuel, *My Last Sigh*, 217–18.

99 **The central plot:** "*L'Age d'Or* (1930)."

100 **The Noailleses debuted the film:** Delon, *La 121ème Journée*, 93.

100 **They decorated the lobby:** Paul Hammond, *L'Âge d'Or* (London: British Film Institute, 1997), 58–60.

100 **But now, in the middle:** Hammond, *L'Âge d'Or*, 60–61.

101 **The show resumed:** Benaïm, *Marie Laure de Noailles*, 203–04.

101 **Members of the Surrealists delighted:** Hammond, *L'Âge d'Or*, 64.

101 **Charles in particular:** Mare and Boudin-Lestlenne, *Charles et Marie-Laure de Noailles*, 253.

101 **Noailles stepped from her bedroom:** Benaïm, *Marie Laure de Noailles*, 268.

102 **Noailles's personal escape:** Lord, *Six Exceptional Women*, 93.

102 **Starting with James:** Benaïm, *Marie Laure de Noailles*, 271, 266, 385.

102 **She became a fashion icon:** Mare and Boudin-Lestlenne, *Charles et Marie-Laure de Noailles*, 272.

102 **She published a collection:** Mare and Boudin-Lestlenne, *Charles et Marie-Laure de Noailles*, 303–04.

102 **She eventually took up painting:** Mare and Boudin-Lestlenne, *Charles et Marie-Laure de Noailles*, 273.

102 **And she reigned:** Lord, *Six Exceptional Women*, 128, 130; Benaïm, *Marie Laure de Noailles*, 377.

102 **As one colleague would describe:** Francine du Plessix Gray, "The Surrealists' Muse," *New Yorker,* September 24, 2007, www.newyorker.com/magazine/2007/09/24/the-surrealists-muse (accessed December 16, 2020).

103 **"Marie-Laure was a descendant":** Benaïm, *Marie Laure de Noailles*, 271.

103 **A doctor turned ultra-left firebrand:** Delon, *La 121ème Journée*, 80–84, 94–96.

104 **Noailles, on the other hand:** Benaïm, *Marie Laure de Noailles*, 288.

104 **She had attempted to flee:** Mary McAuliffe, *Paris on the Brink: The 1930s Paris of Jean Renoir, Salvador Dalí, Simone de Beauvoir, André Gide, Sylvia Beach, Léon Blum, and Their Friends* (Lanham, Md.: Rowman & Littlefield, 2018), 275.

104 **She dined with the remnants:** Gray, "The Surrealists' Muse"; Alistair Horne, *Seven Ages of Paris* (New York: Alfred A. Knopf, 2002), 364.

105 **On November 21, 1940:** Benaïm, *Marie Laure de Noailles*, 313.

105 **Her nose was badly injured:** Lord, *Six Exceptional Women*, 101.

105 **The revolt had begun:** Daniel Singer, *Prelude to Revolution: France in May 1968* (Cambridge, Mass.: South End, 2002), xviii–xix.

105 **Then, two days before:** Singer, *Prelude to Revolution*, 166.

106 **Breton had passed away:** Polizzotti, *Revolution of the Mind*, 605–06.

106 **Amid the red velvet seats:** Kate Bredeson, *Occupying the Stage: The Theater of May '68* (Evanston, Ill.: Northwestern University Press, 2018), 52, 59.

106 **In the streets beyond:** Johan Kugelberg and Philippe Vermés, *Beauty Is in the Street: A Visual Record of the May '68 Paris Uprising* (London: Four Corner, 2011), 184, 185, 195.

106 **From the back seat lumbered:** Edgar Schneider, "C'est la Vicomtesse au 'Happening' de l'Odéon," *Paris Presse*, May 18, 1968.

107 **But her exploits:** Lord, *Six Exceptional Women*, 152.

107 **As one of the nearby street posters:** Harold Rosenberg, "Surrealism in the Streets," *New Yorker*, December 21, 1968, 52–55, www.newyorker.com /magazine/1968/12/28/surrealism-in-the-streets (accessed December 7, 2020).

107 **So, respectfully but firmly:** Lord, *Six Exceptional Women*, 153.

107 **The following year, de Gaulle:** Fenby, *France: A Modern History*, 402.

107 **Two years later:** Lord, *Six Exceptional Women*, 85–86.

107 **He would live another eleven years:** "Camellia Sasanqua 'Vicomte de Noailles,'" La Maison du Camélia, www.la-maison-du-camelia.fr/camelias -sasanqua/camelia-vicomte-de-noailles/ (accessed December 18, 2020).

107 **She also left behind two daughters:** Carlo Perrone, interview with the author, October 11, 2019.

108 **The manuscript went to:** Carlo Perrone, interview with the author, October 11, 2019.

108 **In November 1982:** Carlo Perrone, interview with the author, October 11, 2019.

CHAPTER EIGHT: Trouble in Bibliopolis

109 **Lhéritier took a sip:** Frédéric Castaing, interview with the author, December 15, 2016.

110 **Castaing had been born:** Emily Evans Eerdmans, *The World of Madeleine Castaing* (New York: Rizzoli International, 2010), 7.

110 **Growing up:** Frédéric Castaing, interview with the author, April 11, 2019.

111 **He learned how to use:** Rendell, *History Comes to Life,* 14–15, 21–26.

111 **At last count:** "Booksellers," International League of Antiquarian Booksellers, www.ilab.org/page/booksellers (accessed March 21, 2022).

112 **Booksellers and publishers had first begun congregating:** Chabbal, "Les Librairies Parisiennes," 2.

112 **This was where, in the 1920s:** Ernest Hemingway, *A Moveable Feast: The Restored Edition* (New York: Scribner, 2009), 35–36.

112 **In one of the row houses:** John Baxter, *Saint-Germain-des-Prés: Paris's Rebel Quarter* (New York: Harper Perennial, 2016), 128–29.

112 **Halfway up the lane:** Gérard Durozoi, *History of the Surrealist Movement* (Chicago: University of Chicago Press, 2002), 1.

113 **Inspired by the shop's success:** Sylvia Beach, *Shakespeare and Company* (New York: Harcourt, Brace, 1959), 20, 52.

114 **There he could judge customers' reactions:** Frédéric Castaing, interview with the author, April 11, 2019.

114 **The rare-book sale:** Observations by the author, November 8, 2016.

115 **He did business with fashion designer:** Jérôme Dupuis and Laurent Léger, "L'Incroyable Histoire du 'Madoff' Français," *L'Express,* November 3, 2018, www.lexpress.fr/actualite/societe/l-incroyable-histoire-du-madoff-francais_2043901.html (accessed November 15, 2019).

116 **In a hermetic letters market:** Bonnardot, *The Mirror of the Parisian Bibliophile,* xxvii.

116 **Vrain had become one of:** "ARISTOPHIL film de presentation," YouTube video, 7:32:52, Aristophil, June 7, 2012, www.youtube.com/watch?v=S_AbE2uKfpg (accessed September 12, 2020); Vincent Noce, "Aristophil Gavé en Lettres d'Or," *Libération,* February 1, 2013, www.liberation.fr/societe/2013/02/01/aristophil-gave-en-lettres-d-or_878630/ (accessed May 18, 2021).

116 **In 2005, before becoming:** Frédéric Castaing, *Rouge Cendres* (Paris: Ramsay, 2005).

117 **When a reporter:** Erwan Seznec, "Lettres et Manuscrits, Étranges Investissements," *Que Choisir,* March 31, 2011, www.quechoisir.org/actualite-lettres-et-manuscrits-etranges-investissements-n10453/ (accessed November 20, 2019).

117 **In November 2012:** Radia Sadani, "Bruxelles: Soupçons d'Escroquerie dans le Marché des Manuscrits," *RTBF,* November 28, 2012, www.rtbf.be/info/societe/detail_bruxelles-soupcons-d-escroquerie-dans-le-marche-de-l-art?id=7883105 (accessed November 20, 2019).

117 **The following month, France's:** "L'Autorité des Marchés Financiers Appelle les Épargnants à la Plus Grande Vigilance en Matière de Placements Atypiques Proposés au Public," Autorité des Marchés Financiers, Decem-

ber 12, 2012, www.amf-france.org/technique/multimedia?docId=workspace://
SpacesStore/41202e80-6bd2-4a4b-87a6-ed12bdf401bc_fr_1.0_rendition (accessed November 20, 2019).

117 **Aristophil had always provided:** Francis Triboulet, interview with the author, November 10, 2016.

117 **He had long been friendly:** Frédéric Castaing, interview with the author, July 11, 2019; Alain Nicolas, interview with the author, July 9, 2019.

118 **Castaing didn't care:** Horlans, *Affaire Aristophil,* 82.

118 **In 1985, Castaing had traveled:** Frédéric Castaing, interview with the author, December 15, 2016.

118 **In 2013, the sound of drums:** Dupuis and Léger, "L'Incroyable Histoire du 'Madoff' Français."

119 **The year before, he had spent:** Horlans, *Affaire Aristophil,* 25.

119 **On November 13, when he learned from his daughter:** "EuroMillions Results for Tuesday 13th November 2012," Euro-Millions.com, www.euro-millions.com/results/13-11-2012 (accessed November 21, 2019).

119 **He won €169 million:** Grégory Leclerc, "Le Gagnant à 169 Millions d'Euros de l'Euromillion se Confie à Nice-Matin," *Nice-Matin,* November 13, 2013, www.nicematin.com/faits-societe/le-gagnant-a-169-millions-d-euros-de-l-euromillion-se-confie-a-nice-matin-332241 (accessed November 21, 2019).

119 **Lhéritier didn't go public:** Dupuis and Léger, "L'Incroyable Histoire du 'Madoff' Français."

119 **He had more than enough:** Horlans, *Affaire Aristophil,* 158.

120 **He talked about the history:** Gérard Lhéritier, "Discours Inauguration Hôtel de La Salle" (speech, April 24, 2013), transcript provided by Lhéritier.

120 **To derail the Belgian investigation:** Horlans, *Affaire Aristophil,* 161.

120 **Closer to home:** Jean-Pierre Rondeau, interview with the author, January 30, 2020; Lhéritier declined to respond to these allegations.

120 **Bloggers who questioned:** Rémi Mathis, interview with the author, November 8, 2011; Hugues Ouvrard, interview with the author, January 30, 2020; Lhéritier declined to respond to these allegations, noting, "They are incomprehensible and delusional. So it's impossible for me to answer them."

120 **In response to *Que Choisir*'s:** Judgment of the Tribunal de Grande Instance de Paris, March 25, 2013, no. 13/00538; Erwan Seznec, interview with the author, September 9, 2019.

120 **Payback arrived:** "Exceptionnel Ensemble de Manuscrits Littéraires de Marcel Aymé et de Marguerite Duras," *La Gazette Drouot,* www.gazette-drouot.com/ventes-aux-encheres/13882-exceptionnel-ensemble-de-manuscrits-litteraires-de-marcel-ayme-et-de-marguerite-duras (accessed July 20, 2020).

121 **Lhéritier had told his staff:** Gérard Lhéritier, interview with the author, July 18, 2019.

121 **A few months later:** Frédéric Castaing, interview with the author, December 15, 2016.

CHAPTER NINE: Citizen Sade

122 **While imprisoned in the Bastille:** Lever, *Sade,* 350.

122 **He described Charenton:** Lever, *Sade,* 351.

123 **"Good day, good works":** Lever, *Sade,* 357.

123 **Sade emerged into a Paris:** Gray, *At Home,* 311.

124 **Gone was the patchwork:** McPhee, *Liberty or Death,* 88.

124 **Even the quantification:** Emmet Kennedy, *A Cultural History of the Revolution* (New Haven, Conn.: Yale University Press, 1989), 348.

124 **"I have lost my taste":** Lever, *Sade,* 360.

124 **But Renée-Pélagie wanted nothing:** Lever, *Sade,* 361–63.

125 **Doing so wouldn't be easy:** Suzanne Desan, "Making and Breaking Marriage: An Overview of Old Regime Marriage as a Social Practice," in *Family, Gender, and Law in Early Modern France,* ed. Suzanne Desan and Jeffrey Merrick (University Park: Pennsylvania University Press, 2009), 14–17.

125 **Renée-Pélagie surely considered:** Gray, *At Home,* 302.

125 **Sure enough:** Lever, *Sade,* 368–69.

125 **Two years later:** Suzanne Desan, *The Family on Trial in Revolutionary France* (Berkeley: University of California Press, 2006), 123.

126 **He also took up:** Lever, *Sade,* 390.

126 **Devastated by years:** Georges Lefebvre, *The Great Fear of 1789: Rural Panic in Revolutionary France* (Princeton, N.J.: Princeton University Press, 2014), x–xi.

126 **Sade was right:** Lever, *Sade,* 432.

127 **Several companies rejected:** Lever, *Sade,* 376, 379–81, 383.

127 **Considering himself an expert:** Gray, *At Home,* 317.

128 **Scandalized, critics denounced:** Lever, *Sade,* 384–85.

128 **Lurid accounts like these:** Gray, *At Home,* 371.

128 **On June 24, 1791:** Gray, *At Home,* 325–26.

129 **Or so went the story:** Gray, *At Home,* 326–27.

129 **Sade, however, not only refused:** Lever, *Sade,* 439.

129 **He volunteered for:** Schaeffer, *The Marquis de Sade,* 428.

130 **He took charge of renaming:** Gray, *At Home,* 312–13.

130 **He composed essays:** Lever, *Sade,* 440–41; Schaeffer, *The Marquis de Sade,* 426.

130 **Impressed, his colleagues appointed:** Lever, *Sade,* 440.

130 **But deep down:** Lever, *Sade,* 404.

130 **While he went through the motions:** Lever, *Sade,* 424, 420.

130 **After having his prison-cell letters:** Lever, *Sade,* 439.

131 **He composed a missive:** Lever, *Sade,* 428.

131 **He edited prison-cell compositions:** Bongie, *Sade,* 226.

131 **After the mass slaughters:** Lever, *Sade,* 430.

131 **And when Marie-Antoinette:** Gray, *At Home,* 333.

131 **At times, Sade felt safe:** Lever, *Sade,* 416–17.

132 **Outside, the darkened streets:** Pernoud and Flaissier, *The French Revolution,* 248.

132 **"It went as pleasantly":** Lever, *Sade,* 442.

132 **But he hadn't forgotten:** Lever, *Sade,* 444.

132 **He would soon get the chance:** Lever, *Sade,* 444.

132 **On August 2:** Lever, *Sade,* 443.

133 **Calling Jesus:** Schaeffer, *The Marquis de Sade,* 436–37.

133 **Robespierre, well on his way:** Gray, *At Home,* 338.

133 **A week after Sade's speech:** Lever, *Sade,* 461.

133 **The Great Terror had reached:** Colin Jones, *The Great Nation* (New York: Columbia University Press, 2002), 496.

134 **The bailiff's list that day:** Lever, *Sade,* 465.

134 **He'd been arrested:** Lever, *Sade,* 457.

134 **He'd been unmasked:** Gray, *At Home,* 338.

134 **After his arrest:** Gray, *At Home,* 344.

134 **On July 25:** Lever, *Sade,* 465–66.

135 **One by one, the convicts:** Daniel Gerould, *Guillotine: Its Legend and Lore* (New York: Blast, 1992), 23.

135 **As the bailiff had collected:** Schaeffer, *The Marquis de Sade,* 446.

135 **As he wrote to Gaufridy:** Gray, *At Home,* 347.

136 **For the first time:** Gray, *At Home,* 350.

136 **In the months to come:** Lever, *Sade,* 505–06.

136 **In 1795, the widow:** Lever, *Sade,* 476–77.

136 **Over the next several years:** Gray, *At Home,* 377–78.

137 **The work made an impression:** Lever, *Sade,* 498–99.

137 **But their serenity:** Lever, *Sade,* 512.

CHAPTER TEN: The Purloined Scroll

138 **The police moved:** Herbert Mitgang, "Sale of French Publisher Raises Bookmen's Fears," *New York Times,* January 18, 1981, www.nytimes.com/1981/01/18/books/sale-of-french-publisher-raises-bokmen-s-fears.html (accessed September 13, 2021); Patrick Besson, "La Chronique de Patrick Besson," *Le Point,* August 27, 2020, www.pressreader.com/france/le-point/20200827/281556588208293 (accessed September 13, 2021).

138 **Grouet admitted to:** Carlo Perrone, interview with the author, October 11, 2019.

139 **On the floors below:** "Third Generation," *Maus Frères SA,* www.maus.ch /en/practice/third-generation/ (accessed January 13, 2021).

139 **The retail kingdom:** "Established in Geneva in 1902," *Maus Frères SA,* www.maus.ch/en/about/ (accessed January 14, 2021); Clive H. Church and Randolph C. Head, *A Concise History of Switzerland* (Cambridge: Cambridge University Press, 2013), 230.

139 **Nordmann, with his neatly combed:** Jacques Chamay, "Hommage: Gérard Nordmann N'Est Plus," *Journal de Genève et Gazette de Lausanne,* February 10, 1992, 28.

139 **Like many prominent:** Julianne Slovak, "The Billionaires," *Fortune,* September 11, 1989.

140 **Perrone explained:** Carlo Perrone, interview with the author, December 2, 2016.

140 **Here, bookshelves rising:** Charles Méla, interview with the author, January 8, 2021.

140 **During his first meeting:** Rainer Michael Mason, ed., *Eros Invaincu: La Bibliothèque Gérard Nordmann* (Paris: Fondation Martin Bodmer, 2004), 10, 321.

140 **His discoveries included:** Mason, *Eros Invaincu,* 322–23; John De St. Jorre, "The Unmasking of O," *New Yorker,* August 1, 1994, 43.

141 **Nordmann had each:** Mason, *Eros Invaincu,* 14.

141 **He financed reprints:** Mason, *Eros Invaincu,* 322.

141 **And once, after purchasing:** Patrick Kearney, "Demande d'Entretien Concernant Gérard Nordmann," email, October 12, 2020.

141 **He had never been particularly interested:** Swiss Federal Tribunal decision, May 28, 1998, 5C.16/1998, 4–5.

141 **Working with a prominent Swiss bookbinder:** *Les Collections Aristophil: Vente Inaugurale,* auction catalog (Paris: Aguttes, 2017), 55.

141 **He and his Jewish family:** "French Collection," *Economist,* December 8, 2006, www.economist.com/news/2006/12/08/french-collection (accessed January 15, 2021).

142 **In the late 1940s:** Pauvert, *Sade's Publisher,* 113–14.

142 **At the legal hearing:** Jean Jacques Pauvert, *Nouveaux (et Moins Nouveaux) Visages de la Censure, Suivie de l'Affaire Sade* (Paris: Les Belles Lettres, 1994), 69.

142 **Many of the era's most esteemed:** Pauvert, *Sade's Publisher,* 192–93.

142 **He found Pauvert guilty:** Pauvert, *Sade's Publisher,* 197, 208.

143 **Inspired by the Pauvert case:** Amy S. Wyngaard, "Translating Sade: The Grove Press Editions, 1953–1968," *Romanic Review* 104, nos. 3–4 (May–November 2013), 313–14, 324.

143 **In 1836, fourteen-year-old:** Gustave Flaubert, *Bibliomania: A Tale* (London: Rodale, 1954), 10.

143 **He based the work:** Basbanes, *A Gentle Madness,* 33–34.

144 **That included Sir Thomas Phillipps:** Werner Muensterberger, *Collecting: An Unruly Passion* (Princeton, N.J.: Princeton University Press, 1994), 75.

144 **After years of court battles:** Cour d'Appel de Paris decision, December 8, 1988, no. 7708/87.

144 **More important, the court declared:** Cour de Cassation, Chambre Criminelle decision, June 11, 1990, no. C 89-80.467.

145 **In 1954, a conference:** Sharon Waxman, *Loot: The Battle over the Stolen Treasures of the Ancient World* (New York: Times Books, 2008), 2–7.

145 **Attempts to return:** Marc-André Renold, "Cross-Border Restitution Claims of Art Looted in Armed Conflicts and Wars and Alternatives to Court Litigations," study commissioned and supervised by the European Parliament's Policy Department for Citizens' Rights and Constitutional Affairs at the request of the JURI Committee, May 2016.

145 **There was only one problem:** J. Murray Luck, *A History of Switzerland: The First 100,000 Years; Before the Beginnings to the Days of the Present* (Palo Alto, Calif.: Society for the Promotion of Science and Scholarship, 1985), 740.

145 **The idea of good faith:** Marc-André Renold, interview with the author, December 13, 2019.

145 **The justices considered:** Swiss Federal Tribunal decision, May 28, 1998, 5C.16/1998, 3–4.

146 **What's more, a French manuscript:** Alain Nicolas, interview with the author, July 9, 2019.

146 **The justices also took:** Swiss Federal Tribunal decision, May 28, 1998, 5C.16/1998, 1998, 3–5.

146 **On May 28, 1998:** Swiss Federal Tribunal decision, May 28, 1998, 5C.16/1998, 16–17.

146 **Six years earlier:** Mason, *Eros Invaincu,* 10.

147 **On a hill overlooking Geneva:** "A Spiritual Edifice," YouTube video, 26:17, Fondation Martin Bodmer, June 17, 2015, www.youtube.com/watch?v=BZvirZAstJI (accessed January 19, 2021).

147 **Throughout the space:** "The Collections," Fondation Martin Bodmer, www.fondationbodmer.ch/en/the-collections/ (accessed June 19, 2021).

147 **This is the Bibliotheca Bodmeriana:** Charles Méla, interview with the author, January 8, 2021; Carol Vogel, "$7 Million Michelangelo," *New York Times,* January 29, 1998, www.nytimes.com/1998/01/29/arts/7-million-michelangelo.html (accessed January 10, 2021).

147 **The foundation turned to the heir:** Charles Méla, interview with the author, January 8, 2021.

148 **At the conclusion:** Florence Darbre, interview with the author, January 13, 2021.

148 **Preservation is as ancient:** Michele Valerie Cloonan, *Preserving Our Heritage: Perspectives from Antiquity to the Digital Age* (Chicago: Neal-Schuman, 2015), xxiv.

148 **In 1966, the Arno River:** Sheila Waters, *Waters Rising: Letters from Florence* (Ann Arbor, Mich.: Legacy, 2016), 4–11.

148 **By the time Darbre:** Florence Darbre, interview with the author, January 13, 2021.

150 **Shortly before his death:** Charles Méla, interview with the author, January 8, 2021.

150 **On a warm spring day:** Clive Aslet, "Erotic Sale of the Century (Wife Says It's Got to Go)," *Daily Telegraph,* April 20, 2006, www.telegraph.co.uk /culture/art/3651695/Erotic-sale-of-the-century-wife-says-its-got-to-go .html (accessed January 20, 2021).

150 **Catalogs for the event:** Judith Benhamou, "Le Must de la Bibliothèque Érotique," *Les Echos,* April 7, 2006, www.lesechos.fr/2006/04/le-must-de-la -bibliotheque-erotique-567466 (accessed January 20, 2021).

150 **Signs placed:** *Secret Museums: In Search of Hidden Erotic Art,* directed by Peter Woditsch (Icarus Films, 2009), online.

150 **Nordmann's eleven-volume edition:** "[ASHBEE, Henry Spencer (1834– 1900)?]. My Secret Life. Amsterdam Not for publication [imp. Auguste Brancart?, vers 1890?]," Christie's, www.christies.com/en/lot/lot-4698934 (accessed January 21, 2021).

150 **A set of 102 lewd illustrations:** "[CHAUVET, Jules-Adolphe?]—Suite de 102 figures galantes ou libres, attribuées à Chauvet (vers 1875) pour illustrer les Mémoires de J. Casanova," Christie's, www.christies.com/en/lot/lot -4839916 (accessed January 21, 2021).

150 **The original manuscripts:** "REAGE Pauline [Dominique Aury (1907– 1998)]. Histoire d'O et Retour à Roissy Manuscrits autographes," Christie's, www.christies.com/en/lot/lot-4699236 (accessed January 21, 2021); Corydon Ireland, "A Collection Unlike Others," *Harvard Gazette,* November 7, 2012, www.news.harvard.edu/gazette/story/2012/11/a-collection-unlike-others/ (accessed January 21, 2021).

151 **Pietro Aretino's groundbreaking:** "[L'ARÉTIN (Pietro Aretino, 1492– 1556). Sonnetti lussuriosi. Venise: Giovanni Tacuino da Tridino? vers 1527]," Christie's, www.christies.com/en/lot/lot-4698928 (accessed January 21, 2021).

151 **By the end:** "Bibliothèque Erotique Gérard Nordmann—Première Partie," Christie's, www.christies.com/en/auction/biblioth-que-erotique-g-rard -nordmann-premi-re-partie-20695/ (accessed January 20, 2021); "Bibliothèque Erotique Gérard Nordmann—2ème Partie," Christie's, www

.christies.com/en/auction/biblioth-que-erotique-g-rard-nordmann-2-me
-partie-20800/ (accessed January 20, 2021).

CHAPTER ELEVEN: Erased from the Minds of Men

152 **The well-to-do:** Lever, *Sade,* 527–28.
152 **Even more damning:** Lever, *Sade,* 514, 547.
153 **After Sade was detained:** Lever, *Sade,* 514, 518–19.
154 **This time at Charenton:** Lever, *Sade,* 546, 554.
154 **As always, he wrote:** Lever, *Sade,* 548–549.
154 **Most notably:** Lever, *Sade,* 527–31.
155 **In May 1813:** Lever, *Sade,* 557, 559.
156 **His ex-wife:** Lever, *Sade,* 547.
156 **His youngest child:** Gray, *At Home,* 392.
156 **For a while, Sade enjoyed:** Lever, *Sade,* 543–44.
156 **That left Sade's middle child:** Lever, *Sade,* 552.
157 **In November 1814:** Lever, *Sade,* 549.
157 **Armand would eventually:** Gray, *At Home,* 409.
157 **In fact, the septuagenarian:** Schaeffer, *The Marquis de Sade,* 511–12.
157 **Even in the twilight:** Lever, *Sade,* 550–51.
157 **Sade's health had been deteriorating:** Lever, *Sade,* 542–43.
158 **His condition didn't stop him:** Lever, *Sade,* 563–64.
158 **A phrenologist:** Lever, *Sade,* 566–67.
159 **According to his last wishes:** Gray, *At Home,* 410.

CHAPTER TWELVE: The Grand Bargain

160 **Bruno Racine sat by:** Bruno Racine, interview with the author, December 12, 2019.
160 **The bulk of the institution's:** "François-Mitterrand," Bibliothèque Nationale de France, www.bnf.fr/en/francois-mitterrand (accessed December 13, 2019).
160 **In his previous job:** Alan Riding, "Arts, Briefly; A Shake-Up in Paris at the Pompidou Center," *New York Times,* March 29, 2007, archive.nytimes.com/query.nytimes.com/gst/fullpage-9407E5DD1030F93AA15750C0A9619C8B63.html (accessed December 13, 2019).
160 **Since assuming the helm:** Bruno Racine, interview with the author, April 9, 2019.
161 **Soon he had amassed:** Elaine Sciolino, "It's a Sadistic Story, and France Wants It," *New York Times,* January 21, 2013, www.nytimes.com/2013/01/22/books/frances-national-library-hopes-to-buy-sades-120-days.html (accessed December 13, 2019).

161 **Racine sprang into action:** Nathaniel Herzberg, "Caché, Volé, Racheté: L'Histoire Folle d'un Manuscrit de Sade," *Le Monde,* October 1, 2012, www .lemonde.fr/livres/article/2012/10/01/cache-vole-rachete-l-histoire-folle-du -manuscrit-de-sade_1767353_3260.html (accessed December 13, 2019).

161 **At the same time:** Vincent Noce, "Caché, Disparu, Volé, Racheté, Le Manuscrit Mythique de Sade Revient en France," *Libération,* April 3, 2014, www.next.liberation.fr/livres/2014/04/03/cache-disparu-vole-rachete-le -manuscrit-mythique-de-sade-revient-en-france_992764 (accessed December 13, 2019).

162 **Racine, meanwhile, began working closely:** Bruno Racine, interview with the author, April 9, 2019.

162 **In the middle of:** Sciolino, "It's a Sadistic Story."

162 **That's when Racine's phone:** Bruno Racine, interview with the author, December 12, 2019.

162 **Behind the scenes:** Corinne Hershkovitch, interview with the author, December 11, 2019.

163 **Not long before:** "Contrat de Vente entre Nathalie Nordmann, Alain Nordmann, Serge Nordmann, et Aristophil SAS."

163 **Working with Aristophil:** "Protocole de Vente du Manuscrit 'Les 120 Journées de Sodome,' de Sade," memo signed by Carlo Perrone and Gérard Lhéritier, February 26, 2014.

163 **In total, Lhéritier wound up:** Gérard Lhéritier, interview with the author, December 6, 2016.

163 **Along with financial compensation:** "Protocole de Vente du Manuscrit 'Les 120 Journées de Sodome,' de Sade."

163 **He offered to donate:** Philippe Durand, "SADE—Synthèse de la position de la BNF," email, December 20, 2013.

163 **Thanks to the donation:** "Loi N° 2003-709 du 1er Août 2003 Relative au Mécénat, aux Associations et aux Fondations," www.legifrance.gouv.fr /affichTexte.do?cidTexte=JORFTEXT000000791289 (accessed December 16, 2019).

164 **The complication could be traced:** Gérard Lhéritier, interview with the author, July 20, 2019.

165 **On the morning of March 25:** "Grâce à Aristophil le Manuscrit du Divin Marquis de Sade Revient en France," YouTube video, 2:52, Aristophil, April 7, 2014, www.youtube.com/watch?v=x-7JFXCS5es (accessed December 16, 2019).

165 **The national press hailed:** "L'Épilogue Français des " 'Cent Vingt Journées de Sodome,' " *Le Point,* April 3, 2014, www.lepoint.fr/livres/l-epilogue -francais-des-cent-vingt-journees-de-sodome-03-04-2014-1808871_37.php (accessed December 16, 2019).

165 **Recounting its convoluted provenance:** Noce, "Caché, Disparu, Volé, Racheté."

165 **Lloyd's of London insured:** Jean-Claude Vrain to Gérard Lhéritier, April 14, 2014.

165 **At the weekly French newsmagazine:** Jérôme Dupuis, interview with the author, May 22, 2020.

166 **Dupuis began in 2001:** Jérôme Dupuis, "Le Mystérieux Itinéraire du Voyage," *L'Express,* May 5, 2001.

166 **In 2011, he reported that Patrick:** Jérôme Dupuis, "Le Plagiat de PPDA," *L'Express,* January 4, 2011, www.lexpress.fr/culture/livre/le-plagiat-de -ppda_949676.html (accessed December 17, 2019).

166 **By that point, Dupuis:** Jérôme Dupuis, interview with the author, May 22, 2020.

167 **In the middle of his investigation:** Jérôme Dupuis, interview with the author, November 8, 2016.

168 **In May 2013:** Jérôme Dupuis, "Vente de Manuscrits: L'Étrange Système Aristophil," *L'Express,* May 7, 2013, www.lexpress.fr/culture/livre/vente-de -manuscrits-l-etrange-systeme-aristophil_1247044.html (accessed December 17, 2019).

169 **The most obvious red flags:** Tamar Frankel, *The Ponzi Scheme Puzzle: A History and Analysis of Con Artists and Victims* (New York: Oxford University Press, 2012), 171–73.

169 **As Boston University law professor:** Frankel, *The Ponzi Scheme Puzzle,* 28–29.

169 **As one bookseller told Dupuis:** Dupuis, "Vente de Manuscrits."

170 **Five months after Dupuis's exposé:** Horlans, *Affaire Aristophil,* 215–16.

170 **A few months earlier:** *Winner: The Magazine of Success,* no. 8, July 2013.

170 **Then, in January 2014:** "Dans les Coulisses d'Aristophil: Fouquet's, Jets Privés et ISF . . . Les Argumentaires d'Aristophil," Bibliophilie.com, September 17, 2015, www.bibliophilie.com/dans-les-coulisses-daristophil -fouquets-jets-prives-et-isf-les-argumentaires-daristophil/ (accessed December 18, 2019).

170 **The firm also threw:** Dupuis and Léger, "L'Incroyable Histoire du 'Madoff' Français."

170 **Lhéritier, meanwhile, was quietly:** Francis Triboulet, interview with the author, November 10, 2016.

170 **It didn't seem to matter:** Dupuis and Léger, "L'Incroyable Histoire du 'Madoff' Français."

170 **Or that Lhéritier's confidant:** Horlans, *Affaire Aristophil,* 269.

171 **Or that in February 2014:** Horlans, *Affaire Aristophil,* 215–16.

171 **As part of the fête:** "D.A.F. de Sade: Justine et Autres Romans," *La Pléiade,*

www.la-pleiade.fr/Catalogue/GALLIMARD/Bibliotheque-de-la-Pleiade
/Justine-et-autres-romans (accessed December 19, 2019).

171 *Le Figaro* and *The Paris Review:* Alexandre Devecchio, "Michel Onfray:
Sade, Marine Le Pen, L'École et Moi," *Le Figaro,* September 26, 2014, www
.lefigaro.fr/vox/politique/2014/09/26/31001-20140926ARTFIG00442-michel
-onfray-sade-marine-le-pen-l-ecole-et-moi.php (accessed December 19, 2019);
Paulin Césari, "Pour en Finir Avec Sade," *Le Figaro,* November 14, 2014,
www.lefigaro.fr/arts-expositions/2014/11/14/03015-20141114ARTFIG00220
-pour-en-finir-avec-sade.php (accessed December 19, 2019); Sarah Moroz,
"Horrific Practices," *Paris Review,* December 2, 2014, www.theparisreview
.org/blog/2014/12/02/horrific-practices/ (accessed December 19, 2019); Cath-
erine Golliau, "Pourquoi Sade Nous Fascine," *Le Point,* September 25, 2014,
www.lepoint.fr/culture/pourquoi-sade-nous-fascine-25-09-2014-1866575_3
.php (accessed December 19, 2019).

171 **The French writer Michel Onfray:** Michel Onfray, *La Passion de la Méchanceté* (Paris: Éditions Autrement, 2014), 12–13.

171 **In Geneva, the Bodmer Foundation:** Marianne Grosjean, "À la Fondation
Martin Bodmer, on a Sade dans la Peau," *Tribune de Genéve,* December 6,
2014, www.tdg.ch/culture/fondation-martin-bodmer-sade-peau/story
/31893574 (accessed December 19, 2019); Delon, *La 121ème Journée,* 163.

171 **Most notably, just around:** *Sade: Attacking the Sun,* Musée d'Orsay, www
.musee-orsay.fr/en/events/exhibitions/in-the-museums/exhibitions-in-the
-musee-dorsay/article/sade-41230.html (accessed December 19, 2019).

172 **The show's title:** Sade, *120 Days of Sodom,* 154.

172 **Lhéritier refused:** Gérard Lhéritier, interview with the author, December 6, 2016.

172 **In the center:** Gérard Lhéritier, interview with the author, December 6,
2016.

172 **Lhéritier, dressed in:** "Sade et l'Éventail des Libertinages," YouTube video,
12:12, Les Nautes de Paris, October 1, 2014, www.youtube.com/watch
?v=Fgum6vvB2_Q (accessed September 4, 2020).

173 **As the festivities stretched:** Tony Perrottet, "Who Was the Marquis de
Sade?," *Smithsonian Magazine,* February 2015, www.smithsonianmag.com
/history/who-was-marquis-de-sade-180953980/?page=2 (accessed September 4, 2020).

173 **Hundreds agreed to:** Sylvie Le Gall, interview with the author, May 2,
2019.

173 **So on April 14:** "Corpus Scriptural Prestige," signed by Sylvie Le Gall,
April 14, 2014.

173 **And with that, Le Gall:** Gérard Lhéritier, "Plus de questions!," email, January 16, 2017.

173 **The Aristophil exhibit proved:** Jenny Awford, "The Original *Fifty Shades*

of Grey Goes on Display," *Daily Mail,* September 19, 2014, www.dailymail
.co.uk/news/article-2762859/Marquis-Sade-s-The-120-Days-Sodom-goes
-display.html (accessed September 4, 2020).

173 **After years of fighting:** Carlo Perrone, interview with the author,
December 2, 2016.

173 **Racine attended the show:** Bruno Racine, interview with the author,
April 9, 2019.

174 **In Strasbourg, Sylvie:** Sylvie Le Gall, interview with the author, May 2,
2019.

CHAPTER THIRTEEN: The Divine Marquis

175 **The bare branches:** Mahon, *The Marquis de Sade and the Avant-Garde,* 99.

175 **Despite the cult of Sade:** Hobart Ryland, "Recent Developments in Research on the Marquis de Sade," *French Review* 25, no. 1 (October 1951):
10–12.

175 **The gentleman who opened:** John Brunton, "Revolution in Their
Blood," *Advertiser,* July 8, 1989.

176 **Starting with Armand:** Gray, *At Home,* 418.

176 **And for generations:** Thibault de Sade, interview with the author, February 1, 2021.

176 **But now, thanks to:** Thibault de Sade, interview with the author, February 1, 2021; Hugues de Sade, interview with the author, November 9, 2016.

177 **The French intellectual Simone:** Simone de Beauvoir, "Must We Burn
Sade?," in Donatien Alphonse François Sade, *The 120 Days of Sodom and Other
Writings,* trans. Austryn Wainhouse and Richard Seaver (New York: Grove,
1966), 4.

177 **The writer Pierre Klossowski:** Pierre Klossowski, "Nature as Destructive
Principle," in Sade, *The 120 Days of Sodom and Other Writings,* 65; Mitchell
Dean and Daniel Zamora, "Did Foucault Reinvent His History of Sexuality
Through the Prism of Neoliberalism?," *Los Angeles Review of Books,* April 18,
2018, www.lareviewofbooks.org/article/did-foucault-reinvent-his-history
-of-sexuality-through-the-prism-of-neoliberalism/ (accessed February 2,
2021).

177 **Thanks to the unrestrained lust:** Angela Carter, *The Sadeian Woman and the
Ideology of Pornography* (New York: Pantheon, 1978), 26.

177 **As the French author Albert Camus:** Albert Camus, *The Rebel: An Essay
on Man in Revolt* (New York: Vintage International, 1991), 47.

177 **Max Horkheimer and Theodor W. Adorno:** Max Horkheimer and Theodor W. Adorno, *Dialectic of Enlightenment: Philosophical Fragments* (1947; repr.,
Stanford, Calif.: Stanford University Press, 2002), 69.

178 **In France and the United States:** Will McMorran, "Introducing the Mar-

quis de Sade," *Forum for Modern Language Studies* 51, no. 2 (April 2015), 141–42; Wyngaard, "Translating Sade," 313–14, 325–26.

178 **As French literary theorist:** Roland Barthes, *Sade, Fourier, Loyola* (New York: Hill and Wang, 1976), 137.

178 **In April of that year:** Roger Shattuck, *Forbidden Knowledge: A Landmark Exploration of the Dark Side of Human Ingenuity and Imagination* (San Diego: A Harvest Book / Harcourt Brace, 1996), 256–58.

179 **The literary critic George Steiner:** Sade, *120 Days of Sodom,* xxv.

179 **As English novelist:** Sade, *120 Days of Sodom,* xxv.

179 **In the dimming light:** Tony Perrottet, "The Marquis de Sade Is Dead! Long Live Pierre Cardin!," *Slate,* December 17, 2008, www.slate.com /human-interest/2008/12/the-marquis-de-sade-is-dead-long-live-pierre -cardin.html (accessed February 4, 2021).

180 **Cardin declared that his goal:** Nathalie Feld, "Les 'Américains' du Village François de la Mode," *France-Amérique,* October 13, 2010, www.france -amerique.com/en/les-americains-du-village-francais-de-la-mode/ (accessed February 3, 2021).

180 **Others balked:** Tony Perrottet, "Ever Wonder What Pierre Cardin Has Been Up To?," *Wall Street Journal,* June 23, 2011, www.wsj.com/articles /SB10001424052702304186404576388143793160396 (accessed February 3, 2021).

180 **To allow the festivities:** "Pierre Cardin Renonce à un Projet de Golf dans le Vaucluse," *Agence France-Presse,* July 16, 2010.

181 **A 1965 *New York Times* review:** Alex Szogyi, "A Full Measure of Madness," *New York Times,* July 25, 1965.

181 **The 1965 Broadway debut:** Steintrager, *The Autonomy of Pleasure,* 284–87.

181 **Then, in 1975, the Italian:** Delon, *La 121ème Journée,* 157–59.

181 **Finally, in 2000, Hollywood returned:** Steintrager, *The Autonomy of Pleasure,* 292.

182 **In 1990, on the 250th:** Delon, *La 121ème Journée,* 14.

182 **Across town, the trendy:** Daniel Rogov, "The Divine Marquis," *Jerusalem Post,* May 31, 1990.

182 **On occasion, he spoke out:** Susan Heller Anderson, "Saving Château and Writings of Marquis de Sade," *New York Times,* December 7, 1981, www .nytimes.com/1981/12/07/style/saving-chateau-and-writings-of-marquis-de -sade.html (accessed February 3, 2021); "De Sade Prize Whips His Family into Frenzy," *Australian,* August 3, 2001.

182 **But more than any other venture:** Thibault de Sade, interview with the author, February 2, 2021.

182 **With prim composure:** Thibault de Sade, interview with the author, April 15, 2019.

183 **He had learned the value:** Frank Kools, "Franse Kruistocht Tegen Ont-wrichting," *Trouw,* October 20, 1995.

183 **His oldest brother, Elzéar:** Adam Sage, "My Family Has Been Punished Enough, Claims de Sade's Heir," *Times* (London), December 20, 2014, www .thetimes.co.uk/article/my-family-has-been-punished-enough-claims-de -sades-heir-boptbhkkl7g (accessed February 4, 2021).

183 **The middle brother, Hugues:** Hugues de Sade, interview with the author, November 9, 2016.

183 **But Thibault was the one:** Thibault de Sade, interview with the author, February 2, 2021.

184 **Thanks to his studies:** Sade, *120 Days of Sodom,* 59.

184 **The marquis, he and other:** Jean-Christophe Abramovici, interview with the author, November 11, 2016.

184 **"The manuscript":** Thibault de Sade, interview with the author, April 15, 2019.

CHAPTER FOURTEEN: The Prisoner by the Sea

185 **The police arrived:** Gérard Lhéritier, interview with the author, December 6, 2016.

185 **The commander refused:** Horlans, *Affaire Aristophil,* 30–32.

186 **Aristophil collapsed:** Mélanie Delattre, Christophe Labbé, and Laure Rougevin-Baville, "Descente de Police au Musée des Lettres et Manuscrits," *Le Point,* November 18, 2014, www.lepoint.fr/justice/descente-de-police-au -musee-des-lettres-et-manuscrits-18-11-2014-1882159_2386.php (accessed January 22, 2020).

186 **The French media jumped:** Vincent Noce, "La Justice Écorne Aristophil, le Roi du Manuscrit," *Libéracion,* November 20, 2014, www.next.liberation .fr/arts/2014/11/20/la-justice-ecorne-aristophil-le-roi-du-manuscrit_1146972 (accessed January 22, 2020); Eric Treguier, "L'Empereur des Manuscrits Finira -t-Il Comme Madoff?," *Challenges,* November 27, 2014, www.challenges .fr/entreprise/gerar-lheritier-aristophil-finira-t-il-comme-madoff_132277 (accessed January 22, 2020).

186 **In early March 2015:** Benoit Huet, "Legal documents," email, January 26, 2017.

186 **For the organized-fraud charge alone:** Article 313-2, Code de Procédure Pénale, Legifrance, www.legifrance.gouv.fr/affichCode.do?idSectionTA=LE GISCTA000006165331&cidTexte=LEGITEXT000006070719 (accessed January 23, 2020).

186 **Lhéritier wasn't the only one:** Horlans, *Affaire Aristophil,* 55–59.

187 **Through his contacts, Dupuis scored:** Jérôme Dupuis, "Le Grand Krach des Manuscrits," *L'Express,* November 12, 2015, www.lexpress.fr/actualite /societe/justice/le-grand-krach-des-manuscrits_1734536.html (accessed January 16, 2020); Dupuis and Léger, "L'Incroyable Histoire du 'Madoff' Français."

187 **As one of the company's brokers:** Dupuis and Léger, "L'Incroyable Histoire du 'Madoff' Français."

187 **Dupuis discovered an example:** Dupuis, "Le Grand Krach des Manuscrits."

188 **Vrain alone was responsible:** *Jean-Claude Vrain v. Maxime Saada, Donatien Lemaitre, and Frédéric Castaing,* 16189000087 Judgment 2, Tribunal de Grande Instance de Paris, 17th Correctional Chamber, September 17, 2019.

188 **"Members of the French trade":** Name withheld upon request, interview with the author, February 21, 2019.

188 **Former French prime minister:** "Villepin, ou l'Éclatante Réussite du Bibliophile," *Le Canard Enchaîné,* March 18, 2015; Dupuis and Léger, "L'Incroyable Histoire du 'Madoff' Français."

188 **And news that the police:** Jérôme Dupuis, "Pourquoi PPDA a Été Placé en Garde à Vue," *L'Express,* November 26, 2015, www.lexpress.fr/actualite /societe/justice/pourquoi-ppda-a-ete-place-en-garde-a-vue-hier_1739610 .html (accessed January 23, 2020).

188 **Three months after the raids:** Horlans, *Affaire Aristophil,* 107–10.

189 **"The press now call me":** Gérard Lhéritier, interview with the author, December 6, 2016.

191 **"The minister of culture":** Gérard Lhéritier, "Le don," email, March 19, 2017.

191 **"It might take two":** Gérard Lhéritier, interview with the author, December 8, 2016.

191 **The odds of him:** "EuroMillions Odds & Statistics," EuroMillions, www .euromillions.online/euromillions-odds-statistics/ (accessed January 23, 2020).

191 **In 1991, the American mobster:** Kevin Cullen, "US Orders Lottery to Hold Bulger's Winnings," *Boston Globe,* July 18, 1995, www.archive.boston .com/news/local/massachusetts/articles/1995/07/18/us_orders_lottery_to _hold_bulgers_winnings/ (accessed January 23, 2020).

192 **"It sounds like an American":** Gérard Lhéritier, "La loterie," email, January 29, 2018.

192 **As the sun set:** Gérard Lhéritier, interview with the author, December 6, 2016.

193 **The company's bankruptcy proceedings:** Nicolas Lecoq-Vallon, interview with the author, December 10, 2016.

193 **Seeking other alternatives:** Benoît Huet, interview with the author, December 10, 2016; Alain Poncet, interview with the author, November 11, 2019.

193 **An organization called ADILEMA:** Philippe Julien, interview with the author, December 10, 2016.

193 **The largest group:** Nicolas Lecoq-Vallon, interview with the author, December 10, 2016.

193 **One association made headlines:** Erwan Seznec, "Affaire Aristophil: Une Association d'Aide aux Victimes au Financement Trouble," *Que Choisir,* May 25, 2015, www.quechoisir.org/actualite-affaire-aristophil-une -association-d-aide-aux-victimes-au-financement-trouble-n2741/ (accessed January 24, 2020).

194 **"It is a sad affair":** Gérard Lhéritier, interview with the author, December 6, 2016.

194 **Robert Cipollina:** Aude Nehring, interview with the author, November 5, 2016.

194 **Then there was Jean-Claude:** Xavier Deroche, interview with the author, October 30, 2019.

194 **In the spring of 2019:** Horlans, *Affaire Aristophil,* 9, 12.

195 **The one person not responsible:** Horlans, *Affaire Aristophil,* 289.

195 ***Affaire Aristophil* concluded:** Horlans, *Affaire Aristophil,* 305–31.

195 **The book's author was:** Isabelle Horlans declined multiple interview requests.

195 **The book's preface was written:** Dupuis and Léger, "L'Incroyable Histoire du 'Madoff' Français."

195 **And it had been sent to:** Horlans, *Affaire Aristophil,* 245–46.

195 **Many of the logistics:** Christophe Reille, interview with the author, April 15, 2019.

196 **Lhéritier didn't deny:** Gérard Lhéritier, interview with the author, July 20, 2019.

196 **When Lhéritier's criminal defense attorney:** Francis Triboulet, interview with the author, November 10, 2016.

196 **"There's a contract":** Gérard Lhéritier, interview with the author, July 18, 2019.

196 **Two days later:** Gérard Lhéritier, interview with the author, July 20, 2019.

197 **On a warm December afternoon:** Gérard Lhéritier, interview with the author, December 8, 2016.

197 **"He is sixty-eight years old":** Francis Triboulet, interview with the author, November 10, 2016.

198 **"It is incredible":** Gérard Lhéritier, interview with the author, December 8, 2016.

CHAPTER FIFTEEN: The Black Sale

199 **Encased in security glass:** Observations by the author, December 19, 2017.

200 **It stood for Les Collections Aristophil:** Vincent Noce, "An Inestimable Collection," *La Gazette Drouot,* December 10, 2017, www.gazette-drouot .com/en/sale/les-collections-aristophil/88463?showAgenda=false#4957 (accessed February 24, 2020).

200 **Two days before the auction:** Aguttes, "2 Trésors Nationaux," press release, December 18, 2017.

200 **Everything about the scroll:** Ministère de la Culture, "Classement en Tant Que Trésors Nationaux, d'un Manuscrit du Marquis de Sade et d'un Ensemble d'Écrits d'André Breton," press release, December 19, 2017.

201 **In 2009, Aguttes and his team:** Claire Bommelaer, "La Mamounia, pour le Plaisir des Yeux," *Le Figaro,* May 23, 2009, www.lefigaro.fr/culture/2009/05 /23/03004-20090523ARTFIG00226-la-mamounia-pour-le-plaisir-des-yeux -.php (accessed February 25, 2020).

201 **More recently, his firm jockeyed:** "Dinosaurs & Natural History," Aguttes, www.expertise.aguttes.com/en/dinosaurs-natural-history/ (accessed February 25, 2002).

201 **Aguttes now helmed:** Florian Gallant, "19 Ans Après Son Rachat, le Château de Tournoël à Volvic N'A Plus Rien d'une Ruine," *La Montagne,* August 2, 2019, www.lamontagne.fr/volvic-63530/loisirs/19-ans-apres-son -rachat-le-chateau-de-tournoel-a-volvic-n-a-plus-rien-d-une-ruine _13617432/ (accessed February 25, 2020).

201 **At times, Aguttes's chutzpah:** "Painting Probe Leads to Two-Month Sale Ban for Aguttes," *Antiques Trade Gazette,* July 30, 2012, www.antiquestrade gazette.com/news/2012/painting-probe-leads-to-two-month-sale-ban-for -aguttes/ (accessed February 25, 2020).

202 **The company removed hundreds:** Vincent Noce, "Dernière Ligne Droite pour les Manuscrits d'Aristophil," *La Gazette Drouot,* March 24, 2017, www .gazette-drouot.com/article/derniere-ligne-droite-pour-les-manuscrits-d -aristophil/7651 (accessed December 11, 2021).

202 **Hôtel Drouot had been the obvious:** Jean Bruce and Miguel Elliott, *Drouot Vu Par* (Paris: Éditions Binôme, 1999).

203 **Legal reforms had done away:** Doreen Carvajal, "French Auction House Trades Haughty for Hip," *New York Times,* June 1, 2015, www.nytimes .com/2015/06/02/arts/international/french-auction-house-trades-haughty -for-hip.html (accessed February 24, 2020).

203 **The operation lost additional luster:** Amah-Rose Abrams, "Art Handlers and Auctioneers Involved in Shocking Drouot Scam Get Jail Time," *Artnet News,* September 7, 2016, www.news.artnet.com/art-world/jail-sentences -art-handlers-drouot-scam-636716 (accessed February 24, 2020).

203 **Since the Aristophil sales:** Gérard Lhéritier to Valérie Leloup Thomas et al., October 24, 2017; Gérard Lhéritier to Christian Tessiot et al., November 6, 2017.

204 **These documents, he insisted:** Gérard Lhéritier, interview with the author, December 8, 2016.

204 **The U.S. Common Core:** Maria Konnikova, "What's Lost as Handwriting Fades," *New York Times,* June 2, 2014, www.nytimes.com/2014/06/03

/science/whats-lost-as-handwriting-fades.html (accessed February 28, 2020); Liana Heitin, "Why Don't the Common-Core Standards Include Cursive Writing?," *PBS NewsHour,* October 17, 2016, www.pbs.org/newshour /education/scary-clown-rumors-serious-business-schools (accessed February 28, 2020).

204 **In the early 2010s:** Aaron Smith, "How Americans Use Text Messaging," Pew Research Center, September 19, 2011, www.pewresearch.org/internet /2011/09/19/how-americans-use-text-messaging/ (accessed February 28, 2020); Eddie Wrenn, "Could We Forget How to Write? The Typical Adult Has Not Scribbled Anything by Hand for Six Weeks," *Daily Mail,* June 22, 2012, www.dailymail.co.uk/sciencetech/article-2163175/Could-forget -WRITE-The-typical-adult-scribbled-hand-weeks.html (accessed February 28, 2020).

204 **And while every day 215 billion:** Council on Library and Information Resources, *A Report from the Task Force on Technical Approaches for Email Archives* (Washington, D.C.: Council on Library and Information Resources, August 2018), 1; John Mazzone and Samie Rehman, *The Household Diary Study: Mail Use and Attitudes in FY 2017* (Washington, D.C.: United States Postal Service, March 2018), 20, www.prc.gov/docs/105/105134/USPS_HDS_FY17 _Final%20Annual%20Report.pdf, accessed February 28, 2020.

204 **As important texts evolved:** Kirschenbaum, *Track Changes,* 220.

205 **Now that public figures had:** Rachel Foss, interview with the author, February 3, 2020; Stephen Enniss, interview with the author, January 28, 2020.

205 **As a rare-book dealer:** Barry R. Levin, "Manuscript Collecting: An Endangered Species," International League of Antiquarian Booksellers, November 27, 2013, www.ilab.org/index.php/articles/manuscript-collecting -endangered-species (accessed February 28, 2020).

205 **"In people's basements":** Gérard Lhéritier, interview with the author, December 8, 2016.

206 **"L'adjugé!":** Observations by the author, December 20, 2017.

207 **Nearly a third:** Aguttes, "Bilan de la Vente Inaugurale du 20/12/2017," sales report, December 22, 2017.

208 **As the headline:** Jérôme Dupuis, "Le Marché Dit Sa Cruelle Vérité sur le Scandale Aristophil," *L'Express,* December 21, 2017, www.lexpress.fr /culture/livre/le-marche-dit-sa-verite-cruelle-sur-le-scandale-aristophil _1970797.html (accessed February 26, 2020).

208 **"The atmosphere was like":** Serge Plantureux, interview with the author, December 20, 2017.

208 **A sequence of seven:** Michael Stillman, "2018: It Was a Very Good Year (for Books and Paper at Auction)," Rare Book Hub, February 2019, www .rarebookhub.com/articles/2560 (accessed February 27, 2020).

208 **The strong sales persisted:** Opérateurs de Ventes pour les Collections Aris-

tophil, "Récapitulatif des Ventes 1 à 28 des Collections Aristophil du 20 Décembre 2017 au 4 Décembre 2019 à Drouot," sales report, December 5, 2019.

208 **Disappointing results:** "Mozart Manuscript Fails to Sell at Paris Auction," *ArtDaily,* June 21, 2018, www.artdaily.cc/news/105539/Mozart-manuscript -fails-to-sell-at-Paris-auction#.XlgQx6hKg2w (accessed February 27, 2020); Claire Parker, "Rare Einstein Manuscript That 'Almost Miraculously' Survived Sold for More Than $13 Million in Paris Auction," *Washington Post,* November 22, 2021 (accessed November 27, 2021).

209 **France's national library obtained:** Opérateurs de Ventes pour les Collections Aristophil, "A Session d'Automne des Collections Aristophil Totalise 8,8m€," press release, November 21, 2018; J. M. Sultan, "Une Lettre de Vincent van Gogh au Critique Qui A Reconnu son Génie Exposée à Amsterdam," *Passéisme,* May 15, 2019, www.passeisme.com/articles/une-lettre-de -vincent-van-gogh-au-critique-qui-a-reconnu-son-genie-exposee-a -amsterdam/ (accessed February 27, 2020).

209 **In November 2019:** Alison Flood, "Brontë Society Secures Last of Charlotte's Minute Teenage Books," *Guardian,* November 18, 2019, www .theguardian.com/books/2019/nov/18/bronte-society-secures-last-of -charlottes-minute-teenage-books (accessed February 27, 2020).

209 **The miniature manuscript sold:** Horlans, *Affaire Aristophil,* 269.

209 **After three years of auctions:** Vincent Noce, "More Grief for Aristophil Investors as French Government Seizes Hundreds of Documents," *Art Newspaper,* May 28, 2019, www.theartnewspaper.com/news/aristophil-investors -face-further-setback (accessed February 27, 2020).

209 **In March 2019, Dupuis dropped:** Jérôme Dupuis, "L'État Lorgne sur les 130,000 Manuscrits d'Aristophil," *L'Express,* March 25, 2019, www.lexpress .fr/culture/l-etat-lorgne-sur-les-manuscrits-d-aristophil_2069353.html (accessed September 16, 2020).

210 **He noticed that for one:** Mélanie Delattre, Christophe Labbé, and Laure Rougevin-Baville, "Descente de Police au Musée des Lettres et Manuscrits," *Le Point,* November 18, 2014, www.lepoint.fr/justice/descente-de-police-au -musee-des-lettres-et-manuscrits-18-11-2014-1882159_2386.php (accessed March 5, 2020).

210 **Like everyone in his field:** Frédéric Castaing, "Question sur l'avenir de la collecte d'autographes et de manuscrits," email, February 10, 2002.

210 **Now signs were emerging:** Béatrice de Rochebouët, "Aux Enchères, des Lettres de Proust ne Trouvent Pas Preneur," *Le Figaro,* October 8, 2019, www.lefigaro.fr/culture/encheres/proust-mis-au-pied-de-la-lettre-20191008 (accessed February 27, 2020).

210 **When an auction of Sade:** Thibault de Sade, interview with the author, February 2, 2021.

210 **"Aristophil has left a stain on the world of autographs"**: Frédéric Castaing, interview with the author, July 11, 2019.

211 **Every day, in fact**: Lever, *Sade,* 281.

211 **"This affair will last"**: Frédéric Castaing, interview with the author, July 11, 2019.

EPILOGUE: Entombed

213 **The announcement arrived**: Ministère de la Culture, "Le Ministère de la Culture Annonce l'Acquisition par l'État de Manuscrits Littéraires Majeurs Qui Entrent dans les Collections de la BnF à la Suite de Leur Classement Trésors Nationaux," press release, July 9, 2021.

213 **For Boussard**: Emmanuel Boussard, interview with the author, July 22, 2021.

214 **"It is a pure scam"**: Gérard Lhéritier, "Questions sur le rouleau de Sade," email, May 23, 2021.

214 **For much of the previous year**: Liz Alderman, "Along the Seine, Book-sellers Try to Hold Off an Unhappy Ending," *New York Times,* November 7, 2002, www.nytimes.com/2020/11/07/world/europe/france-paris-seine-books.html (accessed May 22, 2021).

214 **In the Saint-Germain-des-Prés**: Constant Méheut, "In the Latin Quarter, Paris's Intellectual Heartbeat Grows Fainter," *New York Times,* March 22, 2021, www.nytimes.com/2021/03/22/world/europe/latin-quarter-paris-bookstores.html (accessed May 22, 2021).

215 **But in reality**: Stephen Enniss, interview with the author, January 28, 2020; Naomi Nelson, interview with the author, March 5, 2020.

215 **As communication has become digitized**: Leah Price, *What We Talk About When We Talk About Books: The History and Future of Reading* (New York: Basic Books, 2019), 1; Farhad Manjoo, "Welcome to the Post-Text Future," *New York Times,* February 14, 2018, www.nytimes.com/interactive/2018/02/09/technology/the-rise-of-a-visual-internet.html (accessed May 22, 2021).

215 **When Gutenberg invented**: Nicholas A. Basbanes, *A Splendor of Letters: The Permanence of Books in an Impermanent World* (New York: HarperCollins, 2003), 312–15.

215 **In the nineteenth century**: Price, *What We Talk About When We Talk About Books,* 165; Cynthia Monaco, "The Difficult Birth of the Typewriter," *Invention & Technology,* Spring–Summer 1988, www.inventionandtech.com/content/difficult-birth-typewriter-1 (accessed May 22, 2021).

216 **In 1913, Thomas Edison announced**: Price, *What We Talk About When We Talk About Books,* 165.

216 **In the twenty-first century**: Gretchen McCulloch, *Because Internet: Understanding the New Rules of Language* (New York: Riverhead, 2019), 14–15.

BIBLIOGRAPHY

Anderson, James M. *Daily Life During the French Revolution*. Westport, Conn:
Greenwood, 2007.

Apollinaire, Guillaume. *L'Oeuvre du Marquis de Sade*. Paris: Collection des Classiques Galants, 1909.

Asimov, Isaac. *Buy Jupiter, and Other Stories*. Garden City, N.Y.: Doubleday, 1975.

Barras, Paul. *Memoirs of Barras, Member of the Directorate*. Vol. 1, *The Ancient Régime
and the Revolution*. New York: Harper & Brothers, 1895.

Barthes, Roland. *Sade, Fourier, Loyola*. New York: Hill and Wang, 1976.

Basbanes, Nicholas A. *A Gentle Madness: Bibliophiles, Bibliomanes, and the Eternal
Passion for Books*. New York: Henry Holt, 1995.

———. *On Paper: The Everything of Its Two-Thousand-Year History*. New York:
Alfred A. Knopf, 2013.

———. *A Splendor of Letters: The Permanence of Books in an Impermanent World*.
New York: HarperCollins, 2003.

Bataille, Georges. *Literature and Evil*. London: Marion Boyars, 1985.

Baxter, John. *Saint-Germain-des-Prés: Paris's Rebel Quarter*. New York: Harper Perennial, 2016.

Beach, Sylvia. *Shakespeare and Company*. New York: Harcourt, Brace, 1959.

Beachy, Robert. *Gay Berlin: Birthplace of a Modern Identity*. New York: Alfred A.
Knopf, 2014.

Benaïm, Laurence. *Marie Laure de Noailles: La Vicomtesse du Bizarre*. Paris: Bernard
Grasset, 2001.

Benjamin, Mary A. *Autographs: A Key to Collecting*. New York: Dover, 1986.

Berkeley, Edmund Jr., ed. *Autographs and Manuscripts: A Collector's Manual*. New
York: Charles Scribner's Sons, 1978.

Bernier, Olivier. *Pleasure and Privilege: Life in France, Naples, and America 1770–1790*.
Garden City, N.Y.: Doubleday, 1981.

Bloch, Iwan. *Beiträge zur Aetiologie der Psychopathia Sexualis*. Dresden: Verlag von
H. R. Dohrn, 1902.

————. *Marquis de Sade: His Life and Works*. New York: Castle, 1947.

————. *Marquis de Sade's Anthropologia Sexualis of 600 Perversions: "120 Days of Sodom, or the School for Libertinage" and the Sex Life of the French Age of Debauchery from the Private Archives of the French Government*. New York: Falstaff, 1934.

————. *Neue Forschungen über den Marquis de Sade und Seine Zeit: Mit Besonderer Berücksichtigung der Sexualphilosophie de Sade's auf Grund des Neuentdeckten Original-Manuskriptes Seines Hauptwerkes "Die 120 Tage von Sodom."* Translated by Eugene Duhren. Berlin: Max Harrwitz, 1904.

————. *Sex Life in England*. New York: Panurge, 1934.

————. *The Sexual Life of Our Time in Its Relations to Modern Civilization*. London: Rebman, 1909.

Bocher, Héloïse. *Démolir la Bastille: L'Édification d'un Lieu de Mémoire*. Paris: Vendémiaire, 2014.

Bongie, Laurence L. *Sade: A Biographical Essay*. Chicago: University of Chicago Press, 1998.

Bonnardot, Alfred. *The Mirror of the Parisian Bibliophile: A Satirical Tale*. Translated by Theodore Wesley Koch. Chicago: Lakeside, 1931.

Bredeson, Kate. *Occupying the Stage: The Theater of May '68*. Evanston, Ill.: Northwestern University Press, 2018.

Breton, André. *Manifeste du Surréalisme*. Paris: Éditions du Sagittaire, 1924.

Bruce, Jean, and Miguel Elliott. *Drouot Vu Par*. Paris: Éditions Binôme, 1999.

Bullough, Vern. *Science in the Bedroom: A History of Sex Research*. New York: Basic Books, 1994.

Buñuel, Luis. *My Last Sigh: The Autobiography of Luis Buñuel*. New York: Vintage Books, 2013.

Camus, Albert. *The Rebel: An Essay on Man in Revolt*. New York: Vintage International, 1991.

Carter, Angela. *The Sadeian Woman and the Ideology of Pornography*. New York: Pantheon, 1978.

Carter, John. *ABC for Book Collectors*. New Castle, Del.: Oak Knoll, 1995.

Castaing, Frédéric. *Rouge Cendres*. Paris: Ramsay, 2005.

Caws, Mary Ann. *Creative Gatherings: Meeting Places of Modernism*. London: Reaktion, 2019.

Charavay, Étienne. *La Science des Autographes: Essai Critique*. Paris: Charavay Frères, 1887.

Church, Clive H., and Randolph C. Head. *A Concise History of Switzerland*. Cambridge: Cambridge University Press, 2013.

Cloonan, Michele Valerie. *Preserving Our Heritage: Perspectives from Antiquity to the Digital Age*. Chicago: Neal-Schuman, 2015.

Darnton, Robert. *The Forbidden Best-Sellers of Pre-revolutionary France*. New York: W. W. Norton, 1996.

Datz, Stephen. *Stamp Investing*. Loveland, Colo.: General Philatelic Corporation, 1997.

Delon, Michel. *La 121ème Journée: L'Incroyable Histoire du Manuscrit de Sade*. Paris: Albin Michel, 2020.

Denton, Chad. *Decadence, Radicalism, and the Early Modern French Nobility: The Enlightened and Depraved*. Lanham, Md.: Lexington Books, 2017.

Desan, Suzanne. *The Family on Trial in Revolutionary France*. Berkeley: University of California Press, 2006.

Desan, Suzanne, and Jeffrey Merrick, eds. *Family, Gender, and Law in Early Modern France*. University Park: Pennsylvania University Press, 2009.

Dickinson, Edward Ross. *Sex, Freedom, and Power in Imperial Germany, 1880–1914*. New York: Cambridge University Press, 2014.

Dulaure, Jacques-Antoine. *Liste des Noms des Ci-devant Nobles: Nobles de Race, Robins, Financiers, Intrigans, & de Tous les Aspirans à la Noblesse, ou Escrocs d'Icelle; avec des Notes sur Leurs Familles*. Vol. 1. Paris: Garnery, 1791.

Duprilot, Jacques. *Gay et Doucé: Éditeurs sous le Manteau, 1877–1882*. Paris: Éditions Astarté, 1998.

Durozoi, Gérard. *History of the Surrealist Movement*. Chicago: University of Chicago Press, 2002.

Dworkin, Andrea. *Pornography: Men Possessing Women*. New York: Perigee, 1981.

Eerdmans, Emily Evans. *The World of Madeleine Castaing*. New York: Rizzoli International, 2010.

Fenby, Jonathan. *France: A Modern History from the Revolution to the War on Terror*. New York: St. Martin's, 2015.

Fisher, John. *Airlift 1870: The Balloons and Pigeons in the Siege of Paris*. London: Max Parrish, 1965.

Flaubert, Gustave. *Bibliomania: A Tale*. London: Rodale, 1954.

Frankel, Tamar. *The Ponzi Scheme Puzzle: A History and Analysis of Con Artists and Victims*. New York: Oxford University Press, 2012.

Fraxi, Pisanus. *Index Librorum Prohibitorum: Being Notes Bio- Biblio- Icono-graphical and Critical, on Curious and Uncommon Books*. London: privately printed, 1877.

Froulay Créquy, Renée-Caroline-Victoire. *Souvenirs de Marquise de Créquy: 1710 à 1800, Tome Troisième*. The Hague: G. Vervloet, 1834.

Gabin, Jean-Louis. *Gilbert Lely: Biographie*. Paris: Librairie Séguier, 1991.

Garrioch, David. *The Making of Revolutionary Paris*. Berkeley: University of California Press, 2002.

Gerould, Daniel. *Guillotine: Its Legend and Lore*. New York: Blast, 1992.

Gertzman, Jay A. *Bookleggers and Smuthounds: The Trade in Erotica, 1920–1940*. Philadelphia: University of Pennsylvania Press, 2011.

Gibson, Ian. *The Erotomaniac: The Secret Life of Henry Spencer Ashbee*. Cambridge, Mass.: Da Capo, 2001.

Glass, Loren. *Rebel Publisher: Grove Press and the Revolution of the Word*. New York: Seven Stories, 2018.

Goncourt, Edmond de, and Jules de Goncourt. *Journal des Goncourt: Mémoires de la Vie Littéraire*. Vol. 2, *1862–1865*. Paris: G. Charpentier, 1888.

Grau, Günter. *Iwan Bloch: Hautarzt, Medizinhistoriker, Sexualforscher*. Teetz: Hentrich & Hentrich, 2007.

Gray, Francine du Plessix. *At Home with the Marquis de Sade*. New York: Penguin Books, 1999.

Halverson, Krista, ed. *Shakespeare and Company, Paris: A History of the Rag and Bone Shop of the Heart*. Paris: Shakespeare and Company Paris, 2016.

Hamelin, Lancelot, and Luca Erbetta. *Dans les Eaux Glacées du Calcul Égoiste*. Vol. 1, *Le Bal des Matières*. Grenoble: Éditions Glénat, 2018.

Hamilton, Charles. *Collecting Autographs and Manuscripts*. Rev. ed. Santa Monica, Calif.: Modoc, 1993.

Hammond, Paul. *L'Âge d'Or*. London: British Film Institute, 1997.

Hankey, Frederick, Jacques Duprilot, and Jean-Paul Goujon. *Ce N'Est Pas Mon Genre de Livres Lestes . . . : Lettres Inédites à Richard Monckton Milnes, Lord Houghton (1857–1865)*. N.p.: Miss Jenkins, 2012.

Hayden, Deborah. *Pox: Genius, Madness, and the Mysteries of Syphilis*. New York: Basic Books, 2003.

Hemingway, Ernest. *A Moveable Feast: The Restored Edition*. New York: Scribner, 2009.

Hibbert, Christopher. *The Days of the French Revolution*. New York: Harper Perennial, 1980.

Holmes, Richard. *Falling Upwards: How We Took to the Air*. New York: Pantheon, 2013.

Hopkins, David, ed. *A Companion to Dada and Surrealism*. West Sussex: John Wiley & Sons, 2016.

Horkheimer, Max, and Theodor W. Adorno. *Dialectic of Enlightenment: Philosophical Fragments*. Stanford, Calif.: Stanford University Press, 2002.

Horlans, Isabelle. *Affaire Aristophil: Liquidation en Bande Organisée*. Paris: Le Passeur, 2019.

Horne, Alistair. *Seven Ages of Paris*. New York: Alfred A. Knopf, 2002.

Isherwood, Christopher. *Christopher and His Kind, 1929–1939*. New York: Farrar, Straus and Giroux, 1976.

Joline, Adrian Hoffman. *Meditations of an Autograph Collector*. New York: Harper & Brothers, 1902.

Jones, Colin. *The Great Nation*. New York: Columbia University Press, 2002.

Kahan, Benjamin. *The Book of Minor Perverts: Sexology, Etiology, and the Emergences of Sexuality*. Chicago: University of Chicago Press, 2019.

Kearney, Patrick J. *A Catalogue of the Publications of Jules Gay, Jean-Jules Gay and*

Gay et Doucé. Rev. ed. Santa Rosa, Calif.: Scissors & Paste Bibliographies, 2019.

————. *Frederick Hankey (1821–1882): A Biographical Sketch*. Santa Rosa, Calif.: Scissors & Paste Bibliographies, 2019.

Kendrick, Walter. *The Secret Museum: Pornography in Modern Culture*. Berkeley: University of California Press, 1996.

Kennedy, Emmet. *A Cultural History of the French Revolution*. New Haven, Conn.: Yale University Press, 1989.

Kirschenbaum, Matthew G. *Track Changes: A Literary History of Word Processing*. Cambridge, Mass.: Belknap Press of Harvard University Press, 2016.

Krafft-Ebing, Richard von. *Psychopathia Sexualis*. Translated by Charles Gilbert Chaddock. Philadelphia: F. A. Davis, 1894.

Kugelberg, Johan, and Philippe Vermés. *Beauty Is in the Street: A Visual Record of the May '68 Paris Uprising*. London: Four Corner, 2011.

Kushner, Nina. *Erotic Exchanges: The World of Elite Prostitution in Eighteenth-Century Paris*. Ithaca, N.Y.: Cornell University Press, 2013.

Large, David Clay. *Berlin*. New York: Basic Books, 2000.

Le Brun, Annie. *À Distance*. Issy-les-Moulineaux, France: Éditions Carrère, 1984.

————. *Sade: A Sudden Abyss*. San Francisco: City Lights Books, 1990.

Leck, Ralph M. *Vita Sexualis: Karl Ulrichs and the Origins of Sexual Science*. Urbana: University of Illinois Press, 2016.

Lefebvre, Georges. *The Great Fear of 1789: Rural Panic in Revolutionary France*. Princeton, N.J.: Princeton University Press, 2014.

Legman, Gershon. *The Horn Book*. New Hyde Park, N.Y.: University Books, 1964.

Lély, Gilbert. *The Marquis de Sade: A Definitive Biography*. New York: Grove, 1961.

Lerner, Paul. *Hysterical Men: War, Psychiatry, and the Politics of Trauma in Germany, 1890–1930*. Ithaca, N.Y.: Cornell University Press, 2003.

Lever, Maurice. *"Je Jure au Marquis de Sade, Mon Amant, de Nêtre Jamais Qu'à Lui . . ."* Paris: Librairie Arthème Fayard, 2005.

————. *Sade: A Biography*. New York: Farrar, Straus and Giroux, 1993.

Lhéritier, Gérard. *Collection 1870: Ballons Montés, Boules de Moulins*. Paris: Éditions Aristophil, 2000.

————. *Intime Corruption: L'Affaire des Timbres Rares de Monaco*. Paris: L'Archipel, 2006.

————. *Les Ballons de la Liberté*. Paris: Plon, 1995.

Linguet, Simon Nicolas Henri. *Memoirs of the Bastille*. Vol. 2. Edinburgh: privately printed, 1885.

Lord, James. *Six Exceptional Women: Further Memoirs*. New York: Farrar, Straus and Giroux, 1994.

Luck, J. Murray. *A History of Switzerland: The First 100,000 Years; Before the Begin-*

nings to the Days of the Present. Palo Alto, Calif.: Society for the Promotion of Science and Scholarship, 1985.

Lüsebrink, Hans-Jürgen, and Rolf Reichardt. *The Bastille: A History of a Symbol of Despotism and Freedom*. Translated by Norbert Schürer. Durham, N.C.: Duke University Press, 1997.

Mackay, Charles. *Memoirs of Extraordinary Popular Delusions and the Madness of Crowds*. Vol. 1. London: Office of the National Illustrated Library, 1852.

MacLean, Rory. *Berlin: Portrait of a City Through the Centuries*. New York: Weidenfeld & Nicolson, 2014.

Mahon, Alyce. *The Marquis de Sade and the Avant-Garde*. Princeton, N.J.: Princeton University Press, 2020.

Mancini, Elena. *Magnus Hirschfeld and the Quest for Sexual Freedom: A History of the First International Sexual Freedom Movement*. New York: Palgrave MacMillan, 2010.

Marcus, Steven. *The Other Victorians: A Study of Sexuality and Pornography in Mid-Nineteenth-Century England*. New Brunswick, N.J.: Transaction, 2009.

Mare, Alexandre, and Stéphane Boudin-Lestlenne. *Charles et Marie-Laure de Noailles: Mécènes du XX Siècle*. Paris: Bernard Chauveau Édition, 2018.

Marhoefer, Laurie. *Sex and the Weimar Republic: German Homosexual Emancipation and the Rise of the Nazis*. Toronto, Ont.: University of Toronto Press, 2015.

Mason, Rainer Michael, ed., *Eros Invaincu: La Bibliothèque Gérard Nordmann*. Paris: Fondation Martin Bodmer, 2004.

McAuliffe, Mary. *Paris on the Brink: The 1930s Paris of Jean Renoir, Salvador Dalí, Simone de Beauvoir, André Gide, Sylvia Beach, Léon Blum, and Their Friends*. Lanham, Md.: Rowman & Littlefield, 2018.

———. *When Paris Sizzled: The 1920s Paris of Hemingway, Chanel, Cocteau, Cole Porter, Josephine Baker, and Their Friends*. London: Rowman & Littlefield, 2016.

McCulloch, Gretchen. *Because Internet: Understanding the New Rules of Language*. New York: Riverhead, 2019.

McDill, John R. *Lessons from the Enemy: How Germany Cares for Her War Disabled*. Philadelphia: Lea & Febiger, 1918.

McPhee, Peter. *Liberty or Death: The French Revolution*. New Haven, Conn.: Yale University Press, 2016.

Mirabeau, Honoré-Gabriel de Riquetti. *Enquiries Concerning Lettres de Cachet: The Consequences of Arbitrary Imprisonment, and a History of the Inconveniences, Distresses, and Sufferings of State Prisoners*. France: Whitestone, Byrne, Cash, Moore, and Jones, 1787.

Morin, Louis. *Comment le Docteur Boche, pour Justifier à l'Avance les Infamies Allemandes, Accusait de Sadisme Sanglant les Français en Général et les Parisiens en Particulier*. Paris: C. Bosse, 1918.

Muensterberger, Werner. *Collecting: An Unruly Passion*. Princeton, N.J.: Princeton University Press, 1994.

Munby, A. N. L. *The Cult of the Autograph Letter in England*. London: Athlone, 1962.

Murciano, Jean-Pierre. *Juge sur la Côte d'Azur: Missions Impossibles*. Neuilly-sur-Seine, France: Michel Lafon, 2001.

Nadeau, Maurice. *The History of Surrealism*. New York: Macmillan, 1965.

Nelson, Christine. *The Magic of Handwriting: The Pedro Corrêa do Lago Collection*. Cologne, Germany: Taschen, 2018.

Nicolas, Alain. *Les Autographes*. Paris: Maisonneuve & Larose, 1988.

Onfray, Michel. *La Passion de la Méchanceté*. Paris: Éditions Autrement, 2014.

Parker, Kate, and Norbert Sclippa. *Sade's Sensibilities*. Lewisburg, Penn.: Bucknell University Press, 2015.

Paulhan, Jean. *Le Marquis de Sade et Sa Complice*. Brussels: Éditions Complexe, 1987.

Pauvert, Jean-Jacques. *Nouveaux et Moins Nouveaux Visages de la Censure, Suivie de l'Affaire Sade*. Paris: Les Belles Lettres, 1994.

————. *Sade's Publisher: A Memoir*. New York: Paris Writers Press, 2016.

Pearsall, Ronald. *The Worm in the Bud: The World of Victorian Sexuality*. Toronto, Ont.: Macmillan, 1969.

Pernoud, Georges, and Sabine Flaissier. *The French Revolution*. New York: G. P. Putnam's Sons, 1960.

Perry, Heather R. *Recycling the Disabled: Army, Medicine, and Modernity in WWI Germany*. Manchester, U.K.: Manchester University Press, 2014.

Petrarca, Francesco. *The First Modern Scholar and Man of Letters: A Selection from His Correspondence with Boccaccio and Other Friends, Designed to Illustrate the Beginnings of the Renaissance*. New York: G. P. Putnam's Sons, 1909.

Plant, Richard. *The Pink Triangle: The Nazi War Against Homosexuals*. New York: Henry Holt, 1986.

Polizzotti, Mark. *Revolution of the Mind: The Life of André Breton*. New York: Farrar, Straus and Giroux, 1995.

Ponzi, Charles. *The Rise of Mr. Ponzi: The Long-Suppressed Autobiography of a Financial Genius*. Austin, Tex.: Despair, 2009.

Price, Leah. *What We Talk About When We Talk About Books: The History and Future of Reading*. New York: Basic Books, 2019.

Quignard, Marie-Françoise, and Raymond-Josué Seckel. *L'Enfer de la Bibliothèque: Eros au Secret*. Paris: Bibliothèque Nationale de France, 2019.

Rendell, Kenneth W. *History Comes to Life: Collecting Historical Letters and Documents*. Norman: University of Oklahoma Press, 1995.

Riqueti, Honoré Gabriel, Comte de Mirabeau. *Des Lettres de Cachet et des Prisons d'État,* Vol. 2. Hambourg: n.p., 1882.

Roberts, William. *A Portrait of Holywell Street and Its Environs*. Santa Rosa, Calif.: Scissors & Paste Bibliographies, 2019.

Roe, Sue. *In Montparnasse: The Emergence of Surrealism in Paris, from Duchamp to Dalí*. New York: Penguin Press, 2019.

Rosenblum, Joseph. *Prince of Forgers*. New Castle, Del.: Oak Knoll, 1998.

Sade, Donatien Alphonse François de. *Aline et Valcour*. Paris: Gallimard, 1990.

———. *Die Hundertzwanzig Tage von Sodom, oder die Schule der Ausschweifung*. Translated by Karl von Haverland. Leipzig: Privatdruck, 1909.

———. *Juliette*. Translated by Austryn Wainhouse. New York: Grove, 1968.

———. *Justine, Philosophy in the Bedroom, and Other Writings*. Translated by Richard Seaver and Austryn Wainhouse. New York: Grove, 1965.

———. *Letters from Prison*. Translated by Richard Seaver, New York: Arcade, 1999.

———. *120 Days of Sodom*. Translated by Will McMorran and Thomas Wynn. London: Penguin Classics, 2016.

———. *The 120 Days of Sodom and Other Writings*. Translated by Austryn Wainhouse and Richard Seaver. New York: Grove, 1966.

———. *120 Journées de Sodome, ou l'École du Libertinage*. Translated by Eugène Dühren. Paris: Club des Bibliophiles, 1904.

Schaeffer, Neil. *The Marquis de Sade: A Life*. New York: Alfred A. Knopf, 1999.

Schaffner, Anna Katharina. *Modernism and Perversion: Sexual Deviance in Sexology and Literature, 1850–1930*. New York: Palgrave Macmillan, 2012.

Schama, Simon. *Citizens: A Chronicle of the French Revolution*. New York: Vintage Books, 1989.

Shattuck, Roger. *Forbidden Knowledge: A Landmark Exploration of the Dark Side of Human Ingenuity and Imagination*. San Diego: A Harvest Book/Harcourt Brace, 1996.

Silverman, Willa Z. *The New Bibliopolis: French Book Collectors and the Culture of Print, 1880–1914*. Toronto, Ont.: University of Toronto Press, 2008.

Singer, Daniel. *Prelude to Revolution: France in May 1968*. Cambridge, Mass.: South End, 2002.

Steintrager, James A. *The Autonomy of Pleasure: Libertines, License, and Sexual Revolution*. New York: Columbia University Press, 2016.

Thruston, Gates P. *Autograph Collections and Historic Manuscripts*. Sewanee, Tenn.: University Press, 1902.

Trubek, Anne. *The History and Uncertain Future of Handwriting*. New York: Bloomsbury, 2016.

Villeneuve-Trans-Flayosc, Romée de. *Notice sur les Villeneuve Arcs, Trans, Flayosc, Suivie d'un Appendice Où Se Trouvent Relatés les Titres Ayant Existé ou Existant Encore dans la Maison de Villeneuve en Provence*. Lyon: Société Anonyme de l'Imprimerie A. Rey, 1926.

Villeneuve Esclapon, L. Romée de. *Histoire de la Maison de Villeneuve en Provence: Généalogie et Preuves des Nouvelles Générations de 1850 à Nos Jours*. Fontenay-le-Comte, France: Imprimerie Loriou, 1989.

Waters, Sheila. *Waters Rising: Letters from Florence*. Ann Arbor, Mich.: Legacy, 2016.

Waxman, Sharon. *Loot: The Battle over the Stolen Treasures of the Ancient World*. New York: Times Books, 2008.

INDEX

Sade in subentries refers to Donatien Alphonse François de Sade

ABOUT THE AUTHOR

JOEL WARNER is a writer and editor whose work has appeared in *Esquire, Wired, Newsweek, Men's Journal, Bloomberg Businessweek, Popular Science, Grantland,* and *Slate,* among other publications. He currently serves as managing editor of the investigative news outlet *The Lever* and previously worked as a staff writer at *International Business Times* and *Westword.* He is also co-author of *The Humor Code: A Global Search for What Makes Things Funny.* Warner lives with his family in Denver, Colorado.

joelwarner.com
Twitter: @joelmwarner

ABOUT THE TYPE

This book was set in Bembo, a typeface based on an old-style Roman face that was used for Cardinal Pietro Bembo's tract *De Aetna* in 1495. Bembo was cut by Francesco Griffo (1450–1518) in the early sixteenth century for Italian Renaissance printer and publisher Aldus Manutius (1449–1515). The Lanston Monotype Company of Philadelphia brought the well-proportioned letterforms of Bembo to the United States in the 1930s.